Sport and British Jewry

MANCHESTER
1824
Manchester University Press

Sport and British Jewry

Integration, ethnicity and anti-Semitism, 1890–1970

David Dee

Manchester University Press

Published by Manchester University Press
Altrincham Street, Manchester M1 7JA, UK
www.manchesteruniversitypress.co.uk

British Library Cataloguing-in-Publication Data is available

Library of Congress Cataloging-in-Publication Data is available

ISBN 978 0 7190 9657 0 paperback

First published by Manchester University Press in hardback 2013

This paperback edition first published 2014

The publisher has no responsibility for the persistence or accuracy of URLs for any external or third-party internet websites referred to in this book, and does not guarantee that any content on such websites is, or will remain, accurate or appropriate.

Printed by Lightning Source

For my family

Contents

List of figures   *page* ix
Acknowledgements   xi
List of abbreviations   xiii

Introduction   1

1 Integration and Anglicisation   14
   Introduction
   Anglicisation through sport: the Jewish youth movement,
      1895–1914   17
   Competitive sport and immigrant integration, 1899–1939   38
   'Too Semitic' or 'thoroughly Anglicised'? The life and
      career of Harold Abrahams   53
   Conclusions: sport and Anglicisation   70

2 Religion and ethnicity   88
   Introduction
   'All on the side of the more athletic form of
      Sabbatarianism': physical recreation and the
      Jewish Sabbath   90
   The new 'golden age' of Jewish professional boxing   109
   Creating a 'new Jew'? Sport and Maccabi Great Britain,
      1934–70   123
   Conclusions: sport and Jewish ethnicity   139

3 Anti-Semitism   158
   Introduction
   The British Union of Fascists and the 'sporting' Jew,
     1935–39   160
   'There is no discrimination here, but the Committee never
     elects Jews': anti-Semitism and golf   174
   Kicking discrimination into touch? Sport as a response
     to anti-Semitism   196
   Conclusions: sport and anti-Semitism   208

   Conclusion   224
   Select bibliography   230
   Index   249

List of Figures

1 The gymnastics teams of the West Central Jewish   *page* 26
   Working Lads' Club, pictured c.1900. This team
   would go on to dominate gymnastics competitions
   held by the London Federation of Working Boys'
   Clubs during the 1900s. Taken from the
   Jewish Chronicle. Exact date unknown.
2 The football team of the Stepney Jewish Lads' Club,   33
   pictured in 1913 with the 'Jewish Athletic Association
   Football League' First Division trophy. Taken from the
   Jewish Chronicle. Exact date unknown.
3 The victorious London Jewish Lads' Brigade Prince of   45
   Wales' Boxing Shield team, pictured receiving the Shield
   from the Prince of Wales (later Edward VIII) in London,
   1921. Image courtesy of Manchester Archives and
   Local Studies.
4 The Manchester Jewish Lads' Brigade Prince of Wales'   47
   Boxing Shield winning team, pictured in 1926. Image
   courtesy of Manchester Jewish Museum.
5 Jewish Manchester City fans eagerly awaiting a First   100
   Division home game against Grimsby Town, pictured in
   1936. Image courtesy of Manchester Jewish Museum.
6 *The Maccabi Code*, published by the British Maccabi   127
   Association in 1936. Image courtesy of Tyne and
   Wear Archive Services.
7 *Golf Illustrated* cartoon, 1910.   178
8 *Golf Illustrated* cartoon, 1910.   180

Acknowledgements

Many people have offered advice, assistance and guidance with this publication. I must express special thanks to Panikos Panayi for his insightful and detailed comments on various drafts of this work and for his general support as my mentor and friend. Similarly, Matt Taylor, Dick Holt and Tony Kushner also made many useful and constructive suggestions on this work in its previous incarnations.

I would also like to express my gratitude to various former and present colleagues at De Montfort University not directly involved with the book. Thanks go to Dil Porter, Tony Collins, Jean Williams, Neil Carter, Kathy Burrell, Jeff Hill, James Panter, Pippa Virdee, Kenneth Morrison, John Martin, Mark Sandle, Chris Lash and Chris Goldsmith for their general advice, assistance and reassurance over the past four years. I must also thank Gavin Schaffer, Anthony Clavane, Nathan Abrams, Mike Huggins, Martin Polley and Matthew Llewellyn for their advice with regard to my research for this publication.

I am also appreciative of the assistance offered by all of the friendly and helpful staff at the various archives, libraries and record offices that I visited across Britain during my research. I would also like to express my gratitude to the Arts and Humanities Research Council for providing the finance to make this research possible and to the team at Manchester University Press for their help and assistance.

Finally, and most importantly, I must thank my immediate family. My mum and dad, my brother Ian and my sister Caroline have all been a significant source of encouragement and support. My partner Caroline is also deserving of a very special mention for being such an incredible source of reassurance and friendship over the past eight years.

Abbreviations

AAA	Amateur Athletic Association
AJY	Association for Jewish Youth
BMA	British Maccabi Association
BUF	British Union of Fascists
BUSC	University of Birmingham, Special Collections
CAC	Churchill Archives Centre, Churchill College, Cambridge
JAA	Jewish Athletic Association
JLB	Jewish Lads' Brigade
LCC	London County Council
LFWBC	London Federation of Working Boys' Clubs
MJM	Manchester Jewish Museum
NA	National Archives, Kew
SJAC	Scottish Jewish Archives Centre, Glasgow
TWAS	Tyne and Wear Archive Services
UCLL	University College, London, Library
UoSSC	University of Southampton Special Collections

Introduction

In 2006, a 68-page booklet entitled *Living and Giving: The Jewish Contribution to the UK* was published as part of the commemorations surrounding the passing of 350 years since Jewish re-admission to the United Kingdom.[1] The openly and outwardly celebratory publication sought to document Jewish involvement in British life since 1656 and contained essays by a variety of well-known British Jewish professionals and intellectuals. It argued that 'hardly an economic, social or cultural area remains untouched by the Jewish contribution' and that many Jews have become 'role-models' and 'leading figures in their fields'.[2] Whilst Jewish 'achievements' in British law, science, politics and business were heralded, one chapter within the publication focused on an area of British life less readily associated with the Jewish community – sport and physical recreation.[3]

The author of the chapter conceded from the outset that the inclusion of sport alongside these more traditional fields of Jewish participation may cause some raised eyebrows. Stephen Pollard – journalist, author and, subsequently, editor of the *Jewish Chronicle* – noted in his first line that 'two words which Jews themselves tend not to associate with Judaism are "sports champion"'. Despite this observation, Pollard went on to demonstrate in a brief three-page chapter that Jews had been involved in British sport and had made a significant contribution to that area of the life of the country. Whilst openly admitting that discussion of the topic was 'far from comprehensive', he argued that 'almost every sport has had successful Jewish participants' with Jews having both a 'huge impact behind the scenes' and 'an enormous contribution on the field'.[4]

As Pollard suggested, the idea of Jewish involvement and interest in sport went against the grain of perceptions of British Jews. In the popular mindset, Jews may have been recognisable within Britain as solicitors, barristers, doctors, politicians and businessmen, but not as footballers, boxers and athletes. Indeed, a misconception has long existed that Jews excel where intellect and the mind is key and have little ability or interest in physical professions or pastimes. Throughout British history, stereotypes and perceptions of Jews have often focused on their supposed physical weakness and 'disinterest' in physical and sporting pastimes. As both Edgar Rosenberg and Bryan Cheyette have noted, such a view has long been prominent within British popular culture.[5] It can, for instance, be seen in Shakespeare's Shylock or Dickens' Fagin, whose physical weakness and ugliness is a reoccurring theme within *Oliver Twist*.[6] In the twentieth century, such views have also been evident within wider society. One Mass Observation survey from 1939, for instance, concluded that 'many Gentiles based their dislike of Jews upon a misconception that: "Jews are no good at games or manual labour of any kind, are eager to evade military service and are in the last resort cowards"'.[7]

Such stereotypes are not limited to within Britain. Across Western society, the view that Jews are a people of the book and morally, culturally, spiritually and physically opposed to physical recreation has been common over the course of modern history. As Peter Levine has noted, a 'picture' has long existed in the Western mindset of Jewish communities dominated and symbolised by 'devout Orthodox Jewish men with long beards, yarmulkes and prayer shawls who spoke only in Yiddish and Hebrew, [who] valued the intellect over the physical and devoted their lives to God and the Talmud'.[8]

Such a view builds upon long-standing characterisations of Jews as physically weak, effete and non-athletic – the polar opposite of the stereotyped strong and masculine sportsman. As Gilman has highlighted, the belief is common across much of modern history that Jews had 'a weak constitution' and 'were innately unable to undertake physical labour'.[9] In a wider sense, it is true that Judaism itself values the cultivation of the mind over the body. As one American scholar of religious history has noted, whilst ancient Judaism may have respected physical strength, sport has not been regarded highly in terms of Jewish religious and cultural values, customs and law for over two millennia.[10]

Within Britain, it is incorrect to think that Jews have been apathetic towards – or unsuited to – sporting pastimes. A passing glance at the period before 1890 demonstrates this aptly. For instance, in the Georgian period several English Jews came to prominence in the world of pugilism. Boxers such as Daniel Mendoza (dubbed the 'Star of Israel'), Barney Aaron and Sam Elias dominated the sport and in doing so 'challenged ... accepted prejudices' surrounding 'Jewish cowardice' and physical weakness.[11] In a less direct sense, perceptions of Jews as 'unsporting' were also undermined within the world of British horse-racing during the mid- to late Victorian era. English Jewish families such as the Rothschilds, Cassels and Sassoons became keen race-goers and stable owners from this period onwards, commencing a Jewish connection to the 'Sport of Kings' which remained strong well into the twentieth century.[12]

These two examples from the sporting world demonstrate much more than the fallacy of certain Jewish stereotypes. As well as challenging perceptions of the Jewish community, the involvement of these Jewish sportsmen exerted a direct social and cultural effect on British Jewry, and also influenced relations between Jews and Gentiles more broadly. Endelman, for example, has linked the success of Jewish prize-fighters to trends of Jewish working-class and pauper 'acculturation' occurring at the same time. Seemingly, Jewish involvement in boxing reflected and hastened wider Jewish absorption of the 'habits and tastes' of Gentile working-class society.[13] Various historians of British Jewry writing in the so-called 'Whig' vein have argued that Mendoza and his peers' success facilitated and symbolised Jewish social mobility and acceptance by the English establishment.[14]

Jewish involvement in horse-racing is also believed to have had a significant wider impact on the Jewish community. It has been claimed that the increasing interest of the Jewish 'Establishment' in the sport from the mid-nineteenth century onwards reflected the 'gradual embourgeoisement of Native Jewry' occurring at this time. Interest in 'the Turf' was just another indicator of increasing Jewish integration, evidenced by the growing participation in the 'social affairs' and 'cultural and recreational activities' of English 'respectable society'.[15] This example also demonstrates something about the nature of Jewish/non-Jewish relations at this time. Huggins has noted that the 'acceptance' of Jews into the horse-racing community is evidence of the 'openness' of British sport and high-society to 'outsiders' – showing that sporting interest and achievement was indeed an 'aid' for 'social success' by minorities within Britain.[16]

Evidently, an examination of the period immediately preceding the focus of this volume indicates the importance of sport to the Jewish community of Britain. Given sport's clear ability to illuminate and influence Anglo-Jewish history, therefore, it is surprising that little has been written about the subject in a more modern context – when both organised sport and the Jewish community have grown in size and importance within British society and culture. Despite certain key, yet limited, exceptions, Jewish sport history within Britain since the late Victorian era has been largely ignored by the academic world.[17]

Within the field of Jewish history within Britain, little or no attention has focused on interactions between British Jewry and sport. Indeed, many major scholarly histories of the community almost completely overlook the topic. In Rubinstein's substantial volume on the history of British Jews since medieval times, entitled *A History of the Jews in the English Speaking World: Great Britain*, sport is addressed on only four out of over 500 pages, with the majority of his discussion addressing Daniel Mendoza.[18] Likewise, in his comprehensive examination of the history of British anti-Semitism, *Trials of the Diaspora*, Julius touches on sport only twice. Not only does this suggest that sport is often neglected in academic studies of the community: sport's general omission from this particular volume implies – falsely, as Chapter 3 highlights – that physical recreation was not a prominent arena for Jewish exclusion and discrimination within Britain.[19]

The fact that sport has not generally featured within this canon of literature has been lamented by one of the most high-profile historians of the British Jewish community. In the preface to the 2001 edition of his seminal volume, *The Jewish Immigrant in England: 1870–1914*, Lloyd Gartner criticised the lack of academic emphasis on the history of Jewish 'cultural life' within Britain – particularly their involvement in 'sports'. Gartner noted that, although many 'detailed studies' of British Jewish social, economic and political history have emerged since the 1960 publication of his original volume, physical recreation has attracted little scholarly focus. This is despite his view that 'sports were significant ... not only as a recreation but as a step towards British identity'.[20]

A similar situation is evident with regard to research conducted into Britain's sporting history. Scholars working in this growing field have paid modest attention to Jews – or, indeed, ethnic minorities more generally – in their examinations of the worlds of British amateur and elite sport.[21] As one prominent academic noted in 2003, 'race and racism in British sport' have been 'surprisingly understudied' by scholars involved in the field.[22] Take, for instance, the critically acclaimed 'standard text' within the discipline: Richard Holt's *Sport and the British*.[23] Despite his authoritative command of Britain's modern sporting past, and the book's clear demonstration of sport's importance to British history since before industrialisation, Holt only indirectly touches on the experiences of Britain's immigrant and racial minority population. Other than brief discussions on minority boxers, golfing anti-Semitism and the links between racism and modern football hooliganism, notions of race, immigration and ethnic identity feature only marginally in Holt's discourse.[24]

The paucity of research on this subject within Britain stands in stark contrast to the picture internationally. Since the 1990s, academic interest in Jewish sport history has seen a significant growth. In the United States, where a trend for 'celebrations and compilations of Jewish sporting achievement' stretches back to the 1930s, the publication of Peter Levine's *Ellis Island to Ebbets Field: Sport and the American Jewish Experience* in 1992 represented a watershed moment.[25] Following in Levine's footsteps, a number of important works on the effect of sport on Jewish identity and culture have emerged from American academia.[26] Similar surges of academic focus in the area have also been perceptible within Israel, Continental Europe and Australia.[27] As the editor of a 2008 volume on Jewish sport history noted, publications such as his seemed to be very much 'in tune with the Zeitgeist'.[28]

Although there are some exceptions, much of this body of research has resisted parochialism. Scholars of Jewish sport history have generally not been interested in creating narrow, celebratory chronicles of Jewish sporting 'success' and have instead been driven by a desire to ascertain sport's impact on Jewish social, cultural, economic and political history – both in the Diaspora and in the Jewish homeland.[29] Through their work, greater light is being shed on the considerable effect that Jewish involvement in the sporting world has had on, amongst other things, Jewish integration, identity, religion, gender and nationalism, and on anti-Semitism. In a variety of different environments, physical recreation has been shown to directly affect what it has meant to be Jewish, and what being Jewish means in the eyes of the Gentile community.

Sport and British Jewry represents the first comprehensive attempt to explore this idea in a British context and is the first sustained analysis of the importance of sport in British Jewish history. It goes without saying that the aim of this book is not to provide a celebratory listing or compilation of British Jewish sporting achievement. Similarly, although this examination will go some way towards undermining pre-existing stereotypes surrounding the Jewish community, this is not its central objective. It is much more deeply concerned with ascertaining the impact of sport on processes and debates internal to British Jewry. The volume as a whole, and several of the case studies contained within, will also examine how physical recreation formed and shaped relations – both positive and negative – with the wider non-Jewish community. In short, it is focused on the effect that sport had on British Jews, rather than the impact that Jews had on British sport.

In order to examine the extent of this 'effect', the volume focuses on Jewish interactions with British sport during the period between 1890 and 1970. This is significant for two reasons. Firstly, this eighty year span covers one of the most important periods in the social and cultural history of British Jewry. During the 1890s, Jewish immigration to Britain from Eastern Europe considerably altered the size and social, religious, economic and political character of the community. Up to the 1960s, British Jewish life underwent significant changes as these and subsequent immigrants (such as Central European refugee Jews in the 1930s), together with their children and grandchildren, adapted to and influenced the wider environment. Important general transformations to the ways that Jews viewed themselves, and were perceived by non-Jews, occurred in this time period, which also saw significant social and geographic mobility within the British Jewish community. The book's focus ends in 1970, the end of a decade where British Jewry's integration and secularisation, as well as its decreasing size, were becoming ever more apparent. This was also an era when the Jewish community's status as the most significant minority in Britain (apart from the Irish) ceased due to immigration from the 'New Commonwealth'.[30]

Secondly, this era is also significant in that it represents the zenith of Jewish involvement and interest in British sport. Before the 1890s, as previously demonstrated, there was some involvement from British Jews in sports at the high and low ends of the social and sporting spectrums. Between this decade and the 1960s, however, Jews were much more deeply involved and visible in an assortment of different sporting milieus. As well as participating in a variety of physical recreations at both an elite and amateur level, British Jews also became highly visible in sport in an indirect sense also – as businessmen, administrators and, significantly, sports spectators. Reflecting the situation in the United States, from the late 1960s onwards it is apparent that British Jews have become less directly involved in elite and professional sport.[31] In stark comparison to the period from 1890 to 1970, during the last forty years Jews have virtually disappeared from the highest echelons of professional sport in Britain. In recent years, Jews have been much more likely to be seen in a 'recreational' sporting environment, in the ranks of spectators or in the boardroom of various sporting clubs.[32]

This book is primarily concerned with examining the links between the social and sporting history of the Jewish community during this time. It will highlight and analyse a number of instances where sport has directly impacted on the Jewish community and affected integration, ethnicity and exclusion – the three major themes of this examination. It does not aim to offer a comprehensive coverage of all sports that Jews have been involved or interested in, nor does it purport to examine every British Jewish sportsman or woman who has achieved success at the elite level. What it does do though is examine some of the most significant examples of where sport has altered the way in which British Jews have thought about themselves, or where sport has influenced interactions between the Jewish and Gentile worlds. As will become clear, Jewish involvement in physical recreation was more than just a marginal phenomenon within British Jewish history. In reality, sport had both a notable and noticeable effect on the history of the community between 1890 and 1970 – not least in terms of acculturation, identity formation/erosion and racial discrimination.

Chapter 1 is mainly concerned with examining how physical recreation became intertwined with immigrant 'Anglicisation' during the period between 1890 and 1940. In particular, this chapter deals with efforts to hasten the integration of Eastern

European Jewish migrants who arrived in Britain during the late nineteenth and early twentieth century. As well as demonstrating that physical recreation was seen by the Jewish establishment as a way of facilitating the Anglicisation of immigrant children, the chapter will also show how competitive sport was used to undermine wider notions of immigrant Jewish social and cultural 'aloofness'. The case study of Harold Abrahams, the famous English Jewish sprinter, will reveal that sporting achievement acted as a catalyst for integration. Participation and interest in sport aided immigrant acculturation and helped in the formation of 'English Jewish' characters, mentalities and physiques.

Chapter 2 examines the intricate relationship between sporting participation and the formation and erosion of Jewish identity. It will demonstrate that both direct and indirect involvement in sport between the early twentieth century and the 1960s exacerbated a 'drift' – a diminishing concern for religious observance, Jewish identity and culture and familial and communal authority – amongst sections of the population. The chapter will show how sport impacted negatively on adherence and attitudes towards the Jewish Sabbath. It will also illustrate that professional boxing came to both catalyse and symbolise the growing detachment of second and third generation Jewish immigrants from the culture, religion, authority and expectations of their elders. This chapter will also demonstrate how attempts by Zionist sporting organisations to 're-engage' Jews with their identity and heritage failed, mainly due to the popularity of sporting over 'cultural' activities. Sport was a powerful factor in decreasing the 'Jewishness' of immigrant children and grandchildren and in lessening concern for aspects of Jewish religion, community and ethnicity.

The third chapter will analyse the relationship between sport and British anti-Semitism. It will illustrate how physical recreation acted as both an arena for racism to develop *and* an environment in which a response to anti-Semitism could be formulated and delivered. Through an investigation of the sporting anti-Semitism of British Union of Fascist propaganda during the 1930s, we will see how sport became intertwined with long-standing ideological and stereo-typical notions of Jewish difference – mainly in an attempt to use Jewish sporting 'otherness' as a means of highlighting the 'Britishness' of right-wing ideology and political organisations. A case study of discrimination against Jews in the world of golf will show how social anti-Semitism directed towards the growing Jewish middle classes extended into this often socially 'exclusive' British sport. Finally, this chapter will highlight that sport has acted as a milieu in which Jews could pro-actively respond, in a generally assertive fashion, to the exclusion and stereotyping of Jews. In this sense, sport reflects trends amongst the wider Jewish working class for a more self-assured attitude towards self-defence. In many ways, as this chapter will show, sport strengthened, demonstrated and undermined notions and expressions of anti-Semitic stereotypes and discrimination.

Overall, the book highlights that sport has had a significant impact on British Jewish life from the late nineteenth century through to the 1960s. Jewish involvement in sport is inextricably linked to Jewish integration, the development and erosion of religious and ethnic identity, as well as anti-Semitism over this period. In one sense, physical recreation can provide a useful lens through which to view and analyse these wider processes. Yet it is clear that participation and interest in physical recreation also had a discernible, direct effect on the history of the community as a whole and on the lives of many individuals. As will become clear, analysing Jewish participation and interest in sport deepens our knowledge of the links between sport and minority society, identity and culture, whilst also shedding new light on British Jewish history more generally.

Notes

1   Z. Cooper (ed.), *Living and Giving: The Jewish Contribution to Life in the UK, 1656–2006* (London, 2006). Jews were expelled from Britain by Edward I in 1290 due to various economic and popular anti-Semitic charges against the small Jewish community. They were eventually re-admitted by Oliver Cromwell in 1656, seemingly for religious reasons and economic and trade benefits. C. Roth, *A History of the Jews in England* (Oxford, 1964), chapter 4: 'The Expulsion, 1272–1290'; D. Katz, *The Jews in the History of England: 1485–1850* (Oxford, 1994), pp. 106–136.
2   Z. Cooper, 'Introduction', in Cooper, *Living and Giving*, p. 11.
3   S. Pollard, 'Sport', in Cooper, *Living and Giving*, pp. 61–63.
4   Ibid. p. 63.
5   E. Rosenberg, *From Shylock to Svengali: Jewish Stereotypes in English Fiction* (Stanford, 1960); B. Cheyette, *Constructions of the*

'Jew' in English Literature and Society: Racial Representations, 1875–1945 (Cambridge, 1993).

6   C. Dickens, Oliver Twist (London, 1837). Fagin, who is often referred to simply as 'the Jew', is described at various times during the text as 'shrivelled', 'repulsive' and like a 'loathsome reptile'.

7   Quoted in S. Smith, 'Sex, Leisure and Jewish Youth Clubs in Interwar London', Jewish Culture and History, 9, 1, 2007, p. 13. For a wider analysis of race and racism in the Mass Observation movement, see T. Kushner, We Europeans? Mass Observation, 'Race' and British Identity in the Twentieth Century (Aldershot, 2004).

8   P. Levine, Ellis Island to Ebbets Field: Sport and the American Jewish Experience (Oxford, 1992), p. 5.

9   S. Gilman, The Jew's Body (London, 1991), pp. 40–52.

10 J. Gurock, Judaism's Encounter with American Sports (Indianapolis, 2005), pp. 15–19.

11 F. Felsenstein, Anti-Semitic Stereotypes: A Paradigm of Otherness in English Popular Culture (Baltimore, 1999), pp. 229–230. For more on Mendoza, see R. Ungar, 'On Shylocks, Toms and Buck: Images of Minority Boxers in late Eighteenth and early Nineteenth Century Britain', in M. Berkowitz and R. Ungar (eds), Fighting Back? Jewish and Black Boxers in Britain (London, 2007), pp. 19–33; H. Ribalow, Fighter from Whitechapel: The Story of Daniel Mendoza (New York, 1962).

12 T. Endelman, Radical Assimilation in English Jewish History (Bloomington, 1990), pp. 74–75. The Rothschilds were also keen hunters, an activity which was particularly encouraged by Nathaniel Rothschild (1812–70) as it had 'aristocratic' and 'royal' connections. Davis has noted that the family's decision to locate themselves in the Vale of Aylesbury during the mid-nineteenth century was primarily designed to enable the family to combine their passion for hunting with an active business life in London. R. Davis, The English Rothschilds (London, 1983), pp. 92–93.

13 T. Endelman, The Jews of Georgian England: 1714–1830 (Philadelphia, 1979), p. 219.

14 Rubinstein has claimed that Jewish involvement in Georgian boxing was 'an important medium of upward social mobility for the down-trodden and also an excellent vehicle for gaining popular recognition and acceptance by these groups'. W. Rubinstein, A History of the Jews in the English Speaking World: Great Britain (London, 1996), pp. 70–71. Cecil Roth sees the success of Mendoza, Elias and others as an indicator of a wider Jewish move away from 'traditional trades' and occupations and claims that Jewish boxing success 'familiarised countless persons throughout the country with the actuality of the

Jew and convinced them that he could excel in other capacities than as pedlar and old-clothes man'. Roth, *A History of the Jews*, p. 244.

15 Endelman, *Radical Assimilation*, pp. 74–75.

16 M. Huggins, *Flat Racing and British Society, 1790–1914: A Social and Economic History* (London, 2000), pp. 62, 67.

17 The scholarly examinations of various aspects of this topic by academics such as Susan Tananbaum, Tony Collins, Michael Berkowitz and Ruti Ungar will be referred to in the main text. Importantly, there have been recent indications of growing non-academic interest in Jewish sport history in Britain since the late Victorian era. For instance, *Running with Fire: The Story of 'Chariots of Fire' Hero Harold Abrahams* (London, 2011), written by journalist Mark Ryan, has recently been published. Similarly, sports writer Anthony Clavane is currently working on a history of Jewish involvement in association football in Britain.

18 Rubinstein, *A History of the Jews*. Similarly, Todd Endelman only briefly discusses Jewish involvement in sport since the late nineteenth century in his two most recent major works on British Jewry See, for instance, Endelman, *Radical Assimilation*, pp. 174–175; T. Endelman, *The Jews of Britain: 1656 to 2000* (London and Berkeley, 2002), p. 175.

19 A. Julius, *Trials of the Diaspora* (Oxford, 2010), pp. 378–379.

20 L. Gartner, *The Jewish Immigrant in England, 1870–1914* (London, 2001), p. xx.

21 Race and immigration have received more attention from scholars concerned with British sports sociology, although historical aspects of the relationship between race, immigration and sport are largely overlooked, and the Jewish sporting experience is almost completely absent. E. Cashmore's pioneering *Black Sportsmen* (London, 1982), for instance, looked at the reasons for black involvement in sport and investigated personal experiences of racism by various black sportsmen. Cashmore also concluded that sport was an important avenue for social mobility for black youths. See also P. Ismond's *Black and Asian Athletes in British Sport and Society: A Sporting Chance?* (Basingstoke, 2003); B. Carrington (ed.), *Race, Sport and British Society* (London, 2001); B. Carrington, *Race, Sport and Politics: The Sporting Black Diaspora* (London, 2010). A great deal of sociological research concerned with race and sport has focused on football. See, for instance, S. Johal and J. Bains, *Corner Flags and Corner Shops* (London, 1999); L. Back, T. Crabbe and J. Solomos, *The Changing Face of Football: Racism, Identity and Multiculture in the English Game* (Oxford, 2001) and D. Burdsey, *British Asians and Football: Culture, Identity, Exclusion* (London, 2007).

22   M. Cronin, 'Playing Games? The Serious Business of Sports History', *Journal of Contemporary History*, 38, 3, 2003, p. 499. Similar admissions have been made by leading academics interested in British sport history since the late 1980s. For instance, in 1988, Jones argued that 'we need to know more' about the 'particular role of ... ethnic minorities in sport' and highlighted the dearth of material linked to immigration and sport. S. Jones, *Sport, Politics and the Working Class: Organised Labour and Sport in Interwar Britain* (Manchester, 1988), p. 198. As recently as 2008, in his authoritative account of the history of British football, Taylor criticised the fact that 'race' had 'not made anything like the mark on British sports history as on the historical mainstream'. M. Taylor, *The Association Game: A History of British Football* (London, 2008), pp. 8–9.

23   R. Holt, *Sport and the British* (Oxford, 1989). Holt's work has sold over 14,000 copies, easily the most academically and popularly successful publication from within the field.

24   Ibid. pp. 275, 302–303, 351.

25   Levine, *Ellis Island*.

26   For instance, S. Riess (ed.), *Sports and the American Jew* (New York, 1998); Gurock, *Judaism's Encounter*; J. Kugelmass (ed.), *Jews, Sports and the Rites of Citizenship* (Chicago, 2007).

27   In Israel, see for instance, H. Harif and Y. Galily, 'Sport and Politics in Palestine, 1918–1948: Football as a Mirror Reflecting the Relations between Jews and Britons', *Soccer and Society*, 4, 1, 2003; H. Kaufman, 'Jewish Sports in the Diaspora, Yishuv and Israel: Between Nationalism and Politics', *Israel Studies*, 10, 2, 2005; H. Kaufman and M. Bar-Eli, 'Processes That Shaped Sport in Israel during the Twentieth Century', *Sport History Review*, 36, 2, 2005; A. Helman, 'Sport on the Sabbath: Controversy in 1920s and 1930s Jewish Palestine', *International Journal of the History of Sport*, 25, 1, 2008. For an indication of the body of research on Jewish/Israeli sport history published in Hebrew, see Kaufman, 'Jewish Sports', pp. 164–167. For Continental Europe, see M. Brenner and G. Reuvani (eds), *Emancipation Through Muscles: Jews and Sports in Europe* (London, 2006). For Australia, see A. Hughes, 'The Jewish Community', in P. Mosely (ed.), *Sporting Immigrants: Sport and Ethnicity in Australia* (Sydney, 1997), pp. 103–116; A. Hughes, 'Sport in the Australian Jewish Community', *Journal of Sport History*, 26, 2, 1999, pp. 376–391.

28   E. Mendelsohn (ed.), *Jews and the Sporting Life* (Oxford, 2008), p. viii.

29   It is the case that several 'commemorative' volumes of Jewish sporting 'stars' and 'achievements' have been produced by non-academics. The most well known publication of this kind is the oft-quoted B. Postal,

J. Silver and R. Silver (eds), *Encyclopaedia of Jews in Sport* (New York, 1965). More modern examples of 'celebratory tomes' of Jewish sporting achievement are R. Slater, *Great Jews in Sports* (New York, 2003); B.P. Robert Stephen Silverman, *The 100 Greatest Jews in Sports: Ranked According to Achievement* (New York, 2003); J. Siegman, *Jewish Sports Legends* (Washington, 2005).

30 P. Panayi, *An Immigration History of Britain: Multicultural Racism since 1800* (London, 2010), pp. 37–44. On the growing awareness of the integration and secularisation of the community, see S. Lipman and V. Lipman (eds), *Jewish Life in Britain: 1962–1977* (London, 1981).

31 In America, Levine has shown that the post-World War Two period has seen a rapid decline in Jewish participation in collegiate or professional sport. The modern era, however, has witnessed a rise in 'recreational sport' i.e. sport for leisure, amongst the Jewish community. Levine, *Ellis Island*, p. 237. See also, E.S. Shapiro, 'From Participant to Owner: The Role of Jews in Contemporary American Sports', in Mendelsohn, *Jews and the Sporting Life*.

32 Certainly, by the late 1960s and 1970s, Jewish participation in British sport was much more evident through indirect means, or for pure leisure purposes, rather than in an elite or competitive sporting respect. This is particularly evident in professional boxing. By the late 1950s, British Jewish boxers had virtually disappeared from the national and international scene, yet remained prominent as trainers, managers and promoters well into the 1980s. See S. Shipley, 'Boxing', in T. Mason (ed.), *Sport in Britain: A Social History* (Cambridge, 1989), pp. 102–104. In football, the first Jewish club directors and chairmen began to appear during the 1950s, beginning a long trend for British Jewish involvement in the business side of the 'beautiful game'. Harry Zussman, who had earned his fortune as a shoe manufacturer, became Leyton Orient Chairman in 1947, commencing a long Jewish association with the administration of the London club. Likewise, Leeds United had a string of Jewish directors and chairmen during the 1960s, 1970s and 1980s, including Albert Morris, Manny Cussins, the furniture magnate, and Leslie Silver. See A. Clavane, *The Promised Land: The Re-Invention of Leeds United* (London, 2010). Both Tottenham Hotspur and Arsenal have had considerable Jewish representation on their boards since the late 1980s. *Jewish Chronicle*, 1 May 1972, 26 May 1972, 17 May 1991. Jews have also been prominent in the national and international administration of table tennis and athletics. See: J. Riordan, 'The Hon. Ivor Montagu (1904–1984): Founding Father of Table-Tennis', *Sport in History*, 28, 3, 2008, pp. 512–531; W. Vamplew, 'Gold, Sir Arthur Abraham (1917–2002)', *Oxford Dictionary of National Biography* (Oxford, 2009); *Observer*, 28 May 2002.

1

Integration and Anglicisation

Introduction

British Jewish society, culture and history have been shaped and characterised by immigration. Since re-admission in 1656, Britain has seen successive waves of Jewish immigration from many parts of the world – influxes that, in various ways and to differing extents, transformed the size and nature of the Jewish population of the country. Immediately after re-admission, a small number of Sephardic Jewish merchants and traders hailing primarily from Iberia and the Netherlands came to Britain. Lipman has estimated that between 1700 and 1815, this Sephardic community was joined in Britain by a significant number (around 14,000–16,000) of Ashkenazi Jews originating from Central Europe. This figure may have reached 18,000 by 1830.[1]

The most significant waves of Jewish migration to Britain occurred between the late nineteenth century and the Second World War. Although small numbers of Russian and Eastern European Jews came to Britain during the 1860s and 1870s, the vast bulk of this immigration occurred between 1880 and 1914, in response to repression and economic hardship in Tsarist Russia.[2] Although the 1905 Aliens Act was introduced to kerb the migration of so-called 'undesirable' Jews, this immigrant wave only effectively ended with the opening of hostilities in the Great War. Estimates vary, but it is thought that approximately 120,000–150,000 Jews permanently settled in Britain during this time. This migrant population dwarfed the existing Jewish community within Britain, but paled in comparison to the millions of Jews who made their way to the USA.[3]

In the twentieth century, large numbers of Central European Jewish refugees (including many unaccompanied children on the

Kindertransport scheme) were allowed into Britain during the 1930s on temporary visas to escape growing Nazi repression. This movement was only made possible with the agreement of the British Government to relax tight immigration restrictions introduced in 1919–20 in return for a pledge from leaders of the established British Jewish community that newcomers would not become a charge on the public purse. Historians have estimated that around 50,000–70,000 arrived in Britain in the decade leading up to war, mainly in the period after *Kristallnacht* in November 1938, although many re-emigrated to America and to Palestine after the cessation of hostilities.[4]

Within scholarship concerned with British Jewish history, there have been many debates about the nature of the reception and integration of these immigrants and refugees. Some historians of British Jewry writing in the 'Whig' vein claim that Jewish migrants generally enjoyed a smooth and trouble free acculturation into British society. For these scholars, Britain was an open, accepting and tolerant new home.[5] Jewish historians writing in the 'New' school since the 1980s, however, reject much of what they feel has been an overly positive 'reading of Anglo-Jewish history'. The vast majority of New school scholars have sought to question previous examinations of the nature of migrant integration and produce what they feel is a more accurate picture of the relations between migrants and wider society, and migrants and established Jews.[6]

One key area of focus for the New school has been the immigration to Britain of Russian and Eastern European Jews during the late nineteenth and early twentieth century.[7] Recent scholarship has highlighted the significant role that popular and political anti-Semitism played in shaping British Jewish communal responses to immigration and processes of immigrant integration. In contrast to Whig notions of tolerance and liberalism, New school academics such as Todd Endelman and Lloyd Gartner have shown that, in the face of growing Gentile anxiety over the 'influx' of alien Jews, members of the established community sought ways of promoting and hastening immigrant acculturation in order to protect their own position.[8]

Such programmes and policies are not just evident during the period of Russian and Eastern European Jewish migration to Britain.[9] However, in terms of 'Anglicisation' – a phrase used to describe immigrant assimilation and integration – the most comprehensive research concerns the Eastern European Jewish 'influx'. From the late nineteenth century through to the effective cessation of migration in 1914, Sephardic and Ashkenazi communal and religious elites deliberately tried to hasten immigrant integration through philanthropic and communal initiatives. Within the literature concerned with this part of British Jewish history, there are a number of contrasting historiographical viewpoints.[10] There is, however, some consensus that processes of Anglicisation generally involved some forethought and planning in order to promote the integration and acculturation of migrant Jews. There now exists a broad literature on the period of Russo-Jewish immigration to Britain and much work has been carried out on Anglicising initiatives in communal philanthropy, charity and education and within the youth club environment.[11]

Despite this, little has been written about one of the most significant avenues in which notions of 'Britishness' were imparted to the immigrant groups – sport and physical recreation. This is in contrast to America, where scholars have shown that physical recreation played a pivotal role in the 'Americanisation' of Russo-Jewish immigrants during the late nineteenth and early twentieth century. Levine has highlighted that German Jewish communal elites, determined to minimise the impact of immigration on their own place in American society, used 'organised sport and physical recreation' to 'mitigate the shock of assimilation while furthering the enterprise'.[12] Gurock has similarly demonstrated that, whilst opinion amongst spiritual leaders over the 'Jewishness' and religious suitability of sport was divided, a consensus existed that 'athleticism' and 'physicality' were key American traits that could be imbued in the new arrivals by programmes of organised and supervised sport.[13]

In Britain, some research on the role of physical leisure on processes of Anglicisation has been conducted, yet the direct attention given to sport has often been relatively small.[14] Tananbaum has shown that sport was one tool used by Jewish elites, through the medium of Jewish youth clubs, to aid processes of Anglicisation. She highlights that organised games instilled ideas of Englishness, respectability, rational recreation and moral and cultural improvement into 'foreign' Jewish children.[15] Likewise, Smith has claimed that Jewish clubs 'sought to inculcate English ways into the immigrants, principally through the medium of sport and exercise', whereas Collins has noted that 'sports and ideals of "sportsmanship" – the most English of value systems – were seen as vital components of this crusade to Anglicise the newcomers'.[16]

This chapter will begin to redress this balance by looking at the relationship between sport and Jewish integration in the late nineteenth to early twentieth century. Sport was central to initiatives and organisations – such as the Jewish boys' and girls' clubs created before the First World War – that were founded during this time period to aid the Anglicisation of Jews of immigrant origin. It was also the case – as will be demonstrated with the analysis of the life and career of Harold Abrahams – that sport and integration became interlinked in the lives of individual Jews with no connection to such programmes or institutions. An examination of sport's links to the integration of second generation children, therefore, can provide evidence that Anglicisation was neither inevitable nor driven by social control motivations. Rather, acculturation could be much more selective and haphazard than previously demonstrated, with a middle-class British sporting spirit being assimilated in order to facilitate integration and social mobility.

Key to this chapter is the contention that sport and physical recreation played a prominent role in the Anglicisation of Jews descending from migrants from Eastern Europe. By becoming interested in sport, and by subscribing to notions of sportsmanship, fair play and teamwork, the youngest section of the immigrant community moved closer to the culture and identity of the indigenous population. Through a variety of sporting channels and opportunities, alien Jews, hailing from a culture without a comparable sporting tradition, became more English in their appearance, thought and actions.

Anglicisation through sport: the Jewish youth movement, 1895–1914

From the 1880s through to 1914, immigration transformed British Jewry. During that period, the existing community was joined in Britain by a sizeable population of Russian and Eastern European Jewish migrants. In response to being 'swamped' by a largely working-class, Yiddish-speaking Jewish migrant community, and following an accompanying rise in political and popular anxiety over the effects of the immigration, the Jewish establishment sought ways to catalyse the migrants' integration into British society. When the focus eventually switched to the foreign- and British-born children of the migrants, efforts were expended to help Anglicise them in speech, manner, dress and mores. However, a considerable emphasis was also placed on using sport as an aid to integration. Physical recreation was promoted amongst the alien children as a means of imbuing key notions of Englishness and indigenous culture, character and identity.[17]

The main vehicle for this aspect of the Anglicisation process was the Jewish youth movement. This comprised of the Jewish Lads' Brigade, formed in 1895, and – more importantly in terms of sport – various Jewish working lads' and girls' clubs, founded in the period from the late 1880s through to 1914. These organisations catered for young Jewish boys and girls in their leisure time, outside of school or work, and were created with the aid, financial assistance and leadership of Anglicised English Jews and religious and communal leaders. The clubs provided recreation within a supervised, managed environment. Within this milieu, especially within the various lads' clubs, sport soon came to dominate. Whilst an increasing emphasis was placed by club leaders and managers on the benefits of promoting sporting participation, sporting ideology and rhetoric was principally used to transform and shape the alien children into 'sporting' young Englishmen of the Jewish religion.[18]

Whilst contemporary non-Jewish youth organisations also displayed a similar interest in the physical and psychological 'use' of sport, Jewish clubs faced added pressures due to the perceived wider need to speed up the Anglicisation process.[19] Although Jewish organisations were aware of wider social and cultural concerns, sport was promoted within the Jewish youth movement primarily for reasons dictated by the British Jewish elites. Communal and religious leaders believed that sport could provide 'rational recreation' for young Jews apparently prone to loafing and idleness, improve the physique of 'weak' immigrant children and imbue English ideals of fair play, pluck, manliness and team spirit. Many also feared that the lack of interest in games exhibited by the alien children emphasised their foreignness in a society which attached cultural and social value to sporting pastimes. Sport, in effect, could act as a social panacea, addressing many of the objectives of the Anglicisation process by catalysing the assimilation, integration and acceptance of foreign Jewish children into mainstream society.[20]

Sport within the Jewish youth movement came to be regarded as much more than just a simple leisure activity. Whilst it was viewed as a weapon against the moral and physical degeneration seemingly facing the wider population, it was also utilised by the Jewish elites for their specific aims of aiding the assimilation and acculturation of the Jewish immigrant community. Through sport, physically 'weak' and mentally 'foreign' children would be exposed to public school notions of 'athleticism' and social deference and would be trans- formed into sporting Englishmen. Via the medium of physical pastimes such as football, cricket, boxing and athletics, the young Jews from an alien land and an alien culture would be assimilated and Anglicised.

Immigration and the Anglicisation campaign

Between 1880 and 1914, up to three million Jews emigrated westwards from the Russian Empire and Eastern Europe to avoid severe economic hardship and growing popular and political persecution. Whilst the vast majority made their way to America, a small number – estimated to be between 120,000 and 150,000 – settled in Britain, choosing to reside mainly in London (mostly within the East End), Glasgow, Manchester, Liverpool, Leeds and Birmingham.[21] This largely working-class, Yiddish-speaking immi- grant community joined in Britain an Anglicised, Jewish population; a community which was 'overwhelmingly English in manners, speech, dress, deportment and habit of thoughts and taste'.[22] These Jews – hailing mainly from the eighteenth- and nineteenth-century Sephardic and Ashkenazi immigration waves – numbered around 60,000 in 1881. They had enjoyed relatively rapid social mobility, developed a strong communal and religious infrastructure and had worked successfully to see a number of formal and informal barriers to Jewish participation in law, politics and local Government removed or revoked.[23]

Whilst this Anglicised, established community sympathised with the plight of their foreign 'brethren', over time relations between the old and new communities became increasingly strained. This was due mainly to the fact that Eastern European Jewish immigration was viewed in Gentile quarters as a factor in contemporary social and economic problems. In the face of accusations that the Jewish 'aliens' were exacerbating overcrowding, destitution, unemploy- ment, rent levels and crime in the inner city, British Jewish elites become increasingly convinced that their own status and well-being would be 'threatened' if immigration continued unabated. To this end, a number of repatriation and re-emigration initiatives were commenced during the mid-1880s.[24]

Despite these schemes, little could be done to stem the steady flow of migrants arriving during the 1890s and 1900s. Importantly, although immigration was linked to larger social and economic problems by a growing 'anti-alien' lobby, the new arrivals also had a more direct, localised effect on Gentile perceptions. They often proved 'quite noticeable as an alien feature' in the limited number of urban areas in which they chose to settle. Kadish has claimed that the popular nineteenth-century representation of the 'well heeled acculturated [Jewish] banker or broker' was replaced, almost overnight, with the image of the 'sweatshop worker, talking loudly in Yiddish and practicing exotic religious rituals'.[25]

Awareness of the social 'problem' of immigration quickly grew amongst the Jewish establishment. In August 1891, the *Jewish Chronicle* noted its concern about the potentially negative effect that the 'foreignness' of the immigrants could have on the community as a whole: 'As long as there is a section of Jews in England who proclaim themselves aliens by their mode of life, by their very looks, by every word they utter, so will the entire community be an object of distrust to Englishmen'.[26] This article, a symbolic shift in direction for the established community, signalled the start of a period in which the focus turned to those immigrants residing in Britain permanently to find ways in which their Anglicisation could be aided. In the early 1890s, a network of charitable and philanthropic organisations focused their efforts on pro-actively aiding the immigrant's smooth integration and their assimilation of the basic tenets of the British lifestyle and culture. These groups hoped 'to guide and discipline the immigrants to erase the most unacceptable aspects of their difference' and help nullify increasing Gentile concerns about the growing 'Alien population'.[27]

Attention quickly changed to the foreign- and British-born children of the migrants. This was mainly because 'they were considered more malleable than their parents' who, the established community believed, 'clung stubbornly ... to old-world habits and attitudes'.[28] The realisation that the focus of the Anglicisation drive needed to switch to the younger Jewish refugees is best evidenced by an article published in the *Jewish Chronicle* on 3 February 1893. This demonstrated the increasing belief that 'in ten or fifteen years,

the children of the refugees today will be men and women consti-
tuting, in point of numbers, the great bulk of the Jews of England.
They will drag down, submerge or disgrace our community if we
leave them in their present state of neglect'.

In the first instance, the Jewish authorities placed great hope in
the education system to carry out the Anglicisation of migrant
children.[29] Through attendance at either Board or Jewish day
school, Jewish migrant children would be exposed to the English
language, lifestyle and customs and would be instructed 'in the ways
of English and Anglo-Jewish society'.[30] Within the school environment, young foreign Jews would learn about cleanliness and
manners and, within Jewish 'Day' schools in particular, be subjected
to intense Anglicising pressure by Jewish teachers, administrators
and benefactors.[31]

Outside of school, the pressure on migrant children to become
Anglicised was also evident within a number of Jewish youth organisations. Although optimistic that the schooling system would be the
main vehicle for encouraging acculturation amongst alien children,
the Jewish elites were also keen to make sure that efforts in that
sphere were not undone once children left school and entered work.
To this end, the Jewish elites founded a number of recreational
organisations aimed specifically at catering for young Jews in their
leisure time to continue the process of Anglicisation into their
adolescence. In 1895, the Jewish Lads' Brigade was created, with an
inaugural meeting held in the hall of the Jews' Free School. The
founder, a Jewish career officer in the British army, Colonel Albert
Goldsmid (1846–1904), wanted to create a quasi-military youth
organisation along the lines of the Church Lads' Brigade, but with
the specific aim of helping to turn 'working-class and foreign youth
into fit and respectable Englishmen of the Mosaic Persuasion'. By
using military-style drills and similar activities, and by exposing
Jewish immigrant children to Anglicised middle-class Jewish leaders
and volunteers, Goldsmid hoped the Brigade would act as a
'mediator' between Jewish and Gentile life and aid the 'foreign'
children's integration. By 1909, the Brigade had grown to 4,000
members with companies across London and all the main Jewish
provincial communities.[32]

Similar intentions also led to the creation of a number of Jewish
youth clubs across London and Manchester from the late 1880s
through to the First World War.[33] These organisations were

extremely successful at drawing immigrant children through their doors. This is demonstrated by statistics from the Chief Rabbi's office in 1914 which showed that the twelve boys' clubs in London alone had a total membership of 2,750, just under half of all 14–18-year-old Jewish males then living in the capital.[34] This was all, as Feldman has noted, 'an impressive amount of activity', given that a large number of Jewish boys entered occupations with long hours that made attendance at these clubs almost impossible.[35]

All of these clubs were established with the aid, assistance and drive of the Jewish elites. It was common for Jewish youth clubs to be founded and supported by families and individuals at the highest echelons of British Jewish society. The first clubs to open were for Jewish girls, as the community felt they needed protection and guidance more urgently than their male counterparts who were likely to be at elementary school, religious school or work. The Jewish Girls' Club was founded in 1886 on Leman Street, Whitechapel by Lady Magnus and was followed ten years later by the West Central Jewish Girl's Club, founded in Bloomsbury in January 1896 by Lily Montagu.[36] With the aid of Lady Sassoon, the Butler Street Jewish Girls' Club opened its doors in 1902.[37]

The British Jewish establishment also played a pivotal role in the formation of various clubs for Jewish working boys. Take, for instance, the Brady Street Club for Working Boys, founded in 1896 in an old vicarage in Durward Street, Whitechapel by Lord and Lady Rothschild. Similarly, the West Central Jewish Working Lads' Club, which was established in West London in 1898, was founded with monetary assistance from the Montefiore and Mocatta families.[38] Significantly, all of the Jewish clubs were run on a day-to-day basis by middle-class, largely public-schooled, English Jewish workers and volunteers. Many had been actively sought by the club's patrons to serve in these establishments to act as examples of successful integration and social mobility to the young membership. The Victoria Jewish Lads' Club, founded on Fordham Street, Whitechapel, in 1901, was one Jewish club which even went as far as establishing formal links with Jewish public school students by welcoming volunteers from Clifton College in Bristol.[39]

This can be seen as part of the wider trend in late Victorian society for privileged public school and university graduates to 'go down' to deprived areas and engage in social work with the working classes. Yet, other similarities can also be highlighted between the philanthropic endeavours of Jewish and non-Jewish society.[40] Within wider society at this time there was also a growing concern over the problem of 'adolescence', and Jewish youth organisations shared Gentile anxieties over the need for 'rational recreation' to prevent young adults from loafing about the streets and becoming rebellious and wayward. In the Jewish youth movement, however, the 'need' to provide supervised leisure was inherently connected to Anglicisation, as there was a significant concern that the danger of unregulated leisure amongst Jewish immigrant children would hamper the integration process. In effect, Jewish clubs 'tried to offer boys and girls a friendly alternative to the streets where it was thought that mischief and idleness ruined their characters'.[41]

The clubs were seen to be a form of 'social prophylaxis'. By providing rational recreation and character-building facilities and activities, such as libraries, debating societies and lecture groups, it was believed that the clubs would prevent impressionable young Jews from indulging in lives of crime or vice or unsuitable pastimes such as smoking, drinking and gambling.[42] This desire to keep Jews off the streets, and away from the potentially sceptical gaze of Gentile onlookers, was evident in the early reports of all the Jewish clubs. The first annual report of the Brady Street Club, for instance, claimed it was founded to supply the 'pressing want' for suitable leisure facilities amongst Jewish youths whose 'leisure hours were spent in aimless loafing about the streets, or occasional visits to low places of entertainment'. Similarly, in the Manchester Jewish community, lay and religious leaders' concerns over the need for rational recreation led to the establishment of the Grove House Jewish Lads' Club in 1907 to steer children 'away from militant politics and from pastimes, especially gambling, which might bring the community into disrepute'.[43]

Evidently, these organisations saw themselves as 'important vehicles for Anglicisation'.[44] As well as aiding integration of immigrant children through 'rational recreation' and exposing them to the influences of socially mobile English Jewish managers and volunteers, the clubs also believed they could play a more direct role in helping the assimilation of young Jews through sport and physical recreation. Whilst positive leisure activities like reading, debating, singing and attending lectures were all significant in their own right, the most considerable emphasis of these clubs' work was placed on providing sport to shape the physical and psychological character of the alien children. Through sport, the Anglicisation process would be catalysed and strengthened and young foreign- and British-born Jews turned into 'sportsmanlike' Englishmen and women.

'Ironing out the ghetto bend': physical aspects of sporting Anglicisation

The first suggestion of the potential usefulness of sport with regards to Anglicisation appeared in the Jewish day school movement during the mid-1890s. In 1896, the headmaster of the Stepney Jewish School, William Ashe Payne, introduced a weekly programme of sports and gymnastics into his school's curriculum. He felt that planned and supervised physical recreation efficiently and effectively 'rounded out the integration of immigrant youth into English society' by turning 'weakly and pale-faced' immigrant Jews into strong Englishmen. Ashe Payne declared his mission was to 'produce Jews who, while devoted to English sports, would be none the less devoted to their ancestral faith'.[45]

Ashe Payne's introduction of sport and gymnastics into his school's timetable was somewhat revolutionary. Up until 1906, sport was not officially recognised as part of elementary education and most physical training in schools was limited to basic and repet- itive forms of drill.[46] Whilst his ideas concerning regular sport were evidently original, Ashe Payne's promotion of sport to aid Anglicisation drew considerable communal support as well. A series of articles in the *Jewish Chronicle* in June 1896 praised the 'attention given to the physical development of his pupils' and the efforts put into the Stepney School sporting programme.[47] As Black has noted, within a short space of time, 'his [Ashe Payne's] advocacy of broad programmes in athletic and physical education reverber- ated throughout Jewish voluntary schools'. The direct result was twofold; firstly, principals and headmasters with 'strong athletic credentials' like Ashe Payne were actively sought by Jewish-run schools in order to fill vacant posts. Secondly, and as a result of these appointments, the vast majority of Jewish schools began to incorporate gymnastics, athletics and, later, cricket and football into their curriculum.[48]

In a similar manner to the Jewish voluntary schools, the Jewish Lads' Brigade also utilised sporting activities to help aid the physical

Anglicisation of immigrants. From its inception, the JLB was focused on altering the physical characteristics of immigrant Jewish children, as demonstrated by Colonel Goldsmid's famous declaration that the Brigade would work to 'iron out the Ghetto bend' within its membership. Similarly, in 1902, assistant Brigade Commandant, Cecil Sebag-Montefiore noted in the *Jewish Chronicle* that one of the Brigade's main aims was to 'improve the physique and consequently the health of our boys'.[49]

Sporting activities were evident within the Brigade from its earliest days. Whilst the main emphasis remained firmly on drill, marching and gym training, traditional sports were gradually introduced into the organisation's programme from 1896 onwards. For instance, at the London company's summer camps, held in Deal, Kent, sports and games could often take up considerable portions of the daily timetable. The original members' pocket book noted that sports 'were to be encouraged' within the Brigade, whilst the first annual report stated that 'the good effects of the drill are supplemented by those of athletic sports'. It went on to highlight that numerous Brigade sports' clubs were in the process of formation and that swimming and football, under strict supervision of officers, were becoming increasingly popular. Significantly, sport remained a prominent aspect of the Brigade's work well into the 1950s and 1960s.[50]

Whilst sport was supplementary within the JLB and Jewish schools, it was pivotal to the Anglicisation programme of the Jewish youth club movement. This was admitted as such by club leaders. In 1909, one club manager was interviewed by the *Jewish Chronicle* and noted that 'sport is the mainstay of our clubs' and is the 'backbone' of the Jewish boys' club movement.[51] Seemingly, as well as being the clubs' most important tool in its social work, sport was also the key means of attracting and keeping members. As Gartner has noted, 'athletic' activities were the youth clubs' 'staff of life', with sports being the main reason why boys joined and kept attending these establishments.[52] As was admitted in 1903 by the Stepney Jewish Lads' Club, sports teams and activities were effectively 'keeping the club from collapsing'.[53] Similarly, in the West Central Jewish Lads' Club annual reports there are several references to 'the attractions of cricket' playing a significant role in preventing the club from folding during the summer months.[54]

Sport, in one sense, could aid the 'social prophylaxis' function of the clubs. If boys were at these clubs playing in closely supervised and managed games and activities, then they would not be on the streets, loafing, smoking, gambling or drinking. The knowledge that attempts were being made to provide sport as an alternative to these less wholesome leisure pursuits pleased many within the community. As one visitor to the West Central Club noted in 1900, the club's sporting programme would aid the 'physical side' of the club's work and 'counteract the temptations' of street life and unacceptable amusements.[55]

The primary role for sport, however, was in aiding Anglicisation through helping the physical development of 'foreign' children. Physical recreation was consciously promoted within both the Jewish boys' and girls' club movements to improve their apparently poor physique and deportment. This would help individual Jews and would also combat the broader view espoused by some commentators that Jewish migration to Britain represented a threat to the nation's health and physical stock.[56] Although not everyone subscribed to the view that alien Jews were weak and replete with illness, the impression was widespread that migrants were physically different and could undermine British physical 'stock'.[57] Life in

1 The gymnastics teams of the West Central Jewish Working
Lads' Club, pictured c.1900

the *shtetl* (small towns and villages located within the Pale of Settlement), so some observers remarked, had apparently ravaged the physique and health of the average immigrant Jew. In 1901, for instance, Russell and Lewis claimed that Jewish immigrants were 'dirty, poverty stricken and degraded alike in morals and physique by the oppressive conditions of their Ghetto-life in Russia'.[58]

To address this problem, the British Jewish establishment supported the broad introduction of sport into the Jewish youth club movement. This would improve the physical fitness of Jewish children to a level comparable to their non-Jewish peers and help to alleviate general concerns surrounding the physique of the immigrant population. Sport would act as a remedy to any physical problems and help turn 'weak' migrant children into strong and fit Englishmen and women. On a visit to one Jewish club in October 1900, Chief Rabbi Herman Adler praised the sporting efforts of the Jewish youth movement and remarked that whilst 'Ghetto' life for many immigrant Jewish children had had the 'result that their statures had been stunted and their limbs bent ... with such gymnastic facilities as he saw around him, they could grow up manly men, manly in shape and form as well as in actions'.[59]

Sport was also important for Jews in a British environment as it would apparently help change the emphasis amongst them from the brain to the body. In 1906, during a speech to the Stepney Jewish Lads' Club prize-giving ceremony, Lady Battersea (Constance Rothschild) remarked that whilst she was 'ignorant of the games themselves' she was fully aware that sport helped imbue physical 'qualities which were so admired in the Anglo Saxon race and which had, for a certain time, been somewhat lacking in her own people'. She continued and noted that 'sedentary' town life in Russia and Eastern Europe for many immigrant Jews had meant that 'the brain had been cultivated at the expense of the other parts of the body'. For Lady Battersea and many others within the 'Jewish establishment', sport was key to redressing this balance.[60]

There was also a clear desire to promote sport to assuage growing concerns over the physical 'degeneration' connected to contemporary urban life. Amongst British society more generally, the late nineteenth and early twentieth century was a period of growing concern over the physical well-being of the nation. Many voiced their fears over the 'physical unfitness of the slum denizens' after military defeats in the Boer War helped promote the idea that the

urban, industrial environment was having a ruinous physical effect
on the working-class population. A government inquiry, convened
after the failed military campaign in South Africa, led to the publication of the 1904 Report of the Inter-Departmental Committee on
Physical Deterioration. This espoused compulsory school sport and
physical training to rectify physical problems evident in military
recruits and within the youngest sections of the general population.[61]

British Jewry's anxieties over the physical effects of 'slum life'
within the Jewish community must be seen within this context. Yet
their fears were more motivated by the potential effects of 'physical
worsening' on Jewish Anglicisation than by concerns of health,
well-being and physical efficiency within the wider population.
Jewish youth club leaders worried that Jewish deterioration and
weakness, due to their immediate surroundings in British cities,
would further emphasise their 'foreignness' against a backdrop of
increasing non-Jewish concern over fitness and well-being. To this
end, sport was viewed both as an important bulwark against the
potential physical degeneration resulting from Jewish inhabitation
of urban, industrial environments and as an aid to raise Jewish
children to a physical level comparable to that of their non-Jewish
peers. In 1900, the *Jewish World* bemoaned the fact that under
'present economic conditions' many within the immigrant
community were 'forced to crowd in the by-ways of the cities'
where the 'sunshine of manly sports and pastimes was shut out'.
The article went on to applaud the efforts of youth clubs such as the
West Central where, 'under proper guidance and training', Jewish
lads could play sports and games to 'fit themselves [sic] to take their
places as citizens, physically and mentally equipped for the battle of
life'.[62]

Sporting facilities and opportunities within the youth club environment were one way to ameliorate the negative effects of urban
life for Jewish migrants. As White has noted, the areas into which
most of the immigrant Jewish population moved, especially in the
East End of London, were 'starved of sporting facilities'. Public
amenities for sport, apart from swimming baths, were often in short
supply in early twentieth-century urban Britain.[63] The comprehensive sporting programmes offered by the youth clubs, therefore,
would fill this gap and act as an antidote to the physical effects of
city life of young immigrant Jews. The founder of the Oxford and St

George's Jewish Lads' Club, Basil Henriques (1890–1961), noted as much in 1955. In a speech concerning the motivation for opening the club in 1914, Henriques claimed that he wanted to provide a 'refuge from the appallingly overcrowded homes and hideous, monotonous slum streets' and 'give physical recreation to half-starved, poverty-stricken, underdeveloped boys and girls'.[64]

As Henriques noted, girls were also in the minds of Jewish youth club leaders when it came to sporting provision. Within the Jewish girls clubs, it was hoped that opportunities for athletic activities could help to improve the 'stunted' physique of the refugee females and assist in their integration into the wider community. During this period 'all [girls] clubs taught the importance of the healthy body as well as the alert mind and moral character' and drill, gymnastics and exercise to music were offered almost every evening.[65] At the 1906 annual meeting of the Butler Street Jewish Girl's Club, the Chairman, Rufus Isaacs KC, applauded the physical exercise programme of the club and noted his belief that 'recreation or education was of little real value unless combined with physical education. Physical training was essential to girls who lived and worked in that part of the world'.[66]

Some clubs took the mission to improve their members' physiques very seriously. The Victoria Club, for instance, employed its own doctor to look after members who were ill and to collate information on their physical condition. One examination of 150 club members during 1907 led to the conclusion that 'visitors to the club will be somewhat startled by how favourably Jewish lads of the same size and station ... contrast with their Christian brethren'. The equal in terms of 'physique' to non-Jewish children, the average Jewish member of the Victoria Club was adjudged to be 'much cleaner, better dressed, smarter, brighter and comparatively speaking, have an air of general well-being lamentably wanting in the members of some of the Christian clubs in the East End'.[67] In the eyes of non-Jewish commentators, this was definitive proof that the Victoria Club's aims for the 'physical improvement of their members' and for the 'transformation' of foreign Jews into Englishmen was being 'realised'. Seemingly, the policy of Anglicisation through sport and physical recreation was markedly successful.[68]

Similar evidence of the 'physical' achievements of the Jewish youth movement came to light in 1904. In that year, the

Government's report into 'Physical Deterioration' gave many indications that the work of Jewish schools and youth organisations had achieved notable successes with regard to the physiques and health of migrant children. Evidence from General Sir Frederick Maurice claimed that the 'Jewish child, although coming from extremely poor quarters and under very unsavoury conditions, is as a rule a stronger and healthier child than the Gentile'.[69] Inspections of Jewish pupils in schools in Leeds and London led to the conclusion that 'the headmaster and headmistress and teachers all agreed that they were of good physique [and] that they were of higher intelligence than our children'.[70]

The Jewish establishment took great delight in these findings. The *Jewish Chronicle*, for example, applauded the report and took pleasure from its comments that the average Jewish boy was 'physically … very much superior to the average British boys [sic]'. This was extremely important, it noted, considering the 'somewhat lurid accounts of the moral and physical degeneracy of other sections of the people'.[71] In seeking to explain the apparent disparity between the Jewish and non-Jewish child, the inquiry singled out the Jewish youth movement, particularly the Jewish Lads' Brigade, for special praise. When seen in conjunction with evidence from within the club movement, it is clear that the drive to physically Anglicise the alien child, a campaign which relied heavily on sport and physical recreation, had had a notable impact.[72]

Playing the game in the 'right' way: the psychological benefits of sport

As well as having important physical benefits, sport was also believed to be a useful psychological tool for Anglicising migrant children. If young Jews could be encouraged to play sport, they would not only develop strong and healthy bodies, but they would also learn a great deal about British attitudes towards fair play, sportsmanship and teamwork – qualities seemingly lacking in young Jews hailing from countries without developed sporting cultures and traditions. Effectively, whilst organised and supervised games could help alien children look and appear less 'foreign', they could also help them think and act like young Englishmen and women.[73]

In this respect, sport could once again be used to combat sentiments promoted by anti-alienists. Although many arguments against Russo-Jewish migration often focused on its supposedly negative physical effects, some commentators voiced their opinion that influxes of alien Jews could also undermine the British mentality. It was believed that 'foreign' Jews – with their strange and exotic language, attitudes, customs and lifestyles – would prove a distinctly 'alien' element in the areas in which they resided and undermine the 'Britishness' of those living closest to them. Not only did weak and sickly 'aliens' represent a threat to the nation's health, they also represented a 'threat to the character' of the country.[74]

Sport could be useful in promoting strong and healthy British bodies, but it could also act as a way of creating strong and healthy British minds. To achieve this, Jewish youth leaders drew inspiration from both the public schools and the muscular Christianity movement – both of which had stressed the usefulness of physical recreation in maintaining 'Mens Sano in Corpore Sano' (a healthy mind in a healthy body). This ideology, prevalent in British society from the mid-nineteenth century onwards, promoted the idea of physical recreation aiding overall individual development. Sport could not only prepare people physically to play the game of life successfully, but it could also equip them with the character and mental strength needed to become full and contributing citizens of both Britain and her Empire.[75]

Jewish youth club managers and workers, often drawn from the public-schooled middle classes, transferred this ideology into their clubs. As with much of the youth movement's work, in that environment this idea became intertwined with the over-arching need to promote the Anglicisation of immigrant children. At the same time that sport was encouraged as a means of 'social prophylaxis' and as a physical aid to integration, it was also viewed as an important tool in the strengthening of the immigrant Jew's character and as a means of Anglicising the mentality of the alien child. Through supervised and organised sport within the youth movement, Jews would develop the correct 'sporting' attitude and acquire a distinctly English character and mentality.[76]

One important hurdle to overcome, however, was that there initially seemed to be little interest in sport amongst the immigrant population. During the earliest period of the youth movement's work, Anglicised club leaders frequently claimed that Jews born abroad or into immigrant families were conspicuous for their indifference towards physical recreation. In the first annual report of the Brady Street Club, for instance, reference was made to the fact that 'a considerable proportion of the boys have an undoubted aversion to physical exercises in any form' and the report's author deplored the finding that 'a true sportsmanlike spirit ... is practically non-existent among East End Jewish lads'.[77]

That young, immigrant Jews exhibited little interest in sporting activities concerned youth leaders greatly. It was argued that a lack of 'sporting' attitude had severe implications for wider Anglicisation efforts. Indifference shown towards sport would only serve to emphasise the young Jews' 'foreignness' in a 'culture which ... always placed a premium on athletic achievement' and where sport was so closely linked to notions of English identity and culture.[78] A Board school headmaster testified to the 1903 Royal Commission on Alien Immigration that he felt one reason why Jewish boys were 'not comparing favourably' with their non-Jewish peers was that 'through no fault of their own they have not had the same privileges ... these children have not had the same advantages in learning cricket, swimming, football and pastimes of that sort'.[79]

Similar fears were evident amongst Jewish youth workers. In 1911, before he embarked upon his own career working with immigrant Jewish children, Basil Henriques noted his belief that 'there was something fundamentally lacking in the children of the foreign born refugees from Russia and Poland'. Henriques went on to observe he felt that immigrant children 'would never become Anglicised to the extent of ordinary British boys and girls because they had not had the opportunity for games as we know them here' and 'had no sporting instincts' like English children. Henriques and his fellow youth club managers felt that, without helping Jewish children to develop an interest in sport comparable to that of the non-Jewish population, immigrant Jewish children would 'remain temperamentally alien'.[80]

Indifference towards sporting activities was distinctly 'un-English', but was a problem which could be addressed through the medium of the youth movement. By encouraging young Jews to participate in the vast sporting programmes offered by the Jewish schools, Jewish Lads' Brigade and the Jewish youth clubs, and by actively seeking managers and volunteers with 'athletic credentials', a new 'sporting instinct' would be gradually created.[81] Indeed, in the period up to 1914, participation in club sports grew considerably within the Jewish movement, with interest often outstripping financial and manpower resources available.[82]

2 The football team of the Stepney Jewish Lads' Club, pictured in 1913

Whilst a growing interest in sport was gratifying, attention also focused on the mental benefits that sporting activities could offer. Although youth leaders clearly believed that sport could make immigrant Jews similar to the non-Jewish population in terms of both physique and leisure interests, it was also true that they believed strongly in the potential utility of sport to mould their members' characters. Through organised and supervised play, key notions of 'Englishness' could be inculcated into the young Jews and aid their psychological development into sportsmanlike, English Jews.[83]

The idea of utilising sporting participation to alter behavioural patterns and 'mould' character was first developed within the English public school system during the early to mid-nineteenth century. In these private educational establishments, sport was viewed as a weapon against disciplinary problems and as a means of shaping and forming character. As Mangan has noted, 'physical exercise' was viewed by public school educationalists as a 'highly effective means of inculcating valuable … educational goals'.

Through emphasising 'physical and moral courage, loyalty and co-operation, the capacity to act fairly and take defeat well, [and] the ability to both command and obey' on the sports pitch, 'a grand breed of men for the service of the British nation' was produced by the public schools with sportsmanship and fair play as their main moral characteristics.[84]

Upper- and middle-class Jews who 'went down' to urban areas carried with them a set of sporting and psychological values formulated in the public school environment. They, according to Bunt, 'believed with a great fervour' that the moral code they absorbed on the football and cricket pitches of the prestigious schools could be 'grafted onto the young Jews recently arrived from the Ghettoes of Europe' in order to aid their Anglicisation. Their 'determination to translate barely literate young Russian and Polish Jews into well-washed Anglo-Jewish sportsmen' led to a significant emphasis being placed on sporting participation, where notions of the public school formation of 'Englishness' could be transferred to young, impressionable members through supervised and managed play.[85]

The key ideals believed to be important in the creation of an 'English' mentality would be inculcated through sport in a strictly supervised milieu. If instructed and managed correctly, it was believed that young Jews would naturally absorb the moral and social lessons offered through sport and gain vital psychological benefits. For instance, two key aspects of Englishness that youth club leaders passionately advocated amongst members were 'fair play' and 'sportsmanship' – seen to be central tenets of middle- and upper-class social and national identity. To this end, club leaders often offered advice on the need for a sporting attitude and implored members to demonstrate 'true sportsmanship' when on the field of play. One article from the Brady Club magazine, *The Bradian*, in 1903, reminded members that 'the aim of everyone who plays a game of any kind, such as cricket or football, is to be known as a good player and a good sportsman'. The article, the essence of which was seen elsewhere within other Jewish youth clubs, continued by offering advice on conduct on the pitch and asked members to 'play the game' in order to 'derive great pleasure and physical benefits'.[86]

When club members appeared to be 'unsportsmanlike' in their conduct, they drew the disdain of managers and leaders and were subsequently admonished. In 1904, the *Stepney Jewish Club Chronicle* noted its disappointment over the behaviour of members during football matches against other clubs. Reports claimed that 'rough' play and poor sportsmanship, on the part of both players and spectators, not only was in breach of rules of 'sporting conduct' but did 'not say much for the boys as sportsmen'.[87] Conversely, however, when members displayed an exemplary attitude during sporting activities, managers were buoyed by the apparent progress being made in changing behavioural patterns. One entry into the logbook of the Victoria Jewish Lads' Club in July 1901 recorded an unsuccessful cricket match yet positively noted that 'the fielding was quite good, the bowling "ditto" ... batting still the weakest point, a lot of the hitting being very fluid. But the most satisfactory feature is the fact that the team seems to be able to play a losing game without getting discouraged'.[88]

Whilst the demonstration of an individual 'sporting' attitude was vitally important, Jewish club sports also worked to emphasise notions of deference to social superiors and respect for authority. Whereas, within the English public school system, complying with the will of the referee or the team captain was linked to ideas of class and the maintenance of social stability, in the Jewish youth movement this was not the case. As Kadish has noted with regard to the Jewish Lads' Brigade, English Jewish youth workers did not have an 'interest in perpetuating the English class system within the Jewish community', as they themselves had benefited significantly from social mobility.[89]

Instead, the idea of sporting respect for authority was linked to Anglicisation. It was hoped that respect for elders on the field of play would transfer into wider society, with Jewish immigrant children showing deference to authority and displaying the kind of behaviour expected of obedient English boys and girls. Complying with the will of the referee, umpire or captain was expected from young Jews during club sport, whilst disobedient and disorderly behaviour was deplored and held to be indicative of a 'foreign' mentality. In 1901, for instance, managers at the Victoria Club noted their concern at a 'disinclination to recognise the Captain's authority' during cricket matches and recorded their 'hope these failings will soon be conspicuous by their absence'. Likewise, one week later, another Victoria Club manager logged 'Very successful day at cricket ... the behaviour of the boys on the field was very good, but there is still a tendency not to accept the Umpire's decision as final'.[90]

It is important not to understate the significance that was attached to showing respect and deference on the sports field. Even before sporting sections were fully organised, some Jewish clubs felt the need to provide strict instructions and rules regarding the principle of 'authority' during sporting contests. The Notting Hill Jewish Lads' Club, founded in 1908, noted in the first issue of its club magazine in April 1911 that whilst 'it is rather early to talk about any details' regarding the newly established club cricket team, 'the new season presents a rather favourable opportunity for the giving of a few hints to players'. Members were advised, firstly, 'never argue with the Umpire, it will not make him alter his decision and it is unsportsmanlike', secondly, 'always go at once to whatever position in the field you are placed' and finally, 'Remember, the Captain's orders must be obeyed at once'. Evidently, playing the game was not enough for club managers keen to see both a sense of submission and a sense of duty from 'foreign' members towards their supposed superiors.[91]

Members often acknowledged the positive effects that the Jewish clubs' emphasis on sport had had on the development of their characters and as a means of social training. One West Central Jewish Lads' Club member later recalled that he felt his involvement in club sport had helped him mature mentally, as well as physically. He noted

> It [club sport] was really a training for citizenship. It sounds like a little thing, but if you lost a football match, you learned to say 'Well played' to your opponents and go on your way. No bitterness, no fighting and no arguments and that is hard for a pugnacious boy to do. However, we were told that was the way it had to be. If you lose, you lose. Someone is going to beat you. Those lessons were priceless.[92]

In the period immediately preceding the First World War, sport played a pivotal role in the acculturation of Jewish immigrant children. This was acknowledged as such by the Jewish clubs themselves. In February 1914, after completing fourteen years of service to the Jewish youth of the East End, the Stepney Jewish Lads' Club produced a booklet outlining what it saw as its major achievements. The publication made reference to the club's work in aiding the Anglicisation process and claimed that the 'object of the club is to develop its members morally, mentally and physically in order that, with wise direction, they may be able to make the best use of their powers and improve their position'.[93]

In the eyes of the booklet's authors, there was one aspect of the club's programme which had accounted for Stepney's successes more than any other: sport and physical recreation. On the one hand, a plethora of organised and supervised games helped to improve the 'physical condition of the working lad' and improved his 'character and moral welfare'. Yet because sport had been a positive use of his leisure time, the 'foreign' member had also become a much more responsible citizen. After proudly listing the sporting activities offered by the club, the booklet noted that 'In all these physical exercises the sturdy characteristics of the British race are inculcated into the lad of foreign extraction which ... is resulting in the production of a man capable of rising to almost any position that opportunity offers'.[94]

Clearly then, those leaders and managers involved in the running of the Stepney Jewish Lads' Club, as in similar institutions, believed that sport and physical recreation had had a positive Anglicising effect on foreign, immigrant children. Not only did the Jewish youth movement value sport as a vital means of filling young Jews' leisure time, but it also viewed physical recreation as an aid to the trans-formation of alien children into sporting young British Jews. Exercise taken, and lessons learnt, on the football or cricket pitch, in the gymnasium or boxing ring would prepare these children's bodies and minds for the integration process. In theory, this would ensure their future well-being and success in British society.

In the minds of the British Jewish community, sport was one tool available to them in their struggle to assimilate a 'foreign' immigrant population. This would prevent the deterioration of their own favourable position within English society and seemingly ensure the integration and acceptance of the migrants. Through sporting activities, administered, supervised and funded by the Jewish elites, British sporting values would be transferred to the 'foreign' Jews. By utilising ideologies emanating from the public school system, Anglicised Jewish youth workers hoped that key aspects of the immigrant children's 'difference' would be gradually erased.

What the case study of the Jewish youth movement's sporting programme also demonstrates, however, is that sport and physical recreation was viewed as much more than just a simple leisure activity. Games such as football and cricket were believed to be inextricably linked to notions of national and cultural identity and

there is much evidence to show that the British Jewish elites understood sport in a much deeper way than just simple 'play'. Physical
pastimes and recreations were consciously linked to concerns
arising out of the contemporary environment and promoted for
ends, other than simple leisure, specific to a particular minority
community. In essence, the significance attached to sport during the
Anglicisation process demonstrates the centrality of physical recreation both to a sense of 'Britishness' and to the formation of British
Jewish identities.

Competitive sport and immigrant integration, 1899–1939

A great deal of importance was attached to sport for acculturating
immigrant children, yet it was also the case that competitive play
more specifically was valued as an aid to integration. Whilst
teaching young Jews how to play the game and helping them enjoy
the various benefits of sport assumed a central position within the
youth movement, over time the need to expand opportunities for
competition developed. Competitive sport was viewed as an indirect
aid to Anglicisation and a tool to address wider social and cultural
concerns arising out of Jewish migration to Britain.[95]

In one sense, sporting competition *against* non-Jews was increasingly seen as a weapon against charges of immigrant 'aloofness' and
unsuitability for integration. By meeting non-Jews on the sports
field, in the gymnasium or in the boxing ring, Jewish immigrant
children could work to undermine ideas of Jewish isolation
prominent in the period of Eastern European immigration. Through
sport, especially in gymnastics and boxing, Jews also had the opportunity to change perceptions of the Jewish immigrant community
and demonstrate that they were physically suitable for acceptance
into the mainstream population.[96]

Great significance was also placed on encouraging competition
between Jews to aid integration. For various reasons – be it Sabbath
observance or the timetabling of sport within Board schools – Jews
often found it difficult to participate in competitions and tournaments organised by Gentile authorities. To minimise this problem,
efforts were made to maintain as 'equal' a standard of sporting
provision as possible – ensuring that Jews would not miss out on the
various benefits of regular, competitive play. The Jewish Athletic
Association, formed in 1899, played a pivotal role in this respect,

developing leagues, tournaments and sporting programmes for Jewish children and young adults. Through the JAA's work, sport continued to assist migrant acculturation.[97]

In both of these instances, competitive sport was seen to be another tool available to the Jewish elites in their quest for immigrant Anglicisation. Competitive sport was not promoted simply for leisure purposes, but for the clear social and cultural benefits it could also seemingly bring. The overriding mission was to use sport against other Jews or Gentiles to further demonstrate the 'Englishness' of the immigrant children and their suitability for integration into the mainstream society. Through competitive play, Jews could challenge some of the main critiques surrounding assimilation, show themselves as suitable material for British society and further the Anglicisation programme of the youth movement.

Undermining Jewish 'isolation'?

As we have seen, during the period of Russo-Jewish migration to Britain, 'anti-alienist' arguments were wide-ranging. Whilst some commentators focused on the negative effect of 'aliens' on Britain's physical and psychological well-being, others claimed that the migrant's presence was problematic due to their 'indifference' towards integration. From the late 1880s onwards, but especially in the years immediately preceding the 1905 Aliens Act, certain non-Jewish observers lamented the supposed 'isolation' of the newcomers from wider society. It was argued that racially, socially and culturally, the Eastern European and Russian Jews were indifferent towards the majority population and culture. In short, they allegedly represented a clear threat to the cohesion of the local and national identity and community.

Criticisms often focused on what some saw as the immigrants' inherent 'clannishness' and apathy towards the wider population. In 1887, for example, the St James' Gazette published an editorial that claimed that the immigrant newcomers 'never forget that they are Jews and that other people are Gentiles'. It argued that as 'long as they [Jews] may live among us, they will never become merged in the mass of the English population'.[98] The right-wing writer Arnold White was similarly convinced that the immigrant Jewish community lacked a desire to integrate. In his 1899 book, The Modern Jew, White claimed that the Russian and Eastern European Jews were 'a community proudly separate, racially distinct and existing preferentially aloof'.[99] In evidence given to the Royal Commission on Alien Immigration in 1903, the first stages of Government inquiries that led to immigration legislation in 1905, White reiterated his belief that Jewish immigrants 'belong to a race and cling to a community that prefers to remain aloof from the mainstream of our national life'.[100]

Such fears were also present in the highest echelons of the Edwardian political establishment. Many Conservative politicians of the time lamented the apparent isolation of the immigrant community and noted their anxiety over the potential impact of its continued 'detachment' from mainstream society. Indeed, the Conservative Prime Minister, Arthur Balfour, claimed during the committee stages of the Aliens Bill in 1905 that

> a state of things could easily be imagined in which it would not be on [sic] the advantage of the civilisation of the country that there should be an immense body of persons who, however patriotic, able and industrious, however much they threw themselves into national life, remained a people apart.[101]

Such criticisms presented the British Jewish establishment with a new problem surrounding Jewish migration. As well as Anglicising immigrants and helping them acculturate British values and traits, effort was also needed to encourage migrants to interact more, and participate more fully, with wider society. Importantly, however, many communal initiatives along these lines were misguided. During the early 1890s, for example, 'optimistic attempts' were made to try to disperse and redistribute the immigrant community; the idea being to force alien Jews to integrate more into the non-Jewish population.[102]

As with the wider Anglicisation campaign, the focus of the Jewish elites once again turned to the immigrant children. It was felt that their experiences could help to undermine the 'self-imposed alien-ation from English society' which supposedly existed amongst their parents and grandparents.[103] Once again, compulsory education would play a pivotal role in this process. In Board schools, Jewish children would mix in an educational and social environment with their non-Jewish peers – interaction and integration which would help lessen their isolation from wider society. Many contemporary observers applauded the efforts of schools in integrating immigrant children into their establishments. In 1901, novelist, historian and social investigator, Walter Besant (1836–1901) discussed the immigrant Jewish population and claimed 'as for their children, you may look for them in the board school, they have become English, both boys and girls ... [they] are English through and through'.[104] In 1902, one Board school headmaster in London's East End applauded the fact that 'Jewish boys soon become anglicised and cease to be foreigners'.[105]

Many Jewish philanthropists were keen for social interactions between Jew and non-Jew to continue after school.[106] It was hoped that the numerous youth clubs that they had helped to form would provide an environment for Jewish and Gentile children to mix, to play and to socialise together. Indeed, Lady Rothschild, the founder and patron of the Brady Street Club, initially wanted the organisation to be non-denominational.[107] Unfortunately for her and other club patrons, Gentile children generally chose to frequent their own clubs and youth organisations away from 'Jewish' areas within the capital. In the Brady Club's first report it was noted that 'at the present moment the Jewish element so largely preponderates that the Club may be looked upon as Jewish in all but name'.[108]

As with much of these clubs' Anglicising efforts, a great deal of emphasis was placed on sport and physical recreation. In this case, sport was seen as a means of encouraging 'association' and aiding the development of 'mutual' good feeling amongst Jewish and non-Jewish children. It was hoped that sporting contact with non-Jewish clubs would help to demonstrate the success of the Anglicisation campaign and highlight the desire of young Jews for integration and interaction with the wider community. Sports like cricket and football 'provided a medium through which gentile and Jewish children could come together' and help break down religious, cultural and social barriers between children of different ethnic backgrounds.[109]

During the earliest years of the club movement, efforts were made to organise regular sporting contests with non-Jewish teams. Both the Brady Street and West Central clubs, for instance, entered into regular contests against non-Jewish club and school teams in sports such as football, cricket, gymnastics and boxing – a fact proudly recorded in their annual reports.[110] Despite this, more regular contact with non-Jews in the sporting arena was sought and it was for this reason that several Jewish clubs based in the capital joined the London Federation of Working Boys' Clubs during the 1900s.[111]

Gaining membership of the Federation was viewed positively by club leaders as it meant access to a number of organised sporting leagues and tournaments throughout the year. As well as an important means of improving the quality of the sports teams within the Jewish youth club movement, participation in these events was also a useful way of improving contact between Jewish and non-Jewish children and changing perceptions of the Jewish community. In its 1902 annual report the Brady Street Club applauded 'the benefits derived from the affiliation of the club to the Federation' commenced in 1900. It highlighted that, as well as 'giving great stimulus' to club sport, in Federation events 'Jewish and non-Jewish working boys have been brought into contact with one another in friendly rivalry and friendly intercourse, and this has tended to do away with much racial prejudice'.[112]

Whilst competing against non-Jews encouraged 'association' between races, competitive sport also had other benefits for Anglicisation. Many club leaders saw opportunities for play against non-Jews as a chance to demonstrate, first-hand, that their members were as sporting, strong and fit as their Gentile peers – the idea being that Jews were, despite criticisms from certain quarters, suitable material for integration. Notions about competitive sport having a 'missionary' role are evident in the reports of the West Central Jewish Lads' Club. In 1902, the club claimed that their affiliation to the London Federation of Working Boys' Clubs 'has proved advantageous in many ways'. As well as helping club managers gain vital insights into the work and sporting programmes of non-Jewish clubs, membership of the Federation 'opened many competitions to members and has shown the members of non-Jewish clubs that our lads can hold their own in athletics and games and are not deficient in sportsmanlike feeling'.[113]

The wider community believed strongly in the 'missionary' effects of sport against non-Jewish peers. The Jewish establishment regularly applauded the efforts of Jewish clubs in Federation sports. In 1906, the *Jewish Chronicle* noted that Jewish successes in annual Federation events such as swimming, boxing and athletics were 'extremely gratifying' and showed the Jewish community in a positive light. Worryingly though, the editorial also noted an increasing tendency for non-Jewish clubs to 'hold aloof from contests' against Jews in certain sports due to 'repeated defeats'. The newspaper argued that 'the decline of these pleasant and friendly rivalries would be regrettable' because 'the competition between Jewish and Gentile lads creates a healthy spirit of camaraderie and good fellowship'.[114]

One sport in which non-Jews had suffered 'repeated defeats' at the hands of young Jews was gymnastics. As with the contemporary non-Jewish youth movement, gym training and competition grew in popularity amongst the Jewish clubs and the JLB during the 1900s and were believed to offer many physical and mental benefits to young participants. English Jewish club patrons such as Lord Rothschild praised gym training for helping to create 'well-developed chests and limbs' and 'strong, clean and truthful bodies' out of supposedly weak immigrant physiques.[115] With encouragement and considerable financial support, gymnastics became extremely popular in the youth movement – with some Jews even developing an 'obsessive' attitude towards training and competition.[116] Before the First World War, the gymnastics teams of the Jewish youth clubs in London dominated local and LFWBC competitions to the point where some non-Jewish teams refused to compete against them.[117]

It was gratifying for the Jewish press and the Jewish establishment to see immigrant boys enthusiastically taking up gymnastics and performing well in competition against their non-Jewish peers. Yet the success of Jewish club gymnasts also took on a wider significance at this time. Against the backdrop of debates surrounding the Aliens Bill in 1904, which included discussions about supposed immigrant physical weakness, Jewish gymnastic success was 'evidence' of the assimilatory potential of immigrant children. During this year, alongside newspaper reports on the physical 'frailty' of the alien population, a number of prominent politicians made statements suggesting that legislation was needed to protect the physical 'stock' of the nation. The former Liberal MP and *Daily Telegraph* proprietor, Harry Lawson-Levy – himself of Jewish origin – claimed that the continuing 'influx' of Jewish refugees would result in a 'backwards march to physical deterioration' for the country as a whole.[118] Likewise, Liberal MP Sir Henry Norman claimed that continuing Jewish immigration meant that 'it would not be long before the quality of our own people would be seriously impaired'.[119]

The success of Jewish gymnasts against non-Jewish children was seen as a retort to these accusations – as highlighted by the *Jewish*

World in a feature on the Victoria Jewish Lads' Club published in 1904. The article argued that Jewish success in gymnastics took on a special significance 'at a time when the dangers and horrors of alien immigration occupy so prominent a place in the popular imagination' and 'when the columns of certain of the daily papers ring with piteous tales of overcrowding, vice and physical degeneration amongst the alien inhabitants of the East End'. Gymnastic success against local non-Jewish boys was 'no barren honour for a club whose membership is composed almost entirely of aliens or children of alien parentage'. The article, which was accompanied by pictures of the victorious teams, recorded pointedly that 'it was noticeable during the competition how favourably the physique of our alien boys compared with that of their Gentile competitors and little trace of that physical degeneration of which so much has been heard is evident in the photographs'. Importantly, sport also helped transform alien children into Englishmen – the fifteen boys making up the two winning gym teams were said to 'all speak English with no trace of a foreign accent. But for their names and perhaps some facial characteristics, they could pass anywhere as native-born Britons'.[120]

Alongside gymnastics, great value was also placed in success against non-Jews in boxing as an aid to integration. From the earliest days of the Jewish youth movement, boxing training and sparring sessions were promoted as a means of improving physical fitness and strength and as a weapon against an increasing tendency for 'indiscriminate fighting' amongst Jewish boys. As first-hand accounts of the pre-1914 period evidence, pitched physical battles between Jewish and non-Jewish children and adolescents were relatively commonplace. Whilst Jewish elites worried that these fights were physically damaging to the young Jews, they were also concerned with the negative impressions that these confrontations could arouse from non-Jewish sources.[121]

In order to combat the 'fighting' temperament amongst young Jews, Jewish youth leaders turned to boxing. This sport could not only give Jewish boys an outlet for their aggression, but it was also a means of learning self-control and restraint. Boxing also became a significant aspect of the programme of the Jewish Lads' Brigade, whose management viewed the sport as an important means of promoting the fitness and physical toughness of its membership. As the Brigade's 1912 annual report noted, 'greater attention' was gradually given to the sport during the 1900s as a supplement to the main programme of 'physical and military drill'. In both London and Manchester – the respective homes of the two largest JLB battalions – regular internal boxing competitions were organised during the years immediately preceding and after the First World War.[122]

Boxing took on a greater significance for the JLB in the period after 1918, when regular competition against non-Jews was secured with the advent of the Prince of Wales' Boxing Shield. In 1920, the Prince of Wales, in his role as head of the British cadet forces, instigated a national boxing tournament for the various youth organisations affiliated to the British armed forces. The team tournament consisted of local, county and regional rounds before a national final between the Northern and Southern regional winners. The victors had the added incentive of being presented with the Shield by either the Prince himself or another prominent member of the royal family.[123]

Attracted by the prestige of the competition and the opportunity

3 The victorious London Jewish Lads' Brigade Prince of Wales'
Boxing Shield team, 1921

for regular bouts against non-Jews, nearly all JLB companies across the country entered teams into the tournament. However, it was the two largest, the Manchester and London battalions, who experienced the most success. As Kadish has noted, teams representing these two battalions won the Shield an 'almost embarrassing' number of times during the interwar period.[124] Between 1920 and 1939, Jewish teams were victorious on no less than twelve occasions and there were also four 'all-Jewish' finals, with the Shield being contested by representatives of the two largest JLB groups.[125]

Whilst their domination of the tournament was gratifying, success in the Shield also benefited the wider Jewish community. Comment was made on several occasions that domination of the competition helped to underline the success of the physical programme of the Brigade. In achieving their victories, young Brigade boxers were promoting a positive view of Jewish physical fitness and strength – something which was noted by Jewish and non-Jewish observers alike. In 1933, the Manchester JLB claimed that Brigade domination of the competition was 'illustrative' of the superior 'physical fitness' of their members. In 1936, an official for the competition noted that 'other cadet units could not compare, age for age, with the Jewish boys in physique and fitness'. In the same year, a letter was received by the victorious Manchester JLB team from the headquarters of the Cadet Group noting that 'their appearance from the physical viewpoint, both in shape and build, left nothing to be desired'. The author of the letter exclaimed: 'I only wish the entire nation were as physically fit as the winning team of the Manchester Jewish Lads' Brigade'.[126]

Alongside helping to change perceptions of Jewish physicality, the Shield was also valued by leaders of the Brigade as an aid for increasing contact between Jewish and non-Jewish adolescents. After their first success in the tournament in 1921, the London JLB battalion claimed that victory in the 'coveted trophy ... served to bring home to the community the "missionary" value of the Brigade in promoting sympathetic understanding and goodwill between Jews and their fellow countrymen'. Indeed, aware that their domination of the competition may have been diminishing the amount of goodwill and 'sympathetic understanding' gained from participation, the JLB temporarily withdrew its teams from the Shield in 1936 – a decision which (as examined subsequently) was also driven by an awareness of growing popular anti-Semitism at this time.[127]

GUTTENBERG
Photo

Manchester Jewish Lads Brigade Boxing Team.
Winners of the PRINCE OF WALES SHIELD, 1926.

MANCHESTER

4 The Manchester Jewish Lads' Brigade Prince of Wales' Boxing Shield
winning team, pictured in 1926

Offering 'equal' provision: the Jewish Athletic Association
Although sport against non-Jews was valued for the many
Anglicisation benefits it offered, competition between Jews was seen
to be equally as important. By regularly experiencing the energy and
pressure of competition, young Jews would learn how to win and
lose graciously, and how to act and react under stress; they could
also improve their skills more quickly than through just training
alone.[128]

There were also certain wider benefits for the Jewish youth
organisations themselves. Youth leaders like Basil Henriques
believed that the opportunity for competitive sport was vital for all
Jewish and non-Jewish youth clubs. Not only did it give members a
'definite goal in view' (i.e. something to work towards through
attendance at club and involvement in sport), but it was also a key
way to improve and maintain club spirit – 'the keener members can
be made in the prowess of their club team the greater will be their
enthusiasm for the club as a whole'.[129]

For various reasons, Jews could often find their opportunities for competitive sport limited. One important factor in this regard was observance of the Jewish Sabbath. Whilst young Jews themselves became less adherent to Sabbath law from the early twentieth century onwards, most Jewish youth organisations proved initially unwilling to organise or promote sport on the rest day.[130] This had a knock-on effect in that Jewish clubs did not enter teams into Gentile sporting competitions organised for Saturdays – the most popular day for sport within non-Jewish society. As well as being unable to compete in some leagues and tournaments offered by groups such as the London Federation of Working Boys' Clubs, Jews often could not take part in Board school leagues often scheduled for Friday evenings or Saturday mornings either. To add to this, it was also the case that many public sporting facilities were off-limits to Jews on Sundays due to restrictions based around observance of the Christian Sabbath.[131]

Such a situation threatened to undermine the work which had been done with regard to sport within the Jewish youth movement. Towards the end of the 1890s, club leaders and sections of the Jewish elites resolved to address this problem by expanding competitive play and minimising the effect of these various 'barriers'. For this purpose, the Jewish Athletic Association was formed in 1899. Operating mainly in the capital, the JAA was designed to aid the growth of sport amongst immigrant children. It helped the organisation of the sporting programmes of the youth movement and also provided clubs and schools with aid and equipment for sport. Importantly, the Association facilitated competitive sports for young Jews by forming 'Jewish' leagues and tournaments and by working with Gentile authorities to expand sporting provision for Jewish children in Board schools. In short, the overriding objective of the Association was to provide as 'equal' a provision for sport as possible for Jews unable to take part in non-Jewish competitions. Such an aim, as with most of the sporting programmes initiated at this time, was inextricably linked to immigrant Anglicisation and designed to aid integration in whatever way possible.[132]

The JAA was given significant impetus by sections of the British Jewish elites during its early years. When it was founded, the Association was made up of a handful of volunteer administrators, mainly Jewish youth club managers and workers.[133] In 1901, however, the Association was taken under the wing of the

Maccabaeans Society, a group of English Jewish intellectuals and professionals brought together in 1891 to promote Jewish culture and identity. The Maccabaeans – who had also played a pivotal role in the formation of the Jewish Lads' Brigade – had gradually become more interested in the promotion of sport for Anglicisation purposes during the late 1890s. In 1900 a resolution was passed at the Society's annual meeting stating that 'the Maccabaeans should take a more active part in fostering an athletic spirit among Jewish boys and girls belonging to the humbler classes'.[134]

The result of the resolution was the convening of the Maccabaean Athletic Committee. Over a twelve-month period, the Committee conducted a comprehensive investigation of sporting provision in over fifty Jewish clubs and schools. Their report, published in 1901, claimed that greater funding and equipment for sport was needed, more leagues and competitions in various sports were desirable and that Jewish students in Board schools had restricted opportunities for sport due to religious considerations. The Society started a formal connection to the Jewish Athletic Association to address these issues. They believed that bringing sporting provision to a level comparable to that of non-Jewish boys and girls would have a 'distinctly beneficial effect on the physique and health of the poorer classes of the Jewish faith'. Regular financial donations to the Association were made throughout the 1900s by the Society, complementing funding drawn from other sections of the English Jewish community.[135]

The Association began as a loosely constituted and defined body, but over time grew to significant proportions. By 1914, it had 51 affiliated clubs and schools and by 1927 – when the Association was absorbed into the Association for Jewish Youth (an umbrella organisation which catered for Jewish youth provision more generally) – it was reported to have 26,000 individual members; approximately 10% of Anglo-Jewry as it stood in the late 1920s.[136] The primary aim of the Association from its foundation through to the late 1920s was to help provide competitive sport for young Jews. Although not directly interested in promoting religious adherence, the JAA's main tasks were to minimise the sporting impact of Sabbath observance and to create opportunities for competitive play between Jews and Jewish teams – thus protecting the wider Anglicisation mission of the youth movement.[137]

To this end, a large infrastructure of weekly 'Jewish' leagues, tournaments and one-off sports meetings was developed from 1900 onwards. Although individual athletics and swimming meetings could often draw hundreds of competitors and thousands of spectators, it was weekly Association competitions in football, cricket (boys), hockey and basketball (girls) that demonstrated the success of the organisation most clearly.[138] By 1913, for example, it was reported in the *Jewish Chronicle* that 54 teams were regularly participating in JAA competitions – a conservative estimate suggesting that this meant that 600–700 young Jews were playing Association sport on a weekly basis.[139]

As well as working to broaden competitive opportunities for youth club members, the JAA also worked hard to ensure that Jewish schoolchildren in Board schools could enjoy equal provision of sport. When physical recreation was introduced into the elementary school curriculum in the 1900s, many competitive leagues and tournaments were created on Saturdays and during after-school hours – often resulting in those Jews attending *Cheder* (religious classes) or observing the Jewish Sabbath being unable to participate. Aware of the potential effects that this could have on the sporting development of Jewish schoolchildren, the Jewish Athletic Association began negotiating with the London County Council to find ways to ensure Jews did not miss out on sport available to their non-Jewish peers. In 1906, these discussions resulted in arrangements that became known as 'double-sessions' – when Jewish pupils in Board schools were released early on Fridays to participate in sport before the commencement of their Sabbath at dusk. In subsequent years, 'double-sessions' were extended to the winter term, not for sport, but to allow young Jews to travel home before the commencement of their rest day.[140]

The established Jewish community praised the efforts of the JAA in securing this key concession. An article from the *Jewish World* in 1906 gave a typical account of how a sport 'double-session' worked in practice. In this instance, a number of schools local to Victoria Park released Jewish children into the care of teachers and Jewish youth club workers under the auspices of the Association. From 2.30 p.m. until dusk, competitive games in football, tennis, cricket and hockey were held. The on-looking reporter applauded the work of the Association in providing sports to young boys and girls denied the opportunity to play on Saturdays. He noted our whole impression is a most excellent one. There are fully 2000 boys and girls taking part under the best possible conditions, not more than half hour distance from their homes, in exercise that is filling their lungs with something better than the mephitic atmosphere a good many of them breathe in and about their homes. Their bodies are being strengthened and braced for the battle of life.[141]

'Double-sessions' continued through the 1920s and beyond, ensuring that Jewish children of observant parentage had equal sporting opportunities to their non-Jewish peers. In 1923, the idea of abolishing the sessions was debated by the LCC, resulting in an uproar from Jewish parents and the Jewish press. They voiced their concern that such an idea would be 'disadvantageous', both from a physical and educational perspective, for the thousands of young Jews taking part in the sessions at that time.[142] Not only was this idea scrapped, but over time greater concessions for Jews playing sport were secured.[143]

The Association drew many plaudits from the Jewish establishment for its work. One of the JAA's first Presidents, Felix Waley-Cohen, claimed that the organisation 'influenced thousands of young men and women for the better'.[144] In 1903, Colonel Albert Goldsmid said the Association was 'doing very great service to the community' by helping create 'sound minds in sound bodies'.[145] Four years later, Liberal MP and Government minister, Herbert Samuel (1870–1963) noted that 'he thought the good work the Jewish Athletic Association was doing was indisputable ... a work for which not only the community but the country at large should be grateful'.[146] In 1914, the awards evening keynote speaker claimed that, through the Association's efforts, 'there had been a more marked change ... amongst them [immigrant Jewish children] for a desire for outdoor exercise' and that 'the reproach formerly hurled at them of a being a stunted race was being removed by physical improvement through athletics'. S.J. Lazarus concluded that 'the need to train the body as well as the mind had been recognised and looking around him he could see at once the fruits of that policy'.[147]

To some extent, opinion was initially split over the practical and symbolic benefits of a separate 'Jewish' sporting organisation. It was argued that the development of an organisation serving Jews exclusively could send out the wrong messages to non-Jewish society and run counter to the wider aims of the Anglicisation campaign. Take, for instance, renowned Biblical scholar, religious leader and philanthropist, Claude Montefiore.[148] During his involvement with the West Central Jewish Lads' Club, which he co-founded in 1898, Montefiore had been a passionate and vocal advocate of the benefits of sport for immigrant Jewish development and integration. He claimed, however, that the foundation of the JAA concerned him significantly and was 'doubtful over its need and propriety' as he 'was not quite sure whether it was necessary to have separate Jewish associations of that kind'. Promoting sport was important, but not at the cost of appearing isolationist or aloof to the wider population.[149]

Over time, this situation changed and Montefiore claimed he had gradually 'become a thorough convert to the merits and necessity of the Association'. Assured that its foundation and programme were not driven by a deliberate attempt at separatism, Montefiore commented in 1909 that he 'now had nothing but praise to offer the Association for the excellent work it had done and was doing for the boys, girls and lads of London'. He noted that the fact that 'Jewish boys and girls were unable to play on Saturday' due to religious considerations meant that it was logical for an organisation like the JAA, which was working towards ensuring equal sporting provision, to be created.[150]

Whilst we have seen previously that sport was believed to confer important physical and psychological benefits for young immigrant Jews, it is also clear that great significance was also attached to competitive sport in the Anglicisation process. Sporting participation in a tournament, league or organised competition, with other Jews or against Gentiles, was valued in various ways for the assistance it gave to immigrant integration. In the first instance, sporting contact between Jewish children and their non-Jewish peers was a useful medium for helping to minimise the apparent 'aloofness' of the immigrant community. Contact on the football or cricket pitch was seen to be a way of promoting goodwill between minority and majority community, as well as helping demonstrate Jewish desire for integration.

Evidence of the value of sporting competition against non-Jews can be seen by looking at the examples of gymnastics and boxing in the early twentieth century. Competing against and beating non-Jews in the physically demanding environments of the gymnasium or boxing ring was an important vehicle for helping to change perceptions of the Jewish community. These victories also answered criticisms surrounding supposed Jewish physical degeneracy. In reality, the British Jewish elites could not have hoped to achieve such outcomes through sporting competition solely between Jewish participants. Sport effectively took on a 'missionary' role, helping to demonstrate to the wider population that certain stereotypes and preconceptions could be undermined and altered through sporting success.

It is also apparent that considerable attention was given to promoting competitive play between Jewish individuals and Jewish teams. This is especially clear when analysing the foundation and growth of the Jewish Athletic Association, whose sporting and social importance – when reminded of how large the organisation's membership grew – should not be underestimated. Those who founded and managed the Association were clearly anxious that efforts should be made towards offering as 'equal' a sporting provision as possible to young Jews in the capital. In creating, managing and expanding the organisation, the Jewish community demonstrated a keenness to respect religious considerations, but also a desire to prevent strict Sabbath observance from restricting opportunity for competitive play.

The Association's work demonstrates once more that the British Jewish community was pro-actively and consciously utilising sport as a catalyst to processes of integration and acculturation. Whilst the sporting programme of the Association may not have been as directly designed to transform Jewish immigrant children as the sporting initiatives of the youth club movement, there was a clear aspiration to promote sport as an indirect aid to the assimilation of alien children. Jewishness, so the Association demonstrated, should be respected, but not necessarily allowed to be a barrier to sporting participation nor to the continuing Anglicisation of the youngest immigrants.

'Too Semitic' or 'thoroughly Anglicised'? The life and career of Harold Abrahams

Whilst sport was a powerful catalyst in Jewish Anglicisation, integration could also facilitate successful sporting careers. There are many English Jews whose acceptance into the upper echelons of

British society opened up opportunities to play high-level sport
during the late nineteenth and early twentieth century. Take, for
instance, respected judge and golfer Lionel Leonard Cohen (1888–
1973), Oxford cricket 'blue' and England rugby union international
John Raphael (1882–1917) and Nathan Mayer Rothschild (1910–
90), who played county cricket for Northamptonshire in the late
1920s. For all of these 'native' English Jews, social and cultural
Anglicisation, together with private education, played an important
role in opening up avenues for sporting participation. Their privileged and integrated backgrounds – which contrasted with the
immigrant population – opened up social, cultural, economic and
sporting opportunities simply not available to the mainstream of
Jewish society.[151]

Some Jews of immigrant parentage did experience a similar
situation. One of the most well-known and successful 'thoroughly
Anglicised' Jewish sportsmen of all was Harold Maurice Abrahams,
the renowned sprinter and long jumper.[152] Abrahams, the son of a
Lithuanian Jewish immigrant, was a successful public school athlete
and Cambridge athletics 'blue' before going on to win the gold
medal for the 100 metres sprint at the 1924 Paris Olympics. As well
as experiencing significant sporting success, after his athletics career
ended abruptly in 1925 Abrahams went on to become a prominent
figure in British athletics administration, sports journalism and
charity work, and was also a prolific writer.[153]

Until recently, very little was known about the life and career of
the Bedford-born athlete.[154] For many years the only reference point
was the 'figurative reconstruction' of Abrahams in the 1981 film
Chariots of Fire, which depicted Abrahams' rivalry with Scottish
sprinter Eric Liddell in the lead up to the 1924 Games.[155] Much
doubt, however, has been cast over the historical accuracy of the
film. Not only is it alleged that *Chariots* takes historical liberties
with Abrahams' story and contains many factual errors, it has often
been claimed that the film – which casts Harold as a pariah who is
shunned for his Jewishness – displays an exaggerated level of anti-
Semitism directed towards the athlete.[156]

Whilst the depiction of Abrahams in *Chariots of Fire* may reflect
reality more than previously believed, it is wrong to consider the
sprinter solely as the 'outsider' shown in the film. Although his
Jewish heritage was a cause of significant hostility, Abrahams also
enjoyed a significant level of integration and acceptance during his

lifetime – something which led to notable sporting successes and made him the toast of British Jewry. His Anglicisation, however, later became the cause of much resentment amongst the Jewish establishment. By 1936 – a year when Abrahams courted contro-versy over his stance on the Berlin Olympics – he was criticised amongst Jewish circles for having 'lost' all personal, cultural and religious attachment to the community of his birth. Although he did face considerable racism due to his Jewish heritage, the central themes of Abrahams' life, effectively, were Anglicisation and inte-gration. A desire to move into or support British society – and not be defined by his 'Jewishness' – characterised the majority of Abrahams' personal and sporting decisions.

'Too Semitic'? Abrahams and Chariots of Fire

Although Harold Abrahams was a well-known figure during his own lifetime, it is the representation of him in the 1981 film *Chariots of Fire* which informs much of popular memory of the sportsman, journalist and sports administrator. Released three years after Abrahams' death in 1978, *Chariots* depicts the preparations and Olympic fortunes of two young British sprinters in the early 1920s – Abrahams and Scottish runner, Eric Liddell. In the film, both are shown as talented athletes troubled by problems caused by their religious identities. Liddell, a devout Christian, runs to please God and wrestles with the effect of his religious beliefs and conscience on his sporting career. Abrahams, a British Jew, is depicted as running to overcome anti-Semitism and is fanatical in his training because of his desire to provide a retort to the bigotry he faces. The film climaxes with both athletes experiencing success in the 1924 Olympic Games, triumphing both over the rivalry that existed between them and over the social, cultural and religious hurdles they each faced.[157]

The film was a commercial and critical success. Based on a screenplay written by Colin Welland and directed by Hugh Hudson, *Chariots* grossed nearly $60m US dollars worldwide and won four awards at the 1981 Oscars. As one of the most well-known films depicting sporting history, it is no surprise that *Chariots of Fire* has attracted significant academic attention. Most scholars – whilst applauding the film's entertainment value – have been critical of the movie and of the willingness of the writer and director to use 'cinematic license' in the portrayal of the subject matter. Cashmore, for instance, has claimed that the film is a 'chronicle of the 1920s' and an 'allegory' of the early 1980s, rather than a truthful reconstruction of this part of British social, cultural and sporting history.[158] Likewise, Carter has claimed that *Chariots* is guilty of a 'falsification of historical reality' and is a 'mythical rather than historical film'.[159]

The majority of criticism has focused on the alleged 'significant distortion in the character portrayal of Abrahams' within the film.[160] As well as highlighting many small factual errors, such as portraying Abrahams as über-confident of victory, *Chariots*' depiction of Abrahams as 'too Semitic' in his attitude and demeanour and its representation of him as a sporting and social 'outcast' have also been called into question.[161] For some academics – as well as many of Abrahams' family and friends – *Chariots* overemphasises anti-Semitism and wrongly presents Harold's Jewishness as a hurdle to his acceptance by his Cambridge peers.[162]

Although the nature of the discrimination towards the athlete may not be entirely accurate within the film, recent research does indicate that Abrahams faced – or at least perceived he faced – considerable anti-Semitism during his Cambridge years.[163] Indeed, it has previously been shown that the Oxbridge environment could be often less than welcoming to Jewish students.[164] This hostility, however, was nowhere near as severe as that which Abrahams faced during his time at public school.[165] Many years later, Harold noted that he experienced a 'demon anti-Semitism' during his time at Repton, something which 'provided one with the driving force to succeed in athletics'. According to the sprinter, the 'keen sense of inferiority' he felt due to his Jewish background pushed him to take up running at public school more seriously.[166]

In contrast to past analyses, the film may therefore be more accurate in the portrayal of Abrahams as a Cambridge 'outsider' than previously suggested. Significantly, *Chariots* helped to filter a particular view of Harold – as an 'outcast' succeeding in the face of Establishment hostility – into the popular imagination. Speaking in 1989, businessman and major donor to production costs of the film, Mohammed Al-Fayed, claimed he was 'inspired by a man who was the victim of severe racial prejudice' and that he was 'fascinated by the story of a man subjected to grave prejudice and English snobbery'.[167] Similar sentiments were evident amongst the Jewish community. In her review of *Chariots* in the *Jewish Chronicle* in

April 1981, Pamela Melnikoff claimed that the film skilfully demonstrated that 'the subtle anti-Semitism he [Abrahams] encountered at
Caius College stung him into a stubborn and aggressive determination to "show them"'. Melnikoff also claimed that Abrahams was
driven by a desire to 'erase' the 'popular belief' that Jews and sport
didn't mix in order to 'raise the status of the Jew in the eyes of the
mocking world'.[168]

Arguably, another theme running throughout the movie hints at a
more important aspect of Harold's life and career than anti-
Semitism – 'Anglicisation'. At various points within the movie, it is
suggested that Abrahams is 'really more English than Jewish'.
Whether it is the symbolic solo rendition of 'He is an Englishman',
the Anglican Masses which begin and end the film or Abrahams'
annoyance at his Cambridge masters' suggestion that he does not
run for his country (all of which have little basis in historical fact),
the picture is painted that Abrahams was somewhat Anglicised.
Significantly, the film also suggests that wealth and social standing
did more to open up opportunities for Abrahams than his
Jewishness did to close doors for him. In essence, *Chariots* claims
that, as well as being an 'outsider', Abrahams is also something an
accepted figure within the British elites.[169]

An analysis of Abrahams' family, educational and sporting background points to the fact that integration and Anglicisation were
much more important in his life and career than anti-Semitism.
Harold Maurice Abrahams was born in Bedford on 15 December
1899 to Isaac and Esther Abrahams. Isaac, a Lithuanian Jew, had
moved to Britain during the 1870s. Despite speaking and writing
very little English, he successfully established himself as both a
money lender (he founded the Bedfordshire Loan Company in
1885) and a trader in jewellery and precious stones. Isaac, who
arrived in Britain 'all but penniless' before the wave of Eastern
European immigration in the 1880s and 1890s, married a Welsh
Jewess from Merthyr Tydfil, Esther Isaacs, and had six children:
two daughters and four sons, of which Harold was the youngest.[170]

Drawing considerable pride from his own naturalisation in 1902,
Isaac Abrahams exhibited a keen desire for his sons to progress up
the social ladder and integrate fully into the higher echelons of
English society. This demonstrated itself most strongly through his
'burning convictions' that his sons should all benefit from public
school and Cambridge education. He believed that private

education of this kind was pivotal in making fine, upstanding young Englishmen out of his four boys. Isaac's 'new wealth' enabled him to fund private and university education for his three eldest sons before Harold Abrahams entered Repton public school in 1914 and eventually Caius College, Cambridge in 1919 to read law.[171]

Although the Abrahams were a minority at a time when most Jewish Oxbridge pupils were the sons of long-established British Jews, they were part of a growing wider trend.[172] In Britain, the end of the nineteenth century saw increasing numbers of Jews progressing through private education. Whilst Jews may have at various times been regarded as 'outsiders' to the upper echelons of British society, entrance into the prestigious public school and Oxbridge 'set' was an important symbolic and facilitative factor in Jewish integration into elite social circles. As Weber has noted, 'by 1914, Oxbridge had become for its Jewish students what it had traditionally been for their Gentile fellow students; the finishing school for its social elites'.[173] Although the number of Jews benefiting from private education was relatively small, this trend is an indicator of a clear desire for integration amongst more socially mobile immigrant Jews such as the Abrahams. Jewish attendance at public school and university was one significant step towards entry into the elites of British society, which was said to have been open to all Jews coming from 'new-wealth' backgrounds.[174]

The integrationist tendencies of the family were also present during their time in private education – as evidenced by their willingness to participate in sport. Whilst attendance at public school and Cambridge demonstrated in itself an Anglicising desire, all of the Abrahams boys became engaged in the sporting environment so closely connected to the British private education system. Adolphe Abrahams, who trained as a physician and was knighted in 1939, was an accomplished athlete during his time at university. Sidney 'Solly' Abrahams, who competed in the 1906 Intercalated Games and 1912 Olympic Games and was later sworn to the Privy Council, was an athletics 'blue' whilst at Cambridge. Lionel Abrahams, who became a successful solicitor and coroner, also enjoyed athletics success during his time at public school.[175]

It is worth noting that sporting involvement was more important as an aid for integration into the contemporary public school and Oxbridge milieu than intellectual or educational prowess. Achievement in these obsessively 'athletic' environments was one sure-fire means of gaining acceptance, even for those pupils from a Jewish background. Julius has noted that if Jews at public school or university were successful at sport then 'they became invisible as Jews' and 'were accepted' by their peers and their masters. In effect, achievement in physical recreation helped Jews pass a 'test of "character"' and minimised their perceived 'difference' amongst fellow pupils.[176] The prestige that Isaac Abrahams' four sons won their schools and colleges through sport, therefore, would have aided their acceptance into these establishments much more than their Jewishness would have hindered their integration.[177]

As the youngest son, Harold drew inspiration from the sporting success and integration of his older siblings. Harold claimed that from an early age he was 'surrounded by this atmosphere of running' and said 'almost literally from my cradle I was guided and encouraged to perform'.[178] In 1963, Abrahams admitted that by the age of six he wanted desperately to earn himself a 'blue blazer' – that proud sign of sporting success and social acceptance – and emulate his older brother Sidney. Undoubtedly, a desire to represent his university 'had a huge impact on Harold' and he was known to have outwardly proclaimed that this was more important to him than representing his country.[179] At Repton, athletics became an 'obsession' for Harold, whilst during his time at Cambridge Abrahams frequently claimed that he was more interested in running than his studies.[180]

Abrahams' entry into the exclusive private education milieu also opened up sporting opportunities outside of school and college. Whilst Harold clearly felt that sporting success would facilitate his integration into the Cambridge 'set', it was also the case that his private education aided his entry into the exclusive world of amateur athletics, dominated at this time by ex-public school and Oxbridge alumni. The original founders of amateur athletics clubs in the Victorian era, and of the Amateur Athletic Association in 1880, were generally privately educated. Whilst athletics gradually achieved a wider social constituency, most participants and administrators within the sport remained of this background well into the twentieth century.[181] As Holt has claimed, whereas working-class participation in professional 'pedestrianism' was well established during the Victorian period, track and field athletics remained an 'almost entirely amateur preserve'.[182]

Abrahams, a privately educated, Anglicised Jew hailing from a family of athletes, was perfectly suitable material for this exclusive world. During his career, he went on to achieve national fame and respectability through his amateur athletic endeavours.[183] After winning his first track race aged only nine, Abrahams went on to win both the 100 yards and long jump events at the prestigious Public Schools Championship in 1918, before going on to experience considerable success as a Cambridge athlete. As well as dominating sprinting at Oxford and Cambridge varsity meetings in the early 1920s, Abrahams was made President of the Cambridge University Athletic Club in 1922, won three events at the Oxbridge versus Yale and Harvard meeting in 1923 and was victorious in that year's Amateur Athletic Championships. His crowning athletic glory was his victory in the 100 metre sprint in the 1924 Olympic Games in Paris.[184]

Whilst Abrahams did face considerable racism during his educational life, his success in sport owes a great deal to his, and his family's, desire to integrate. His family background and attendance at public school and Cambridge – facilitating factors in the lives of many socially mobile Jews and non-Jews – enabled Abrahams' success in the largely middle- to upper-class milieu of British amateur athletics. In an educational sense, Abrahams was following a path more recognisable for Gentiles than Jews at this time. Similarly, in sporting terms, by moving into the sphere of amateur athletics via public school and Cambridge, Abrahams was also firmly entering into an exclusive sporting and social environment not open to less privileged immigrant Jews. Whilst integration into private education aided his sporting career, it was also the case that through sport, he was becoming more Anglicised and was increasingly resembling a middle- to upper-class Englishman, as opposed to a Jew of immigrant parentage.

'An Anglo-Jewish' role model?[185]

In the minds of many observers, there was a clear connection between Abrahams' integration and his sporting success. Whereas *Chariots of Fire* depicted Abrahams as a 'marginalised' figure, in the minds of the contemporary press he was first and foremost an English sportsman from a privileged social and educational background.[186] For example, in the aftermath of the 1924 Olympic victory, the *Daily Mirror* referred to Abrahams as the 'first Englishman to win this race at the Olympic Games' and applauded the efforts of 'the old Cantab'. In a feature length article on Abrahams' career published in 1973, *Athletics Weekly* celebrated 'the day an Englishman won the Olympic sprint crown' and made no mention of Harold's Jewish roots.[187]

Amongst British Jewry, Abrahams was primarily seen as an integrated and successful English Jew. Throughout the 1920s, he featured regularly in the pages of the Jewish press, with his sporting exploits being applauded not just for the effect on wider perceptions of Jews, but also for the impetus given to the youngest within the community. After his victories in the Oxbridge versus Harvard and Yale athletics meeting in 1923, the *Jewish Chronicle* noted that Abrahams was a 'striking instance of the capacity of the Jew in athletics whenever he has had the opportunity of developing his muscles through healthy sport'.[188] Likewise, in the same year the *Jewish World* claimed that Abrahams was a symbolic retort to anti-Semitic stereotypes:

> It has often been said that Jews have produced very few athletes of note, as they are too much engaged in commerce, the arts and finance to take interest in sports ... It is on the track that the Jewish community can look with pride at the wonderful successes of one of its own sons – Harold M Abrahams – who has rightly been described as one of the 'greatest all-round athletes who has ever represented Cambridge University' ... no English team of athletes would be complete without him.[189]

English Jewish communal organisations also rushed to celebrate Abrahams' achievements and to secure the athlete's symbolic involvement in their own activities. In June 1923, Abrahams was the guest of honour at a dinner organised by the Maccabaeans Society. The invitation of Abrahams, who was the youngest Jew honoured in this way by the Society, was a symbolic acceptance of the athlete into the English Jewish elites. Similarly, in 1924, Abrahams was invited to take on the Presidency of the Jewish Athletic Association, a role he accepted and held until the late 1920s. Jewish institutions, which had seen Abrahams celebrated by the English public schools and by Cambridge University, were keen to show that the Jewish community itself welcomed Abrahams' sporting achievements.[190] Seemingly, they were also pleased that Abrahams' success had 'brought lustre on the name of English Jewry' and was also leading to a rise in interest in athletics amongst younger Jews.[191]

For the British Jewish establishment, Abrahams was a perfect and useful example of how Anglicisation could lead to social and sporting integration. In Abrahams, the Jewish elites had someone from an immigrant background who had progressed through the exclusive public school and Cambridge system and who had gained prestige for himself and his community through his efforts in amateur athletics – an example which young immigrant Jews should look up to and try to emulate. When the *Jewish World* suggested offering Abrahams the Jewish Athletic Association Presidency in April 1923, it noted that such an appointment would 'inspire Jewish lads to try and follow in his footsteps ...'; a comment which seemingly referred both to his sporting successes but also to his successful Anglicisation, integration and acceptance.[192]

Whilst British Jewry may have seen Abrahams as an Anglicised figure, he also viewed himself in similar terms. As his biographer has noted, Harold 'had no great desire to defend the Jewish faith and didn't wish to be defined by it'.[193] Although he underwent his Barmitzvah in 1913, Abrahams was generally not observant or interested in Judaism at any point during his adult life. At university, Harold became involved with Christian groups and subsequently was said to have become very keen to lead a secular, 'Christian' lifestyle. In 1936, he took the increasingly common step for Anglicised Jews of marrying outside of the community – in his case to D'Oyly Carte singer Sybil Evers. Later in life he regularly attended Anglican Church services and was buried in a Church of England graveyard alongside his beloved wife in 1978.[194]

Harold's secularity suited his own outlook and lifestyle, but it also apparently aided his sporting career. On several occasions, Abrahams noted to the Jewish community that Anglicisation such as his was needed for a Jew to enjoy elite sporting success. A strong personal, religious or cultural attachment to Jewishness was a hindrance, whereas apostasy could prove helpful to a budding young Jewish sportsman or woman. In a speech made at the Maccabaeans Society dinner in 1923, Harold claimed he was 'unwilling to sacrifice his athletic ambitions for the observance of strict religious laws' and that 'to follow Jewish religious law would rule out athletic distinction'.[195] Similarly, in a speech to the Jewish Athletic Association in 1925, Abrahams claimed that religious observance created a 'difficulty' for young Jews interested in sport as 'most principal athletics events were held on a Saturday' –

something which he had not allowed to prevent him from achieving his own successes.[196]

Abrahams' most comprehensive espousal of the sporting 'need' for Anglicisation came in 1927. In a full page feature entitled 'The Jews in Athletics', published in the *Jewish World*, Abrahams critiqued past Jewish sporting achievements and examined why more Jews had not distinguished themselves in the sporting arena. As well as outlining a number of 'Jewish' characteristics which he felt 'suitable' for sporting competition (Jewish 'quick thinking', their 'high opinion of their own ability' and 'self-assurance' were all highlighted), Abrahams claimed the most important factor in Jewish sporting success was a willingness to Anglicise and to move away from one's religion. Abrahams argued that athletes should be devout to the 'religion' of training and excelling in their sport, not to religious law and customs:

> One must make it clear that a strict adherence to Judaism would prevent one from participating in Saturday competitions and, as a result, the 'strict' Jews could never hope to attain international recognition, since at a conservative estimate ninety per cent of important competitions are held on a Saturday afternoon. A religion (qua such) that is one's philosophy of life (or theistic views) has little if anything to do with the qualities which characterise an athlete. True, clean living and rigid self-denial are the foundations of athletic success, but these could hardly be termed the tenets of one's religion.[197]

In Abrahams' view, religion and sport did not mix. He argued that they even existed in something of a polarised state, as integration and apostasy could apparently help Jews reach the highest sporting echelons.[198] Unsurprisingly therefore, he was also critical of Jewish organisations created exclusively for Jews interested in sport. When asked his opinion of the 'Maccabi' sports movement, he replied 'I am not a supporter' adding that he felt 'people of Jewish origin who are British subjects should play their part in British National Athletics [sic] and not encourage a separatist movement'.[199]

At a time when the growing secularisation of younger Jews was beginning to concern the Jewish elites, it is interesting that Abrahams' comments on religion and sport passed without criticism.[200] During the 1920s, he remained a celebrated and high-profile figure and maintained involvement with a number of Jewish organisations and charities – something which perhaps explains

why his observation on the incompatibility of sport and
'Jewishness' passed without negative comment.

An 'act of treachery': Abrahams and the Berlin Olympics
The Jewish community's impression of Abrahams changed radically
during the 1930s. Although celebrated by the Jewish establishment
during the decade previous, Abrahams became something of a
pariah during the year of the infamous Berlin Olympics. Effectively,
his public actions as both a sports administrator and BBC commentator were seen as a 'cowardly stab in the back'. He was strongly
criticised for outwardly backing the official line on the sporting
'need' for the Games to go ahead, in the face of Nazi repression, and
further inflamed the situation by attending the games as a broadcaster. As one correspondent to the *Jewish Chronicle* remarked
pointedly in May 1936: 'Does Mr Abrahams acknowledge the fact
that no matter how British he may be, no matter to what extent
sport may be his religion, he is yet a Jew?'[201]

Berlin had been awarded the Olympic Games in 1931, after
beating Barcelona in an International Olympic Committee vote.
After Hitler and the National Socialists came to power in 1933 and
began repressing minority groups, international concern grew that
the 1936 Summer and Winter Games, scheduled to be held in Berlin
and Garmisch-Partenkirchen respectively, would be utilised as a
political tool by the Nazis to espouse Hitler's racist ideals and
expansionist ambitions. Subsequently, attempts to organise boycotts
of the Games were widely supported in America and by Jewish
athletes and sporting organisations, although eventually all of the
major sporting nations did send teams to both Olympiads.[202]

In Britain, there was no general desire to rally against the Nazis in
sporting terms amongst officials or the wider public, despite some
concern that Germany would use sport as a political tool.[203] As part
of the wider policy of appeasement, the British Government were
keen for the Games to go ahead – and for a British delegation to be
sent to Berlin – in order to help maintain diplomatic relations with
the Nazi regime. Although in public the Government stressed that a
policy of 'non-intervention' governed its relations with the British
Olympic Association, behind-the-scenes pressure was exerted on the
BOA to ensure that British involvement in the Games proceeded as
planned.[204]

Although there was 'no strong line' against the Games amongst the British public, a campaign in favour of a British boycott was launched by the trade union movement, the Communist Party and the Labour Party, as well as the *Manchester Guardian*.[205] In 1935, the *Manchester Guardian* claimed that allowing the Games to be held in Berlin would be a 'violation of the Olympic principles' as Jews would not be able to compete on 'an equal footing with other athletes'.[206] The idea of a boycott also drew support from the Jewish establishment. For example, in March 1936, the *Jewish Chronicle* noted its support for a motion in favour of a boycott put forward to the meeting of the Amateur Athletic Association by the British Workers' Sport Federation.[207]

In public, Harold Abrahams was a staunch opponent of the boycott movement. At the March meeting, he spoke out against the BWSF's resolution and the wider boycott movement in his position as a senior figure within the AAA. He stressed that it would be harmful to sporting and diplomatic relations if British athletes boycotted the Games, even though sending a team could be construed as condoning Nazi repression:

> I know there is not a single person in this room who does not deplore the conditions in Germany today, but in spite of these conditions, I ask myself whether it is ultimately in the best interests of world sport and better world relationships that the AAA should pass this resolution and withdraw from the Games.[208]

Abrahams had also put forward the same argument to the British Olympic Association in December 1935 – days before they formally accepted the invitation to send a British team to the Games.[209] Abrahams' actions, as both Holt and Mandell have noted, delayed a crucial vote on the resolution and effectively 'killed off' the British boycott movement.[210]

Despite this, it would be wrong to think that Abrahams was entirely comfortable with the Berlin Games going ahead. In reality, there are many indications that he held private reservations about holding the Olympics in a country where the position for minority groups was deteriorating rapidly. During late 1935, Abrahams had been in close contact with leading proponents of a British boycott of the Games. In one letter to Philip Noel-Baker (1889–1982) – politician and former Olympic athlete – Abrahams remarked that a 'strong line' should be taken by 'sporting associations' on the Games and that the 'powers that be' in Britain needed to reconsider the situation in the face of growing oppression of ethnic minorities by the Nazi regime.[211]

Initially, Abrahams supported an idea put forward by Noel-Baker to send a lengthy letter to *The Times* outlining the case for a boycott.[212] However, by early December – just days before Abrahams' opposition to a boycott resolution in a meeting of the British Olympic Association – he had had a significant change of heart. After reading the draft *Times* letter, Abrahams advised Noel-Baker that he 'had no doubt that it was a very inopportune time' to send the letter, that it 'was not quite suitable' and that 'I do not believe anything will be achieved ... [as] there can be little doubt that we shall send a team to Berlin'.[213]

Likewise, although Abrahams publicly opposed a boycott of the Games in meetings with the British Olympic Association, he privately communicated his concerns about the Berlin Games to BOA officials. For instance, in a letter to Colonel Evan Hunter, Secretary of the BOA, Abrahams suggested that the BOA could do more to use its influence to exert pressure on the Nazi regime:

> We are, I think, shutting our eyes to reality if we believe that the mere organisation and support of such institutions as the Olympic Games constitutes the end of our duty in this matter ... I naturally feel very strongly that the total negation of liberty in Germany is a deplorable thing and I believe that a dignified appeal to Herr Hitler, taking the form of a request and not a protest, would tend to do much more good than many people imagine or even hope.[214]

In private, Abrahams was anxious about the Games.[215] In public, however, he maintained strong opposition to the boycott movement throughout late 1935 and 1936. Whilst he clearly understood the nature of the situation for Germany's Jewish population, he remained interested in publicly keeping politics out of sport and ensuring the official line on the Games was followed. Many British sporting officials at this time were, like Abrahams, largely privately educated and of middle- to upper-class background. They believed firmly in the sanctity of sport and the 'amateur ethic of non-intervention' – opposing a boycott as it 'went against the grain' of their public school traditions.[216] In March 1936 Abrahams echoed this sentiment and noted that punishing Germany's political leaders through sporting means and turning the Olympics into a British political issue, was distasteful and hindered 'the furtherance of those ideals in sport ... in which we all believe'.[217]

Abrahams was staunchly criticised by the Jewish community for his public stance on the Games. For one, the *Jewish Chronicle* claimed that his actions were giving 'cachet to the rotten Nazi regime' and betraying British and international Jewry.[218] In 1935, after Abrahams had spoken against a boycott at the British Olympic Association, the President of the Board of Deputies, Neville Laski, wrote to him complaining about his decision: 'It passes the bounds of knowledge that I possess to understand how any national or international Olympic committee ... could think for one moment of holding the Games in Berlin'.[219] One article in the *Jewish Chronicle* in May 1936 called on him to show more than just 'passive sympathy' for his fellow Jews. It noted that, even though Abrahams was now assimilated in all but name, 'it is his duty to do his all to help the German Jews and to secure for them that fairness of treatment which is essential not only in sport but in all walks of life'. A debate in the pages of the newspaper raged throughout the summer of 1936. In September, the editor concluded that whereas previously Abrahams had 'shed lustre on Anglo-Jewry by his remarkable record achievements for Britain in the athletic arena ... his recent attitude ... has called forth resentment, not only from this journal, but by the Jewish community in general'.[220]

Abrahams was also criticised by Anglo-Jewry during the Games themselves. Whilst his opposition to the boycott was believed to be an affront to his Jewish background, he was also attacked by the Jewish community for 'playing into Goebbels' hands' by attending the Games as a commentator for the BBC. Abrahams, who had worked with the BBC since 1924 and had pioneered the art of radio commentary on live events, agonised over attending the Games and sought Government guidance on the matter on several occasions.[221] He later noted that he eventually 'went there with a good deal of misapprehension' and 'unhappiness' and claimed that 'although I hadn't been a practising Jew for years, I was very uneasy about going'.[222]

Abrahams 'knew' that his decision would be 'very much criticised' by some within the Jewish community.[223] Correspondence in the letters column of the *Jewish Chronicle* – a continual 'thorn in his side' during 1936 – attacked him for giving the Nazis a propaganda coup through having a prominent English Jew freely attending, and showing support for the Games.[224] One letter, signed 'A Supporter of the Olympic Ideal', asked pointedly, 'How does Mr Abrahams relish the project [sic] of Nazi party bosses, large and small, bowing to him with all the appearances of friendship due to a loyal supporter and then laughing at him behind his back? For laugh they will'. Again, questions were asked within the Jewish community whether the Anglicised Abrahams was concerned with the international Jewish cause at all, or whether his sympathies lay wholly with the British establishment.[225]

There was some support for Abrahams within the Jewish community, as evidenced by correspondence in the *Jewish Chronicle* in April 1936. One letter, from 'L.C.', agreed with Abrahams' protests at the proposed boycott, claiming that such a move would lead to a 'deepening of misunderstanding' between Germany and the international community.[226] Abrahams himself, both at the time and subsequently, noted that his decisions were not taken lightly and that he 'had no delusions about the situation in Germany' for oppressed Jews and other minorities. In March 1936, Abrahams claimed that he 'did not realise that his action in publicly opposing the boycott might cause hurt to the Jews of this country and be taken by them as an act of treachery'. He added that such was his personality 'If I had been born in Germany, knowing myself as I do, I doubt if I should be alive today'.[227]

Abrahams was more naïve than unsympathetic or ignorant with his decisions surrounding the 1936 Olympics. It is apparent, however, that the approach he took to Berlin was much more indicative of an Anglicised individual than of someone with a strong personal, social and cultural attachment to his Jewish heritage. Although he held private misgivings about the Games and his attendance with the BBC, his decisions were influenced more by his public sense of duty as a senior figure within the British sporting establishment than by his Jewish origins. One contemporary quotation from Abrahams – who also edited the official British report into the Games which, to quote Mandell, was 'remarkable for its utter lack of political discussion' – seems crucial in ascertaining his attitude, position and level of assimilation by 1936.[228] According to the *Jewish Chronicle*, during the controversial meeting of the Amateur Athletic Association in March of that year, where Abrahams had spoken out against a boycott resolution, he symbolically remarked that he approached it [the boycott idea] as an Englishman who had been fortunate to represent his own country at two Olympic Games, as a man who had enjoyed working with his athletic colleagues for over ten years on the Amateur Athletic Association and as a man of Jewish origin.

The hierarchy that Abrahams employed is important to note. Whilst his 'Jewish origin' may have played some role in his decision-making process, Abrahams believed that, as an Englishman, an Olympian and a sports administrator, British involvement in the Berlin Games must go ahead despite wider social and political issues. Though he felt some connection with the community of his birth, it was evidently the case that his motivations and values as an Anglicised Jew clearly lay closer to those of the British establishment – a position also reflected both before and after 1936.[229]

Whilst *Chariots of Fire* has done much to inform and influence public opinion on Harold Maurice Abrahams, the film must be carefully approached by those desiring an accurate historical picture of the Bedford athlete. As Carnes has noted in his volume *Past Imperfect: History According to The Movies*, whilst 'movies inspire and entertain … they do not provide a substitute for history that has been painstakingly assembled from the best available evidence and analysis'.[230] Whilst *Chariots* clearly portrays Abrahams as an 'outsider' figure due to his Jewishness, the best available evidence points to Anglicisation as being much more important in his life and career than anti-Semitism – although Abrahams clearly felt, at various times in his life, that discrimination had been present and had acted as a motivational factor.[231]

In four different ways we can see how it is much more accurate to describe Abrahams as 'thoroughly Anglicised' than 'too Semitic'. Firstly, in Abrahams, we have an example of a sportsman from an immigrant background (although his circumstances were far from typical compared to others from immigrant backgrounds) whose family's pursuance of Anglicisation proved an enabling factor in a highly successful athletic career. Through a public school and Cambridge education, Abrahams, like other socially mobile Jews, entered into an obsessively sporting environment and gained access to the exclusive world of British amateur athletics.

Secondly, Abrahams was held by the British Jewish community to be a useful example of Anglicisation and assimilation. As well as being celebrated by the Jewish establishment as something of an 'English Jewish' hero, Abrahams was consciously portrayed both as justification for the so-called 'Anglicisation' campaign and as evidence of the ability of immigrant Jews to enter into the highest echelons of British social and sporting society. Likewise, and thirdly, during his career Abrahams also claimed that he himself was Anglicised and integrated, and espoused assimilation, with a weakened attachment to religious and cultural Jewishness, as a necessary factor in elite sporting achievement. He argued that being 'too Semitic' was incompatible with sporting achievement.

Fourthly, by examining Abrahams' approach towards 1936, we can clearly see that his social, cultural, political and sporting sympathies were almost wholly English in character. It is inaccurate to believe that Abrahams was indifferent towards the plight of international Jewry. Yet Abrahams, who clearly understood that his actions would be viewed negatively by British Jewry, was motivated by public school, 'amateurist' ideology rather than by allegiance towards an ethnic grouping he had spiritually, culturally and physically left behind him by 1936.

Although racial hostility was present in many different guises and at various times in his life, the picture painted of Harold Abrahams' life and career is one of an Anglicised second generation immigrant Jew as opposed to that of an outsider. This did not mean, however, that he became an accepted, 'Establishment' figure within British society.[232] Yet whilst he may not have been fully integrated into the British social and sporting elites, Abrahams' personality, character and attitude were clearly much more English than Jewish. It is wrong to view his life before, during or after his sporting career as anything other than that of an Anglicised and integrated son of an Eastern European Jewish immigrant.

Conclusions: sport and Anglicisation

It is clearly the case that the experiences of Jewish immigrants in late nineteenth- and early twentieth-century Britain were affected and shaped by sport. In many varied ways, immigrant involvement in physical recreation (or that of second generation immigrant children more specifically) impacted on Jewish integration into all levels of British society. Sport, evidently, became more than just a simple leisure activity and was inherently linked to shaping the aspirations and identities of many young Jews of immigrant heritage. Physical recreation not only helped determine their attitudes towards the 'majority' character and personality, it also directly influenced their entry and reception into mainstream society.

Sport was believed to play a vital role in the Anglicisation of Jewish immigrant children and in the initiatives designed to catalyse their acculturation. Historians of British Jewry have previously examined the direction and content of Anglicisation' programmes driven by the Jewish establishment, but have not generally understood or demonstrated the importance of physical recreation. It is evidently the case that communal leaders attached great significance to the assistance that sport could give to immigrant integration, seeing the promulgation of a 'sporting' attitude as central to these programmes' success. In one sense, the Jewish elites believed strongly in the ability of sport to shape Jews both physically and psychologically to make them appear, act and think like their non-Jewish peers. They also trusted in the power of physical recreation as a tool for breaking down alleged social and cultural barriers and alleviating tensions between Jewish and non-Jewish society.

Such a belief in the power of sport was also evident in the experiences of Jews of migrant parentage in the higher echelons of British society. The case study of Harold Abrahams, an atypical second generation immigrant, reveals that physical recreation was also an important facet of life for more privileged Jews during the early twentieth century. Integration on Abraham's part opened up exclusive sporting opportunities, yet sporting success also aided his acceptance by his public school and university peers and by the British Jewish establishment. Importantly, however, it was also true that Abrahams' integration and acculturation eventually contributed to his alienation from the Jewish community. Seemingly, for this second generation immigrant Jew, Anglicisation through sport, and sport through integration into the British public school and Oxbridge 'set', placed Abrahams in a milieu awkwardly located between Jewishness and Britishness.

In order to improve our understanding of the integration of Jewish immigrants into British society, experiences and attitudes linked to sport and physical recreation need to be much more comprehensively examined. On the one hand, sport evidently affected the formation of second generation migrant identities – a theme which will be more comprehensively discussed in the next chapter. An investigation of the role of sport in both collective and individual Anglicisation also reveals a great deal about the attitudes of communal leaders towards immigrant co-religionists and illustrates the tensions that arose at this time between Jewish and non-Jewish society. Additionally, much significance came to be attached to sport by the British Jewish elites, demonstrating their own strong belief in the links between sport and 'Britishness' and the apparent ability of physical recreation to shape and form 'British Jewish' identities.

Notes

1 V. Lipman, *Social History of the Jews in England: 1850–1950* (London, 1954), pp. 2–5. See also, concerning the growth of the Sephardic community, Roth, *A History of the Jews*, chapter 6.
2 J. Garrard, *The English and Immigration: A Comparative Study of the Jewish Influx 1880–1910* (London, 1971), p. 23.
3 Lipman, *Social History*, pp. 88–89, 102–103.
4 B. Wasserstein, *Britain and the Jews of Europe: 1939–1945* (Oxford, 1979), p. 7. For the higher figure, see L. London, *Whitehall and the Jews, 1933–1948: British Immigration Policy and the Holocaust* (Cambridge, 2000), p. 11.
5 Rubinstein, *A History of the Jews*, p. 28.
6 For a summary, see Endelman, *The Jews*, 'Introduction'.
7 Gartner claimed that this was 'the most actively investigated period in the historiography of the Jews in Britain'. L. Gartner, 'A Quarter Century of Anglo-Jewish Historiography', *Jewish Social Studies*, 48, 2, Spring 1986, p. 114.
8 M.B. Hart, 'The Unbearable Lightness of Britain: Anglo Jewish Historiography and the Problem of "Success"', *Journal of Modern Jewish Studies*, 6, 2, 2007, p. 158.
9 For example, in the Georgian period communal and lay leaders, for their own motivations and to prevent popular anti-Semitism, employed the resources of communal philanthropy to alter immigrant behaviour and characteristics. Endelman has shown in his famous work on this period that contemporary Ashkenazi elites utilised their influence to try to speed up the assimilation of working-class and pauper immigrants. He has noted that the Jewish establishment of the time 'began to view the problem of the Jewish poor as a social issue that required a more communal response' as 'leaders feared that lower class disreputability would strengthen popular hostility, thereby threatening their own advancement'. Endelman, *The Jews of Britain*,

p. 73. See also Endelman, *The Jews of Georgian England*, pp. 196–198, 201–202, 229–231.

10 Gartner, for instance, has argued that the Jewish leadership in Britain were simply hastening a process of 'Westernisation' which would have been the inevitable conclusion of immigrant movement from 'traditional' to 'modern' society. Gartner, *The Jewish Immigrant*, pp. 166, 241–242, 268. Socialist historians of Anglo-Jewry have viewed Anglicisation in terms of social control, seeing philanthropic and 'socialisation' initiatives aimed at encouraging immigrant acculturation as rooted in ideas and practices of class control. See, for instance, B. Williams, 'The Anti-Semitism of Tolerance: Middle-Class Manchester and the Jews, 1870–1900', in A. Kidd and K. Roberts (eds), *City, Class and Culture* (Manchester, 1985), p. 92; J. White, *Rothschild Buildings: Life in an East End Tenement Block 1887–1920* (London, 1980), p. 54. Other historians take a more balanced overview of Anglicisation. Feldman, for instance, contests that 'neither "Westernisation" nor "social control"' adequately 'conveys the contested and fractured process of Anglicisation'. He asserts that neither discourse addresses the complexities and intricacies evident in both the motivations of the Anglo-Jewish elites and the reception of assimilatory ideas and tendencies amongst the immigrants themselves. D. Feldman, *Englishmen and Jews: Social Relations and Political Culture, 1840–1914* (London and Toronto, 1994), p. 112; D. Feldman, 'Englishmen, Jews and Immigrants in London, 1865–1914: Modernization, Social Control and the Paths to Englishness', in R. Dotterer, D. Dash Moore and S. Cohen (eds), *Jewish Settlement and Community in the Modern Western World* (London, 1991), p. 110.

11 See, for instance: Feldman, 'Englishmen'; B. Lammers, '"The Citizens of the Future": Educating the Children of the Jewish East End, c.1885–1939', *Twentieth Century British History*, 19, 4, 2008; E. Black, *The Social Politics of Anglo-Jewry, 1880–1920* (Oxford, 1988), chapter 5: 'Club Life'.

12 Levine, *Ellis Island*, pp. 13, 271.

13 Gurock, *Judaism's Encounter*, chapter 3 'The Challenge and Opportunity of a New World of American Sports'.

14 For instance, in Black's survey of the social interactions of British Jewry, sport is addressed only fleetingly, despite an entire chapter being devoted to 'Club Life: Moulding Youth and Shaping Character'. Black, *Social Politics*.

15 S. Tananbaum, '"Ironing Out the Ghetto Bend": Sports and the Making of British Jews', *Journal of Sport History*, 31, 1, 2004.

16 Smith, 'Sex', p. 6; T. Collins, 'Jews, Anti-Semitism and Sports in

Britain, 1900–1939', in Brenner and Reuvani, *Emancipation Through Muscles*, p. 143.

17 Tananbaum, '"Ironing Out"', pp. 53–69. Tananbaum gives an interesting overview of some aspects of the role that sport played in the Jewish youth movement from the late nineteenth century through to the 1930s and 1940s, although physical recreation forms only one part of a discussion which also touches on ideas of gender, religion and social control.

18 Smith, 'Sex', p. 6.

19 See, for instance, J. Springhall, *Youth, Empire and Society* (London, 1977).

20 S. Bunt, *Jewish Youth Work in Britain: Past, Present and Future* (London, 1975), pp. 46–48.

21 Lipman, *Social History*, pp. 88–89, 102–103.

22 Endelman, *Radical Assimilation*, pp. 73, 94–95.

23 Rubinstein, *A History of the Jews*, p. 75, 93. Perhaps most importantly, in 1858, a special Act of Parliament was passed to allow Lionel de Rothschild to become the first practising Jewish Member of Parliament. The requirement for Jews to take a Christian oath to enter Parliament was dropped in 1866.

24 Endelman, *The Jews of Britain*, p. 171; Rubinstein, *A History of the Jews*, p. 73. For instance, from 1884, the Jewish Board of Guardians began inserting notices in Yiddish in Continental European newspapers warning Jewish refugees from coming to Britain 'because of the depressed state of the labour market'. As well as this policy of 'discouragement', the Board were also responsible for the somewhat controversial repatriation of around 50,000 immigrants back to the Russian Frontier, whilst other organisations such as the Russo-Jewish Committee and the Mansion House Commission also facilitated the 're-emigration' of several thousand refugees to the USA and the colonies. V. Lipman, *A Century of Social Service, 1859–1959: The History of the Jewish Board of Guardians* (London, 1959), p. 93; S.A. Hochburg, 'The Repatriation of Eastern European Jews from Great Britain: 1881–1914', *Jewish Social Studies*, 50, 1/2, Winter/Spring, 1988, p. 49; Gartner, *The Jewish Immigrant*, p. 43.

25 S. Kadish, *'A Good Jew and a Good Englishman': The Jewish Lads' and Girls' Brigade, 1895–1995* (London, 1995), p. 46.

26 *Jewish Chronicle*, 7 August 1891.

27 Feldman, 'Englishmen', p. 99. Free evening classes in English, home visits to aid immigrant women with housework, cooking and shopping, instruction on personal and domestic hygiene and encouraging social interaction between 'old' and 'new' Jews formed the core of a programme focused on 'the task of making the immigrants less foreign'.

28 Endelman, *The Jews of Britain*, p. 174.

29 Lipman, *Social History*, p. 144.

30 G. Alderman, *Modern British Jewry* (Oxford, 1992), p. 140; Lammers, '"The Citizens of the Future"', p. 404. See also R. Livshin, 'Acculturation of Immigrant Jewish Children, 1890–1930', in D. Cesarani (ed.), *The Making of Modern Anglo-Jewry* (Oxford, 1990).

31 G. Black, *JFS: The History of the Jews' Free School, London since 1732* (London, 1998), p. 122.

32 Kadish, '*A Good Jew*', pp. 11, 27–31; Springhall, *Youth*, p. 42.

33 On the Jewish youth club movement in London more generally, see Black, *Social Politics*, chapter 5: 'Club Life ', pp. 133–148.

34 University of Southampton Special Collections, Southampton (hereafter UoSSC), MS132/AJY220/3/6/5, 'Schedules of attendance at Jewish institutions' [1914].

35 Feldman, *Englishmen and Jews*, p. 348.

36 Black, *Social Politics*, pp. 133–140.

37 *Jewish Chronicle*, 12 December 1902.

38 G. Black, *Living Up West: Jewish Life in London's West End* (London, 1994), p. 221.

39 UoSSC MS116/138/4, Brady Street Club for Working Boys, 'First Annual Report: 1896–1897'; University College, London, Library, London (hereafter UCLL), West Central Jewish Working Lads' Club, *First Annual Report* (London, 1899); Bunt, *Jewish Youth Work*, p. 48.

40 On the public school missions and university settlements see G. Stedman Jones, *Outcast London: A Study in the Relationship between Classes in Victorian Society* (Oxford, 1971), pp. 257–259; and G. Himmelfarb, 'Victorian Philanthropy: The Case of Toynbee Hall', *American Scholar*, 59, 3, Summer 1990.

41 Smith, 'Sex', p. 7.

42 Black, *Social Politics*, p. 144.

43 UoSSC MS116/138/4, Brady Street Club for Working Boys, 'First Annual Report: 1896–1897'; B. Williams, *Jewish Manchester: An Illustrated History* (Derby, 2008), p. 83.

44 Tananbaum, '"Ironing Out"', p. 53.

45 *Jewish Chronicle*, 5 June 1896.

46 Holt, *Sport and the British*, pp. 139–142.

47 *Jewish Chronicle*, 5 June 1896, 19 June 1896.

48 Black, *Social Politics*, p. 113.

49 Kadish, '*A Good Jew*', p. 39; *Jewish Chronicle*, 24 January 1902.

50 Kadish, '*A Good Jew*', pp. 27–31; UoSSC, MS223, *First Annual Report of the Jewish Lads' Brigade* (London, 1898), p. 18.

51 *Jewish Chronicle*, 8 January 1909.

52 Gartner, *The Jewish Immigrant*, p. 175. A similar dilemma was faced by non-Jewish youth clubs, with the realisation that the average member was drawn to the club mainly for the sporting opportunities available. As was made clear by Russell and Rigby in 1908, 'outdoor games and athletics' and 'indoor athletic sports' needed to be a significant facet of any youth organisation, Jewish or Gentile, in order to appear attractive to adolescent boys. They acknowledged, somewhat grudgingly in both tone and sentiment, that there existed a 'common belief that the main or sole function of a club, the purpose for which it exists, is the provision of recreation and exercise'. C. Russell and L. Rigby, *Working Lads' Clubs* (London, 1908), p. 115.

53 UoSSC MS172/AJ250/4, *Stepney Jewish Club Chronicle*, 1, 7, September 1903, p. 4.

54 UCLL, West Central Jewish Working Lads' Club, *Fourth Annual Report* (London, 1902), p. 3.

55 *Jewish Chronicle*, 14 October 1900.

56 Such a view had been prevalent since the earliest period of Russian and Eastern European Jewish migration to Britain. For example, in 1886, the *St James' Gazette* published a series of articles on 'Jewish Pauperism' which were subsequently reprinted in mainstream newspapers such as the *Observer*. One article claimed that 'the immigrants were immoral, replete with vice, a heavy charge on the rates ... and steeped to the lips with every form of moral and physical degradation'. *St James' Gazette*, 23 February 1886. Julius, *Trials of the Diaspora*, p. 277, labels this the 'health-threat argument' against alien immigration.

57 Beatrice Potter, for instance, claimed that it was a 'mistake to suppose that the Jew is physically unfit'. See B. Potter, 'The Jewish Community', in C. Booth (ed.), *Life and Labour of the People of London*, Volume I, *East London* (London, 1889), p. 586. On these perceptions see, for instance, C. Holmes, *Anti-Semitism in British Society: 1876-1939* (London, 1979), chapter 3: 'The Health and Morals of the Nation'; B. Harris, 'Anti-Alienism, Health and Social Reform in late-Victorian and Edwardian Britain', *Patterns of Prejudice*, 31, 4, 1997.

58 C. Russell and H.S. Lewis, *The Jew in London: A Study of Racial Character and Present-Day Conditions* (London, 1901), p. 5.

59 *Jewish World*, 12 October 1900.

60 Ibid. 13 April 1906.

61 *Report of the Inter-Departmental Committee on Physical Deterioration* (London, 3 volumes, 1904); G. Searle, *The Quest for National Efficiency. A Study in British Politics and Political Thought: 1899–1914* (Oxford, 1971), chapter 3: 'The Ideology of National

Efficiency'. In the aftermath of the 1904 report, 'Christian' youth organisations such as the Church Lads' Brigade resolved to introduce a stronger physical element to their work, resulting in a much greater emphasis on sport. More generally, physical recreation came to be regarded as an important tool against 'physical worsening'. Springhall, *Youth*, p. 57; M. Rosenthal, *The Character Factory: Baden-Powell and the Origins of the Boy-Scout Movement* (New York, 1986), pp. 131–140.

62 *Jewish World*, 7 December 1900.

63 White, *Rothschild Buildings*, p. 190.

64 UoSSC MS/132/AJ220/3/4, B. Henriques, 'Jewish Youth and Youth Clubs Today', address given to the Annual General Meeting of the Association for Jewish Youth, 23 June 1955. On Henriques more generally, see L.L. Loewe, *Basil Henriques* (London, 1976). On the Oxford and St George's Jewish Lads' Club, see R. Loewe, 'The Bernhard Baron Settlement and Oxford and St George's Club', in A. Newman (ed.), *The Jewish East End: 1840–1939* (London, 1981), pp. 143–146.

65 Black, *Social Politics*, p. 140.

66 *Jewish World*, 1 March 1906.

67 Russell and Rigby, *Working Lads*, p. 347.

68 Ibid.

69 *Report of the Inter-Departmental Committee*, Volume II, *List of Witnesses and Minutes of Evidence*, p. 15.

70 Ibid. pp. 147–148.

71 *Jewish Chronicle*, 19 August 1904.

72 *Report of the Inter-Departmental Committee*, Volume II, p. 151.

73 Bunt, *Jewish Youth Work*, p. 48.

74 For an outline of this debate, see Julius, *Trials of the Diaspora*, pp. 278–279.

75 See Holt, *Sport and the British*, pp. 92–93.

76 Smith, 'Sex', p. 6.

77 UoSSC MS116/138/4, Brady Street Club for Working Boys, 'First Annual Report: 1896–1897'.

78 Black, *Social Politics*, p. 146.

79 *Royal Commission on Alien Immigration*, Volume II, *Minutes of Evidence Taken Before the Royal Commission on Alien Immigration* (London, 1903), p. 690.

80 UoSSC MS132/AJ195/5, R. Henriques, 'Unpublished typescript of a biographical journal of Basil Henriques' [c.1970], p. 161.

81 When the Oxford and St George's Jewish Lads' Club opened in 1914, Basil Henriques noted that 'it is perhaps the athletic man who is more especially needed to transform the newly arrived foreign Jews into

English sportsmen'. UoSSC MS132/AJY200/3/6/5, B. Henriques, *The Oxford and St George's Jewish Lads' Club* (London, 1914), p. 14.

82 There are numerous references in Jewish club reports to financial and staffing limitations eventually limiting the amount of sport that could be offered to members. The 1906 Hutchison House report, for example, noted that financial assistance was urgently needed if the club was to continue offering its hugely popular outdoor sporting programme into the following year. Money from wealthy donors was eventually acquired. *Jewish World*, 2 February 1906.
83 Tananbaum, '"Ironing Out"', p. 54.
84 J.A. Mangan, *Athleticism in the Victorian and Edwardian Public School* (London, 2000), pp. 9, 56.
85 Bunt, *Jewish Youth Work*, pp. 46–47.
86 UoSSC MS132/AJ250/4, *The Bradian*, 5, 1903, pp. 4–5.
87 UoSSC MS172/AJ250/4, *Stepney Jewish Club Chronicle*, 1, 14, January 1904, p. 4; *Stepney Jewish Club Chronicle*, 1, 11, December 1903, p. 5.
88 London Metropolitan Archives, London (hereafter LMA), ACC2996/01, Victoria Club Log Book, 7 July 1901.
89 Kadish, *'A Good Jew'*, p. 44.
90 LMA ACC2996/01, Victoria Club Log Book, 19 May 1901, 26 May 1901.
91 UoSSC MS116/121/AJ301/2, *Notting Hill Jewish Lads' Club Magazine*, 1, 1, April 1911, p. 3.
92 Black, *Living Up West*, p. 230.
93 Stepney Jewish Lads' Club, *How a Jewish Working Boys' Club is Run: An Account of the Stepney Jewish Lads' Club* (London, 1914), p. 5.
94 Ibid. p. 9.
95 Bunt, *Jewish Youth Work*, p. 129.
96 Smith, 'Sex', p. 14.
97 *Jewish Chronicle*, 3 May 1913.
98 *St James' Gazette*, 4 April 1887.
99 A. White, *The Modern Jew* (London, 1899), p. xii.
100 Quoted in Alderman, *Modern British Jewry*, p. 123.
101 Ibid. p. 133.
102 Feldman, 'Englishmen', p. 102.
103 *Jewish Chronicle*, 18 February 1887.
104 W. Besant, *East London* (London, 1901), p. 191.
105 Quoted in Lipman, *Social History*, p. 106.
106 Not all Jewish club leaders and patrons were keen for the 'mixing' of races to be promoted. As Bunt has shown, some within the youth movement feared the effect that encouraging interaction between Jew

and non-Jew in their clubs could have on the overall cohesion of the Jewish community. A deep fear existed in some quarters over the possible effect allowing non-Jewish members into clubs would have on levels of intermarriage and conversion. Bunt, *Jewish Youth Work*, p. 128.

107 The omission of any 'Jewish' reference in the club's title is indicative of the Rothschilds' desire that the organisation should be open to all denominations. M. Lazarus, *A Club Called Brady* (London, 1996), p. 9.

108 UoSSC MS116/138/4, Brady Street Club for Working Boys, 'First Annual Report: 1896–1897'.

109 Smith, 'Sex', p. 14.

110 Lazarus, *A Club*, p. 27; UCLL, West Central Jewish Working Lads' Club, *Third Annual Report* (London, 1901).

111 The Federation of London Working Boys' Clubs was founded in 1887 by a number of boys' clubs, to provide an organisation which could formulate a unified policy and philosophy and provide back-up services for the boys' club movement. The Federation was renamed in the early twentieth century as the London Federation of Working Boys' Clubs, and changed its name again in 1994/95 to the London Federation of Clubs for Young People, to reflect the changing social situation and the increasing inclusion of girls. H.L. Smith, 'Introduction', in H.L. Smith (ed.), *The New Survey of London Life and Labour*, Volume IX, *Life and Leisure* (London, 1935), p. 22. The archives of the movement are held in the London Metropolitan Archives. See LMA 4283.

112 Brady Street Club for Working Boys, *Sixth Annual Report* (London, 1902) reprinted in Lazarus, *A Club*, p. 27.

113 UCLL, West Central Jewish Working Lads' Club, *Fourth Annual Report* (1902), p. 7.

114 *Jewish Chronicle*, 19 March 1906.

115 *Jewish World*, 7 December 1900; *Jewish Chronicle*, 9 February 1900.

116 The *Jewish World* highlighted the example of the gymnastics team of the Victoria Jewish Lads' Club, based on Fordham Street, Whitechapel. In April 1904, the newspaper reported that all of the members of the club's gymnastics team were employed as tailors, upholsterers and sign-makers, and worked from 8 a.m. to 8 p.m. most days, yet 'in spite of these long spells, gymnastics forms one of their chief recreations and if permitted they would remain at the club after closing hour endeavouring to master the intricacies of a difficult exercise or watching and helping the struggles of a younger member. Threat of suspension from the use of the gymnasium is one of the most popular disciplinary measures'. The reporter continued by adding that 'some of the lads, not content with gymnastics five or six

nights a week, spend their Sunday mornings practising in the open air gymnasium at Victoria park', p. 117.

117 Although the Jewish clubs (Brady, West Central, Victoria and Stepney) numbered only four out of over forty affiliated clubs, Jewish gymnasts effectively dominated the Federation's gymnastic tournaments between 1900 and 1914. Lazarus, *A Club*, p. 23. In 1901, the West Central Jewish Working Lads' Club report claimed that in the gymnastics section 'no boy's club was willing during the past year to accept challenges, as they all said that the team representing the Club was too strong'. UCLL, West Central Jewish Working Lads' Club, *Third Annual Report* (1901), p. 7.

118 Lawson-Levy's Jewish heritage makes the fact that this statement was made even more significant. H. Richards, 'Lawson, Harry Lawson Webster Levy, Viscount Burnham (1862–1933)', *Oxford Dictionary of National Biography* (Oxford, 2004).

119 Garrard, *English and Immigration*, p. 18.

120 *Jewish World*, 22 April 1904.

121 See, for instance, the biography of Jewish professional boxer Ted 'Kid' Lewis, whose childhood was regularly interspersed with fights and battles against non-Jewish children. M. Lewis, *Ted 'Kid' Lewis: His Life and Times* (London, 1990), p. 5. Likewise, interviews held in the Manchester Jewish Museum demonstrate that fights between Jewish and non-Jewish individuals and gangs were commonplace in the city through the 1890s and 1900s. Manchester Jewish Museum, Manchester (hereafter MJM), J102, Interview with Jack Goldstone.

122 Manchester City Archives, Manchester Central Library (hereafter MCA), M130/6/1, Jewish Lads' Brigade, 'Annual Report – 1912', p. 6. MCA M130/3, Grove House Lads' Club Managers' and Subscribers' Minutes, 3 November 1919.

123 The Shield started as a competition for London cadet battalions the previous year, but was expanded nationwide in 1920. See MCA M130/6/1, Jewish Lads' Brigade, 'Annual Report – 1919', p. 14.

124 Kadish, 'A Good Jew', p. 126.

125 See Manchester JLB Annual Reports, 1907–27 and 1928–35. MCA M130/6/1; M130/6/2.

126 MCA M130/6/2, Jewish Lads' Brigade, 'Annual Report – 1933', p. 9; *Jewish Chronicle*, 27 May 1936; UoSSC MS223/4/14, *Annual Report of the Manchester Jewish Lads' Brigade* (Manchester, 1936), p. 10.

127 MCA M130/6/1, Jewish Lads' Brigade, 'Annual Report – 1921', p. 7; UoSSC MS223/4/14, *Annual Report of the Manchester Jewish Lads' Brigade* (Manchester, 1938), p. 7.

128 Brady Street Club for Working Boys, *Sixth Annual Report* (1902) reprinted in Lazarus, *A Club*, p. 27.

129 B. Henriques, *Club Leadership* (Oxford, 1943), pp. 128–129.

130 This situation changed over time, especially so during the 1920s. On this and the link between sport and growing secularisation during the first half of the twentieth century, see Chapter 2, below.

131 Bunt, *Jewish Youth Work*, p. 168.

132 *Jewish Chronicle*, 3 May 1913.

133 Although the Association expanded rapidly, by 1913 the management was still composed of just ten unpaid staff. *Jewish Chronicle*, 3 May 1913.

134 Kadish, '*A Good Jew*', p. 11.

135 UoSSC MS126/AJ17/1/1, Ancient Order of Maccabaeans, *Report of the Maccabaean Athletic Committee* (London, 1901), p. 13; ibid. Balance Sheets of the Ancient Order of the Maccabaeans, 1902–10.

136 Bunt, *Jewish Youth Work*, p. 168; *Jewish Chronicle*, 9 January 1914; *Jewish World*, 10 February 1927.

137 Black, *Social Politics*, p. 146.

138 The 1908 JAA sports day, held at Stamford Bridge Athletic Grounds, drew 200 individual competitors and a crowd of over 3,000. *Jewish World*, 26 June 1908.

139 *Jewish Chronicle*, 3 May 1913.

140 *Jewish World*, 1 June 1906; Lammers, '"Citizens"', p. 407; Bunt, *Jewish Youth Work*, p. 168.

141 *Jewish World*, 1 June 1906.

142 Ibid. 17 May 1923.

143 In the 1940s, Local Education Authorities in London began allowing Jews who were members of sports teams to leave school early on Fridays in order to complete their League commitments and be home before the start of the Jewish Sabbath. B. Henriques and I.W. Slotki, *The Jewish Sabbath* (London, 1940), p. 22.

144 Black, *Social Politics*, p. 146.

145 *Jewish Chronicle*, 6 November 1903.

146 *Jewish World*, 29 November 1907.

147 *Jewish Chronicle*, 23 January 1914.

148 For a biographical sketch and detailed discussion of the development of Montefiore's religious thought, see D. Langton, *Claude Montefiore: His Life and Thought* (London, 2002). On his religious views and contribution to the foundation of Liberal Judaism in Britain, see E. Kessler, 'Claude Montefiore and Liberal Judaism', *European Judaism*, 34, 1, 2001, pp. 17–32.

149 *Jewish Chronicle*, 23 December 1909.

150 Ibid.

151 R. Wilberforce, 'Cohen, Lionel Leonard, Baron Cohen (1888–1973)', *Oxford Dictionary of National Biography* (Oxford, 2004); *Jewish*

Chronicle, 30 March 1990.

152 Collins, 'Jews', p. 147.

153 Abrahams was forced to retire from athletics in 1925 after suffering a broken leg whilst competing in the long jump at an athletics meeting. *The Times*, 7 May 1925. After his retirement, Abrahams worked as a barrister, a columnist for *The Times*, held various positions in the British Athletic Board, including Chairman (1948–75), and was elected President of the Amateur Athletics Association in 1976. He also co-authored in 1931, *Oxford versus Cambridge*, a complete record of all of the 7,489 'blues' who had represented their universities at sport. He was appointed CBE in 1957. N. McWhirter, 'Abrahams, Harold Maurice (1899–1978)', *Oxford Dictionary of National Biography* (Oxford, 2004).

154 In 2011, the first official biography of the sprinter was published, entitled *Running with Fire: The True Story of 'Chariots of Fire' Hero*. Written by author and journalist Mark Ryan, the comprehensive volume details Abrahams' life through a broad investigation of archival and newspapers materials and interviews with family and friends.

155 E. Cashmore, 'Bigotry, Manhood and Moral Certitude in an Age of Individualism', *Sport in Society*, 11, 2, 2008, p. 159. It is worth highlighting here the contrast between the relative lack of interest in Abrahams compared to his rival in *Chariots of Fire*, Eric Liddell. A number of biographies of 'The Flying Scotsman' have been published in recent years. For example, S. Magnusson, *The Flying Scotsman: The Eric Liddell Story* (London, 1981); D. McCasland, *Eric Liddell: Pure Gold* (London, 2003); J. Keddie, *Running the Race: Eric Liddell, Olympic Champion and Missionary* (London, 2007).

156 The main proponents of this view are Cashmore, 'Bigotry' and E. Carter, '*Chariots of Fire*: Traditional Values/False History', *Jump Cut: A Review of Contemporary Media*, 28, April 1983.

157 *Chariots of Fire* (dir. Hugh Hudson, 1981).

158 Cashmore, 'Bigotry', p. 159.

159 Carter, '*Chariots of Fire*', p. 14.

160 University of Birmingham, Special Collections, Birmingham (hereafter BUSC), HA/13/1, J. Bromhead, 'Harold Abrahams as Athlete, Author and Amateur', lecture given at University of Warwick, 1988, p. 5.

161 Holt, *Sport and the British*, p. 275.

162 Carter, '*Chariots of Fire*', p. 16. Many friends and family have argued that *Chariots of Fire* displays an 'exaggerated' level of racial discrimination. Abrahams' daughter, Sue Pottle, has repeatedly criticised the film for what she sees as its overemphasis on anti-Semitism during her father's time at university. See, for example, *Daily Express*, 14

September 2007; *Observer*, 9 September 2007. Close friend of Abrahams, Norris McWhirter, has also noted his belief that Abrahams would have felt the suggestion of anti-Semitism at Cambridge in the manner portrayed by *Chariots of Fire* to be 'over-fanciful'. McWhirter, 'Abrahams'.

163 In his biography of Abrahams, Ryan indicates a number of instances in Harold's time at Cambridge, including being 'cold-shouldered' in his application to join the Hawks Club and the apparently two-faced celebration of Abrahams' successes in the 1923 athletics meeting against Oxford University by his fellow teammates (who Harold believed 'probably hated my guts really'), where the sprinter felt discrimination and hostility caused by his Jewishness. He did later concede, however, that he 'may have exaggerated those things' and 'perhaps ... found it [anti-Semitism] when it wasn't really there'. Ryan, *Running*, pp. 39, 41, 80, 141.

164 As Weber has shown, a 'pervasive Gentleman's anti-Semitism' was apparent in the pre-1914 period especially, but was rarely 'overt' or 'violent'. T. Weber, *Our Friend 'The Enemy': Elite Education in Britain and Germany before World War I* (Stanford, 2008), pp. 200–202, 208.

165 Ryan, *Running*, pp. 18–20. It has been suggested that as well as facing a great deal of verbal and social anti-Semitism at Repton, Abrahams may have been subjected to sexual assaults by his peers.

166 BUSC HA/2, H. Abrahams, 'What Makes a Champion' (unpublished [c.1930]). In a BBC radio interview in 1963, Abrahams noted that 'I had to find something where I could score off people and running, of course, you can, you can get first and win and I was determined to do so'. BUSC HA/17/21, Harold Maurice Abrahams interview, BBC Radio, *People Today*, 20 September 1963.

167 *Daily Telegraph*, 22 November 1989.

168 *Jewish Chronicle*, 3 April 1981. Importantly, Abrahams himself later rejected the idea that he had a grand mission to change the nature of perceptions of the Jewish population; claiming 'I didn't run for all the Jews. I ran for myself'. Quoted in Ryan, *Running*, p. 140.

169 Carter, '*Chariots of Fire*', p. 16.

170 McWhirter, 'Abrahams'; BUSC HA/7/1, Memorial Address at Harold Abrahams Funeral, 20 February 1978. For a detailed overview of Harold's early life, see Ryan, *Running*, pp. 3–18.

171 McWhirter, 'Abrahams'.

172 Weber, *Our Friend*, p. 197.

173 Ibid. p. 95.

174 Endelman, *Radical Assimilation*, pp. 76–80.

175 McWhirter, 'Abrahams'; BUSC HA/7/1, Memorial Address at Harold Abrahams Funeral, 20 February 1978.

176 Julius, *Trials of the Diaspora*, p. 378.
177 Holt, *Sport and the British*, pp. 82–83.
178 BUSC HA/17/21, Harold Maurice Abrahams interview, BBC Radio, *People Today*, 20 September 1963; BUSC HA/7/1, Memorial Address at Harold Abrahams Funeral, 20 February 1978.
179 Correspondence of author with E. Bryant [Harold Abrahams' niece], 20 May 2011. Abrahams later noted that 'as far as I was concerned in 1920, I attached far more importance to getting my "blue" at Cambridge than being chosen to represent Great Britain in four events in the [Antwerp] Olympics'. BUSC HA/2, Harold Abrahams, 'Competing at the Olympic Games' [c.1928].
180 BUSC HA/17/21, Harold Maurice Abrahams interview, BBC Radio, *People Today*, 20 September 1963; BUSC HA/2, Transcript of interview with Harold Abrahams, 20 October 1977.
181 J. Crump, 'Athletics' in Mason, *Sport in Britain*, p. 44.
182 For a general survey of amateur dominance, see Holt, *Sport and the British*, chapter 2, 'Amateurism and the Victorians'.
183 Crump, 'Athletics', p. 53.
184 *Athletics Weekly*, 6 January 1973; *The Times*, 7 May 1925; BUSC HA/2 Transcript of interview with Harold Abrahams, 20 October 1977.
185 *Jewish Chronicle*, 1 August 1924.
186 Cashmore, 'Bigotry', p. 162.
187 *Daily Mirror*, 9 July 1924; *Athletics Weekly*, 6 January 1973.
188 *Jewish Chronicle*, 27 July 1923.
189 *Jewish World*, 15 March 1923.
190 *Jewish Chronicle*, 13 April 1923, 1 September 1924; *Jewish World*, 28 June 1923, 2 October 1924.
191 *Jewish World*, 29 November 1923.
192 Ibid. 19 April 1923.
193 Ryan, *Running*, p. 19.
194 *Jewish Chronicle*, 14 February 1913; BUSC HA, Interview with Tony Abrahams; Correspondence with E. Bryant, 20 May 2011.
195 Quoted in Ryan, *Running*, p. 82.
196 *Jewish Chronicle*, 27 November 1925.
197 *Jewish World*, 10 February 1927.
198 This is interesting when compared with Abrahams' rival in *Chariots of Fire*, Eric Liddell, who did achieve success despite being devoutly Christian. Although there were many inaccuracies in the portrayal of the Scotsman in the film, it was true that he did not run in the heats of his favoured event, the 100 metres, because the heats fell on a Sunday. He knew of this several months in advance, however, and not as he boarded the British team boat – as portrayed in the film. Despite

this setback, he was still successful in the 400 metres event at the Games. Seemingly, Abrahams' assertions were aimed mainly at strictly religious Jews, whose aspirations for a successful sporting career would have been hampered by observance of the Jewish Sabbath, dietary laws and other religious practices. Cashmore, 'Bigotry', p. 164.

199 Quoted in Ryan, *Running*, p. 232. Maccabi was founded in Europe in the early twentieth century and had strong links to political Zionism. Underpinning its ideology was the notion of increasing Jewish interest and involvement in sport in order to improve Jewish physical and mental toughness – pivotal in the plans for the creation of a Jewish homeland. Maccabi came to Britain in 1934, with the establishment of the British Maccabi Association and grew considerably. By 1963 it had 6,000 members in Britain, dwarfing any other Jewish organisation catering for children and young adults. See Chapter 2.

200 See Chapter 2 'Religion and ethnicity' below. Jewish communal organisations, which had loudly espoused the need for Anglicisation' during the early part of the twentieth century, were increasingly realising that integration and assimilation had been overly successful and that religious observance amongst young Jews was rapidly declining. Sport, in the minds of communal and religious elites, was one contributory factor in this 'drift' and was said to be weakening the bond between Jews and their religion and culture.

201 *Jewish Chronicle*, 8 May 1936.

202 A. Kruger, 'Germany: The Propaganda Machine', in A. Kruger and W. Murray (eds), *The Nazi Olympics: Sport, Politics and Appeasement in the 1930s* (Chicago, 2003), pp. 18–21.

203 R. Holt, 'Great Britain: The Amateur Tradition', in Kruger and Murray, *The Nazi Olympics*, pp. 70–72.

204 P. Beck, *Scoring for Britain: International Football and International Politics, 1900–1939* (London, 1999), pp. 201–202. See also, M. Polley, 'The British Government and the Olympic Games in the 1930s', *Sports Historian*, 17, 1, 1997, pp. 30–40.

205 Holt, 'Amateur Tradition', p. 70. For more on the British boycott movement, see ibid. pp. 70–86; M. Llewellyn, 'Epilogue: Britannia Overruled', *International Journal of the History of Sport*, 28, 5, 2011; Beck, *Scoring for Britain*, pp. 201–202.

206 *Manchester Guardian*, 6 December 1935.

207 *Jewish Chronicle*, 27 March 1936. The BWSF was the sporting wing of the Communist Party and drew much of its leadership from politicised Jews such as Benny Rothman.

208 Quoted in G. Walters, *Berlin Games: How Hitler Stole the Olympic Dream* (London, 2006), p. 124.

209 Ibid. p. 59. At the 1935 meeting of the BOA, Abrahams argued that if the Games were boycotted then this would lead to a deterioration of international relations. He also felt that a boycott would unnecessarily harm sporting ties to the Nazi regime.

210 Holt, 'Amateur Tradition', p. 72; R. Mandell, *The Nazi Olympics* (London, 1971), p. 80.

211 Churchill Archives Centre, Churchill College, Cambridge (hereafter CAC), NBKR6/54/1, Harold Abrahams to Philip Noel-Baker, 25 September 1935.

212 Ibid. Philip Noel-Baker to L. Montefiore, 30 November 1935. In this letter to L. Montefiore – *Manchester Guardian* athletics correspondent and public advocate of a British boycott of the Berlin Games – Noel-Baker remarked that Abrahams had 'promised to help me in writing such a letter and in editing the draft when I had made it'. The full draft of the letter which Noel-Baker proposed to send to *The Times* can be found in CAC NBKR/6/54/1.

213 Ibid. Harold Abrahams to Philip Noel-Baker, 3 December 1935. Seemingly, Abrahams' decision to recommend to Noel-Baker not to publish the letter was driven by *The Times*' public denouncement of attempts to stop a football friendly between England and Germany, scheduled for 4 December, from taking place. See Beck, *Scoring for Britain*, p. 201 and Chapter 2.

214 Quoted in Llewellyn, 'Epilogue: Britannia Overruled', p. 822; Ryan, *Running*, p. 194.

215 A point which is echoed by Abrahams' biographer. Ryan, *Running*, pp. 212–216. However, evidence also later emerged that Abrahams had been in regular contact with Avery Brundage (American International Olympic Committee Chairman) in the years leading up to 1936. Brundage was a staunch opponent to boycotting Berlin and believed that 'an Olympic boycott on account of the Jews would excite dangerous, possibly uncontrollable anti-Semitic sympathies'. C. Marvin, 'Avery Brundage and American Participation in the 1936 Olympic Games', *Journal of American Studies*, 16, 1, 1982, p. 89.

216 Holt, 'Amateur Tradition', p. 72.

217 *Jewish Chronicle*, 27 March 1936.

218 Ibid. 29 May 1936.

219 Quoted in Walters, *Berlin Games*, p. 60. The Board of Deputies was founded by Jewish communal leaders in 1760 to act as a representative organisation in political, social and cultural affairs.

220 *Jewish Chronicle*, 8 May 1936, 25 September 1936.

221 Abrahams met with Foreign Office officials, including Sir Robert Vansittart and Sir John Simon, on many occasions to discuss his possible attendance at the Games with the BBC. He was told by both

Vansittart and Simon that the Foreign Office had no objection to him going to Berlin. Ryan, *Running*, p. 202.

222 McWhirter, 'Abrahams'; BUSC HA/17/21, Harold Maurice Abrahams interview, BBC Radio, *People Today*, 20 September 1963.

223 BUSC HA/17/21, Harold Maurice Abrahams interview, BBC Radio, *People Today*, 20 September 1963.

224 Ryan, *Running*, p. 212.

225 *Jewish Chronicle*, 8 May 1936.

226 Ibid. 3 April 1936.

227 Ibid. 27 March 1936.

228 Mandell, *Nazi Olympics*, p. 297.

229 *Jewish Chronicle*, 27 March 1936.

230 M.C. Carnes, *Past Imperfect: History According to The Movies* (New York, 1996), p. 10.

231 Holt, *Sport and the British*, p. 275.

232 Indeed, there is much evidence to suggest that he was an extremely controversial character within British sport after his retirement from competition in 1925 and could foster polarised opinions. Abrahams frequently courted controversy over his outspoken views on the 'need' for British athletic specialisation, and on the Olympic Games, and over his suggestions for the modernisation of the British athletic movement. In addition, he was disliked by many within sporting journalism and within British sports administration. Significantly, Bromhead has highlighted the fact that, unlike his brothers, Abrahams was never knighted as a sign of his lack of acceptance amongst the highest social and sporting circles. BUSC HA/13/1, J. Bromhead, 'The Life and Times of Harold Abrahams', lecture given at University of Warwick, 1988. For Abrahams' views on the 'need' for specialisation see *The Times*, 25 April 1926, 18 July 1931. For his views on the Olympic Games see BUSC HA/13/1, Adophe Abrahams Memorial Lecture. Norris WcWhirter claimed Abrahams 'worked against the stolid petty opposition of senior office holders in various governing bodies, often athlete manqués … to raise athletics from a minor to major national sport' during his time with the British Amateur Athletic Board from the 1940s through to his death in 1978. McWhirter, 'Abrahams'.

2

Religion and ethnicity

Introduction

In his discussion of migrant ethnicity since 1800, Panayi argues that the descendants of British immigrant groups gradually 'adopt British norms'. Through interactions with their surroundings, 'hybrid identities' are formed 'using elements of both the homeland and the environment into which they are born'. Over time, the distinctive ethnicity of the immigrant generation is gradually eroded and the 'norms of the homeland' are replaced by 'those of Britain'.[1]

Panayi utilises the example of the Eastern European immigrant Jewish community to demonstrate this process. He argues that after settling in Britain in the decades leading up to the First World War, immigrant Jews, or their children and grandchildren more specifically, gradually cast off the vestiges of the migrant identity. Over time, behavioural patterns, social mobility, intermarriage, assimilation of language, food and dress and increasing secularisation all work to dilute the original immigrant ethnicity. A process of 'cultural adaptation' occurs as generations progress, creating new forms and expressions of individual and collective Jewishness.[2]

This paradigm is also reflected within scholarship directly concerned with British Jewish history. In his book on *Radical Assimilation*, Endelman claims that Jewish ethnicity has been eroded through interactions with the wider community since the seventeenth century. In his analysis, communal unity, religious observance and geographical and cultural cohesion within the Jewish community have all been weakened through life in modern Britain, which has largely been characterised by 'toleration and prosperity'. For Endelman, Jewish ethnicity has undergone substantial change as 'England ... presented Jews with an unprecedented

challenge to the preservation of their religious and ethnic cohesive-
ness'. He claims that 'the weakening of Jewish solidarity runs as a
persistent theme throughout Anglo-Jewish history'.[3]

These themes and processes are especially evident since the
Eastern European Jewish immigration. Mainly from the interwar
period onwards, the second and third generation immigrants
gradually cast off the vestiges of the Old World Judaism that their
parents and grandparents had brought with them. Through interactions with wider society, key aspects of immigrant Jewish ethnicity
were slowly replaced by a hybridised British Jewish identity. After
the Second World War, this 'drift and defection' became more
prominent, as increasing secularity, social mobility and intermarriage and a general weakening of communal and ethnic cohesion
combined to radically alter Jewish identity.[4]

Whilst various social, cultural, political and economic forces
impacted on this process, it also seems that sport had an important
effect on Jewish identity. Outside of Britain, historians of Jewish
sport have made some attempt to analyse the links between physical
recreation and the destruction and construction of Jewish ethnicity.
For instance, Gurock's *Judaism's Encounter with American Sports*
demonstrates the important negative impact that sport had on
Jewish religious identity, leading to the formation of secularised
American Jewish identities during the modern period.[5] Similarly, in
his *Ellis Island to Ebbets Field*, Levine focused on the notion of
sport acting as a 'middle ground', a socio-cultural milieu where the
young immigrant Jews cast off their immigrant identity and where
hybrid forms of American Jewishness were developed and refined.[6]

Although sport has received little direct attention, it has been
touched on in wider discussions of transformation of Jewish identity in
Britain. Endelman, for example, claims the 'enthusiastic' consumption
of 'English popular culture' during the interwar years was an
important factor in promoting religious indifference amongst the
younger immigrant generation. Sport and physical recreation, and
other such 'amusements of urban life', were much more attractive to
immigrant youths than the 'Old World culture of their parents'.[7]
Livshin has shown that social and sporting organisations had a
noticeable impact on Jewish religious observance during the 1920s and
1930s.[8] Likewise, in his examination of Jewish social mobility,
Cesarani has claimed that sport was a 'leisure activity that divided the
Jewish working class along generational lines'. Sport not only both

affected and reflected 'generational and geographical rifts', however, it also had an impact on the 'socialisation' of Jews into mainstream society – thus acting as a corrosive on communal solidarity.[9]

This chapter will further examine how sport has impacted on the transformation of Jewish ethnicity since Russo-Jewish migration. Whereas the previous discussion on Anglicisation focused on conscious efforts and programmes to help the acculturation of 'British' identity, this chapter will show that sport also impacted on Jewish identity in a more fluid and haphazard manner. Without the assistance of the Jewish establishment – indeed, to their growing disdain – young Jews gradually became more interested in sport and less concerned with religious observance, communal cohesion and Jewish culture. Through involvement in sport, many Jews gradually cast off the ethnicity of the immigrant generation and formed new, secularised Jewish identities.

Interest in physical recreation exacerbated a 'drift' away from religion, culture, authority and traditions of the immigrant population. On the one hand, sport contributed to growing religious indifference, especially with regard to attitudes towards the Jewish Sabbath. It also hastened a generational split between the migrants and their offspring and hampered efforts at reinvigorating Jewish religion and culture. Essentially, within three generations of migration, sport had been a significant factor in the erosion and reconfiguration of British Jewish identity.

'All on the side of the more athletic form of Sabbatarianism': physical recreation and the Jewish Sabbath[10]

It is clear that religion – belief and observance – is often a 'fundamental' component of migrant ethnicity.[11] This is especially true for Jewish immigrant communities. Often, religious organisations and customs have been seen as providing a sense of collective identity for Jews hailing from different countries and regions – be it in a British, American or Western context. Although it is historically incorrect to talk of one, unified Jewish community existing within Britain, religion has often been an important aspect of what identified Jews as Jews and what defined Jewish ethnicity.[12]

If a weakening of attachment to religion occurs within a migrant community, there is an accompanying effect on that group's ethnic identity. In the case of British Jewry, there is much evidence to suggest that a marked decline in religious observance has occurred since the late nineteenth century.[13] Whilst the façade of organised religion may have remained relatively strong throughout the twentieth century, there are many indications that concern for faith amongst the Jewish community has steadily declined – a trend reflected amongst other British minority groups and within British society as a whole.[14]

Increasing Jewish secularisation has been most apparent with regard to the British-born offspring of immigrants. From the interwar years onwards, declining levels of religious observance, together with shrinking numbers attending Synagogue or Jewish religious school, have been perceptible. Although some historians have claimed that a strong sense of social and cultural Jewishness was retained, it is apparent that growing numbers of younger Jews were taking little or no interest in the spiritual aspect of their ethnicity.[15] Importantly, such a trend did not go unnoticed and began to cause particular alarm amongst the Jewish establishment from the 1920s onwards. By 1931, religious leaders in Britain were claiming that there was a disturbing 'decline of observance amongst young people in Anglo-Jewry'.[16]

The decline in religious adherence was particularly noticeable with regard to attitudes towards the Jewish Sabbath. Whilst the 'special' nature of the rest day has remained largely intact, fewer and fewer Jews have strictly observed Sabbath laws e.g. prohibiting work, travel, the carrying of money and encouraging attendance at Synagogue.[17] The general trend across the twentieth century has been for a decreasing concern and observance of the Sabbath customs and traditions – with a clear correlation between the progression of generations and declining *Shabbat* (Hebrew term for Jewish rest day) adherence.[18]

Many factors have been highlighted to explain this trend.[19] Alongside economic and cultural changes, however, it is also the case that interest in sport affected attitudes towards the Jewish rest day. Mirroring nineteenth-century trends within British Christian society, Jewish involvement in sport began to exert a visible influence on levels of Sabbath adherence.[20] In contrast to the picture painted by some historians, many Jews ignored Sabbath law and customs in favour of physical recreation on the supposed Jewish 'rest' day.[21] From the 1890s onwards, an increasing number of Jews viewed Saturday as a day for play – or watching professional sportsmen play, rather than a day of spiritual regeneration or prayer.[22]

In the face of growing anxiety, many Jewish individuals and organisations began to play and watch sport on the Sabbath increasingly frequently. Concerns were raised not only for the spiritual well-being of these sportsmen and women, but also for the potential effect that sport on the Sabbath could have on the social togetherness and cohesion of the community more generally. The question was asked: how could Jews be expected to respect themselves, their elders, their community and their religion if they could not respect one of the fundamental principles of their Jewishness? For many, the issue of observance of the Sabbath went to the very core of the health of the British Jewish community.

Most of these calls went unheeded. In the face of growing concern over the 'irreligion' of younger Jews – and appeals for youth organisations to take a lead in 're-Judaising' their members – sport on the Sabbath became more widespread. In short, whilst interest in physical recreation was only one cause of decreasing Sabbath observance, it was an important factor in changing the beliefs and attitudes of a significant proportion of the population. Although it was the source of much anxiety, Jewish participation in sport on Saturdays, in whatever guise, became increasingly prevalent.

Individual Jews

The first indications that sport was impeding on Sabbath observance for some Jews appeared in the nineteenth century. One instance of this emerged within the Jewish establishment. Like their Christian peers, whilst members of the English Jewish elites were publicly observant in religious matters, strict standards of religious adherence were not necessarily maintained in their private lives.[23] This was the case for Samuel Montagu (1832–1911), banker, philanthropist and co-founder of the Federation of Synagogues. Montagu, who according to one biography was a 'strict adherent of Orthodox Judaism', often allowed his household to play tennis on the Sabbath, yet prohibited croquet as he felt a 'chipped mallet constituted work'.[24]

Indications that the wider Jewish population were foregoing traditional Sabbath observance in favour of sport appeared more frequently from the 1890s onwards. In 1898, the *Jewish Chronicle* reported that the Conference of the National Union of Women

Workers had addressed the benefits of strict Sabbath observance for the Jewish community but complained about the propensity of some Jews using the rest day for sport and leisure purposes. Miss Lidgett, a Poor Law guardian from St Pancras, 'considered that the Jews had, by the observance of their Sabbath, strengthened their brain-power, as one day's rest in seven gives increased force to mental action'. She went on to add, however, that more Jews were spending their Saturday 'at play' and that 'a Sabbath spent in tennis, golf and bicycling is not ideal and does not smooth the rigours of the soul'.[25]

Similar concerns were echoed four years later, yet this time came from within the Jewish religious community itself. In 1902, the Reverend John Harris gave a paper entitled 'The Conditions and Needs of Modern English Judaism' at the Liverpool Jewish Social Club.[26] In Harris' eyes, a rise of sport and leisure amongst Jews was acting as a corrosive on the sanctity of the Sabbath. He noted that 'Sabbath after Sabbath, the faces of our friends are not seen in our Synagogues' and went on to ask:

> Are they all engaged in absolutely imperative business? With those so engaged I have sympathy. But what of those who may be found at the time of divine worship on the golf-links, the river or the cricket-field? What of those who may be found on a Friday night in the theatre and the music hall? ... Do these things seem of small moment? It is because we are faithless in small matters that the greater evils befall us.[27]

Although comments such as these indicate that anxieties about Sabbath sport were evident before 1914, concern about this 'problem' became much more widespread from the interwar years onwards. It was at this time that those who had progressed through the sports-obsessed Jewish youth movement reached adulthood. Like their Gentile peers, many were increasingly drawn to sport and leisure opportunities that abounded on Saturday – the main day for such activities within non-Jewish society.[28] As Cesarani has noted, it was during the interwar years, when the 'British-born offspring of the Jewish working class were being socialised into the British working class', that more and more Jews from the immigrant community began exploring sporting opportunities on the Sabbath. Faced with the 'competition' of sporting and leisure activities (cinema, dancing etc.), respect and adherence for the Jewish rest day, and Judaism more generally, 'suffered a dramatic decline'.[29]

What is clear is that whilst many Jews wanted to involve themselves in sporting activities on the Sabbath, some did not want to
appear openly unobservant. In order to avoid an open break with
either familial or communal elders, many young Jews found ways of
minimising their detection and the potential anxiety their sporting
interests could cause. In his account of his East End childhood,
Willy Goldman noted that he regularly played street football on the
Sabbath, but made sure to play away from his own road to avoid
being seen desecrating the rest day by his *Cheder* teacher.[30]
Likewise, Abraham Goldstone, born in Manchester in 1910,
recounted many years later the length he used to go to in order to
play football for his local team without incurring the wrath of his
observant father:

> I remember the time that I used to play football for the team ... and
> my father was very religious at the time and he wouldn't let me play.
> He wanted, all he wanted to do, was to go to the Synagogue on
> Saturdays, you know what I mean. And I was playing football and I
> had to get my football boots out on a Saturday afternoon and I had
> to throw them out of the cellar window to somebody who was
> waiting and then walk out. He says to me 'Wo gehst du?' that means
> 'Where are you going?' and I says 'I'm going to the park'. He says
> 'Okay then, be back in time' and I used to go and play football.

Importantly, Abraham also noted that his experiences were not
unusual and that 'none of the boys' parents knew that they were
playing football'. Indeed, the team used to wash their own jerseys in
order to avoid their parents' detection.[31]

Similar fears were perceptible amongst those Jews who had the
opportunity to play sport for professional teams. Take the example
of Broughton Rangers, a professional rugby league team based in
the centre of Manchester's immigrant Jewish community. During
the interwar years, Broughton had a number of Jewish players on
their books, including Lester Samuels and Reuben Gleskie, who
chose to play as amateurs 'so that they could compete on a
Saturday afternoon with a clear conscience'. Whilst these players
did not want to let Sabbath observance impede on their sport, they
were not willing to fully ignore every tenet of Sabbath law – in this
case trying to avoid the rules preventing work by not publicly
taking remuneration for their efforts.[32] One of the most successful
Anglo-Jewish professional sportsmen, David Hyman 'Harry'

Morris (1897–1985), also had a relaxed attitude to Sabbath observance, despite his adherence to wider Jewish festivals and customs. Morris, who played football professionally for Brentford, Millwall and Swindon Town (for whom he scored a club record 229 goals), regularly played on the Sabbath, but was known throughout his career to refuse to play on High Holy Days.[33]

There were, however, many Jews who openly enjoyed sporting activities on the Sabbath with few, if any, misgivings about the impact of their apostasy on their elders. Jews such as Martin Bobker, born in 1911 in Manchester, were typical of a growing number of second and third generation immigrants who had fully assimilated the leisure and sporting routines of their non-Jewish peers. By the time he was eighteen, Martin, who worked in a waterproof garment factory, said that his 'typical' weekend was distinctly un-Jewish. Starting with a Friday night trip to the Salford greyhound track, followed by billiards and then cards at a friend's house, Martin's 'Sabbath' continued with more billiards on Saturday lunch time, another trip to the dogs and an occasional visit to Maine Road to see Manchester City play football.[34] Similarly, second generation migrant Joe Garman also recounted many years later that his Sabbath often entailed trips to watch professional football matches. Joe claimed 'my lack of orthodoxy suited my own whims' and noted that he never allowed religion to get in the way of his love for sport and leisure activities on a Saturday.[35]

As these two examples show, one of the most popular sporting activities on the Sabbath did not necessarily involve direct participation. During the early twentieth century, spectating at professional sporting contests was an increasingly prevalent activity for Jews on their rest day. Increasingly, and perhaps more commonly than actually playing sport on the Sabbath, Jews were to be found in the terraces of rugby, cricket and football grounds watching others compete. Mirroring similar trends elsewhere, spectator sport was a 'growing passion' for young Jews on a Saturday, much to the detriment of Synagogue attendance.[36]

As early as the 1890s, Jews were already becoming keen sports spectators on the Sabbath. During this decade 'significant numbers' of Jews began going to watch rugby matches in Leeds on Saturday. Such was the strength of support for Leeds Parish Church that the team became locally known as the 'Sheenies' – an anti-Semitic reference to the club's large fanbase.[37] Similarly, Manchester Jewry during the 1900s was also known to include a large number of fans of local rugby league team Broughton Rangers, whose two home grounds, Wheater's Field and (from 1913 onwards) the Cliff, were closely situated to the city's large Jewish immigrant community centred around Cheetham Hill.[38]

Jewish passion for rugby remained strong during the interwar years, a fact which soon came to the attention of communal leaders. In 1928, Professor Selig Brodetsky (1888–1954), renowned Zionist leader and mathematician, wrote of his concern over the number of Jews in Leeds using their Sabbath, not for rest or prayer, but for watching rugby and cricket. He commented that 'the road in which I live in Leeds, leading to and from the famous Headingley ground, is crowded every Saturday by … wandering Jews, upon whom the "packele" [weight, seriousness] of the Torah seems to sit very lightly indeed'. Brodetsky was clearly concerned that a penchant for passive involvement in sport had grave potential consequences for the religious health of the community.[39]

It was association football, however, which was the most popular spectator sport amongst British Jewry. The first indications of Jewish interest in professional football emerged in the pre-1914 period, especially amongst the second generation immigrants. In 1911, Algernon Lesser, a well-known Jewish youth worker, was interviewed for the *Jewish World* about 'Anglicising Methods' and his work with immigrant children. Perhaps to the surprise of some within the community, Lesser noted that boys of the Brady Street Club were becoming keen followers of football and that their enjoyment of indigenous sporting pastimes was beneficial for their ongoing acculturation. He claimed that

> Most non-Jews, and many of our own community also, would be astonished if they were to visit a Jewish boys' club on a Saturday evening and listen to the conversation which goes on among the members. The results of the games in the football leagues that afternoon are most keenly discussed, and loud is the wailing and great the distress among the supporters of the 'Spurs' if Tottenham Hotspur have had to lower their colours.[40]

Despite there being a clear interest in football, it was not until the interwar years that Jews in any considerable numbers began attending matches. Part of the explanation has much to do with the fact that the British-born, second generation – many of whom had progressed through the ranks of the 'sporting' youth movement – were coming of age at this time. In addition, the 'economic advance' experienced by many Jews during the interwar years would also have proved a facilitative factor.[41] The 1920s and 1930s saw considerable numbers of young Jews of migrant parentage moving into 'white collar' employment, meaning they experienced an accompanying rise in free time and expendable income for use on leisure activities such as watching sport.[42]

It is clear that the interwar years saw a considerable rise in Jewish attendance at football matches – something which had significant consequences on levels of observance of the Sabbath. Green points out in his volume on East End Jewry during the interwar years that 'from a day of rest and prayer, Saturday in the Jewish East End was ... becoming a day given to leisure and enjoyment'. Chief amongst the leisure activities chosen was football and 'teenagers and young adults flocked in increasing numbers to see their rival teams play on Saturday afternoons'. Whilst declining levels of observance clearly facilitated greater attendance at football matches, it would have also been the case that football effectively kept some Jews away from their Synagogue – proving a bigger draw than traditional forms of Sabbath adherence. In short, 'as Synagogues slowly lost their clientele, attendances at football matches increased'.[43]

The professional team which appears to have attracted most Jewish support at this time was Tottenham Hotspur FC, a club based in north London.[44] Whilst 'The Spurs' began to attract Jewish interest in the pre-1914 period, it seems that considerable numbers only began attending games at White Hart Lane during the 1920s and 1930s. According to the *Jewish Chronicle*, almost all Jews 'who followed the game [association football]' during the 1920s 'were 'Spurs supporters', and it seems their Jewish fanbase grew considerably during the 1930s as well.[45] By the time that the controversial England versus Germany game was held at Tottenham's ground in December 1935, mainstream newspapers were claiming that up to a third, about 10,000 people, of Tottenham's regular home attendance was made up of Jewish fans.[46] A year earlier, sports writer Trevor Wignall noted in his *Daily Express* column that a recent trip to watch Tottenham Hotspur had seen him surrounded by Jewish fans on the terraces.[47] By the 1970s, due to their large Jewish fanbase, Tottenham supporters adopted the moniker 'The Yids', seemingly as part of a response to being labelled as 'Yids' by rival supporters. The characterisation of Tottenham as the 'Jewish' team still remains strong today.[48]

Many reasons can be put forward to explain why Tottenham garnered so much Jewish support during the first half of the twentieth century. Firstly, it does seem that the social and geographical mobility of Jewish Londoners in the interwar period played a significant role in increasing Jewish support for 'The Spurs'. Jewish settlements in areas like Tottenham, Hackney, Golders Green and Finchley grew considerably in the interwar years as many second generation, socially mobile and increasingly secularised Jews relocated from the East End. For the growing number amongst this community interested in sport, Tottenham Hotspur offered a geographically close option to watch professional football.[49]

Although not solely limited to British Jewry, another influence on growing Jewish support for Tottenham was the age-old footballing fashion of 'glory-supporting' (the practice of choosing a team due to their success, not because of any geographical or familial reasoning). In the early twentieth century, Tottenham were one of the most prominent professional teams in the capital, becoming the first club outside of the Football League to win the FA Cup in 1901. A letter written to the *Jewish Chronicle* from a long-standing Jewish Tottenham fan noted that his own support for the club began after their second FA Cup final victory in 1921: 'I sincerely believed this was God's Chosen Football Club'.[50] There were many Jewish Tottenham fans who had experienced social mobility and economic success and who 'wanted to be associated with an institution like the 'Spurs because it was successful and because they had a certain flair'.[51] It was also the case that many Jewish Tottenham fans claimed their support for the club was made easier by it being one of the capital's easier grounds to access, due to the extensive electric tram network which covered London at this time.[52]

Tottenham Hotspur's bitter north London rivals, Arsenal FC, also began to attract a significant number of Jewish football fans during the 1930s. This decade, which mainly saw Tottenham languishing in the second tier of English football, was an especially successful one for Arsenal, who won multiple League and FA Cup championships. According to the *Jewish Chronicle*, this accounts for why Arsenal 'amassed a loyal group of Jewish fans' during this decade, beginning a Jewish connection to the club which remains strong in the modern day.[53]

Arsenal worked especially hard away from the pitch to develop strong ties with London Jewry. Legendary Arsenal manager, Herbert Chapman, was labelled a 'great friend of the Jewish people' on his death in 1934 for the extensive work he conducted with local Jewish charities. After Chapman's death, two of his successors, George Allison and Billy Wright, worked to maintain the club's links to the Jewish community under their respective regimes. In November 1934, for example, Allison wrote to the *Jewish Chronicle* noting his pleasure at the 'connection' that Arsenal had with London's Jews:

> I am happy to think we have a large number of Jews who derive healthy entertainment and get enjoyment from the demonstrations of sportsmanship which they see at the Arsenal ground. For many years it has been our great pleasure to contribute to Jewish charities and to help those deserving causes which Jewish organisations have 'fathered' and I am conscious of the fact that we are only able to do this to the fullest degree because of the support which we receive from the Jewish community.[54]

Away from London, Jews in some of the main provincial settlements were also becoming keen football followers during the first part of the twentieth century. According to various sources, Leeds United gained a notable Jewish following amongst the city's second and third generation immigrant community from the 1930s, whilst Manchester United also seemingly won over many Jewish football fans in the pre-World War One period.[55] The main Manchester club supported by Jews was Manchester City, founded initially in Ardwick in 1880. Oral interviews held at the Manchester Jewish Museum demonstrate that many young, second generation immigrant Jews became keen and regular Manchester City supporters from the interwar years onwards.[56]

For many young Mancunian Jews, football clearly took precedence over anything resembling a strict Sabbath observance. Religious rituals and customs were gradually replaced with routines based around sport and spending time with other non-observant friends. Sydney Lea, born in Manchester in 1902, recalled that he and a group of Jewish friends became Manchester City season ticket holders during the 1920s. Mirroring footballing rituals elsewhere within British Jewry and the wider population, on Saturday morning the group would go to the Grosvenor Hotel in central

Manchester where they would 'have a couple of drinks and a few games of billiards' before hailing a taxi ('five fellas in, five pence each') to proceed to the ground in the early afternoon. Sydney did not only regularly forego religious customs to support his beloved club, he also curtailed family commitments for important games. In 1923 he even cut short his honeymoon to ensure he could attend City's first game at their new Maine Road stadium.[57]

Football spectating involved a notable degree of religious laxity. Significantly, there is no evidence to suggest that Sydney felt any anxiety over using his Sabbath for sport rather than a stricter observance. For him, and thousands of Jews across the country, Saturday had become a day for sport, not for attending Synagogue or adhering to the seemingly stifling laws and customs associated with the Jewish Sabbath. Like many other young Jews, Sydney was keen not to appear totally unobservant in the company of his family despite being comfortable with his own secularity. On those occasions when he took his father to watch Manchester City – an activity which in itself did not displease his parents – Sydney refrained from one regular activity to avoid incurring his father's disapproval. Many years later, Sydney commented 'well, you see, I used to smoke when I was watching football and the old man being

5 Jewish Manchester City fans, 1936

there I wouldn't want to hurt his feelings ... it being the Sabbath and all'.[58]

This contradictory – or more accurately, selective – attitude towards Sabbath observance emerges elsewhere amongst other Jewish football fans. Whilst some were relaxed and outwardly expressed no concern that their spectating at football matches had ramifications for their faith (which was not necessarily important to them anyway), some believed they could indulge in their passion and still adhere to Sabbath law. In 1934, the *Jewish Chronicle* interviewed a 'well-known member of the community' who was also a keen supporter of Arsenal FC. When asked 'surely you don't attend football matches on Sabbath?', he replied:

> I certainly do, as I don't break Jewish law. I don't pay, I am a season ticket holder. I purchased my pass on a weekday and when I enter the Arsenal ground on Sabbath it is the same as if I was entering a public park, since no money changes hands.

The columnist was confused as to whether this entailed an 'explanation or excuse', yet the gentleman was adamant that regular attendance at professional football was compatible with his interpretation of Sabbath law and customs.[59] One regular attendee at Tottenham Hotspur during the 1960s and 1970s claimed it was 'well known' that Jews who supported the club would often buy season tickets to circumvent Sabbath laws preventing the carrying of money.[60]

This is not to say that football spectating was off-limits to more traditionally observant Jews. Whilst it appears that many of those who followed football did so at the expense of Sabbath services, some Jews managed to combine a visit to the *Shul* (Yiddish term for the Synagogue) with a trip to watch football on the same day. One Jewish Tottenham fan in the 1920s recounted his regular Sabbath routine whenever Tottenham were playing at home:

> In those days, before floodlights were invented, almost all games took place on Saturday afternoons from about two o'clock. It was possible to be in synagogue until the end of *musaf* [additional prayers held on Sabbath and other special services], to nip home for a quick plate of *lokshen soup* [chicken soup], and then board a tram from Aldgate to White Hart Lane. No other ground could offer such ease of access.[61]

What this and all the other examples show is that Jewish sports spectators were making a series of concessions and selections with regard to their faith on a weekly basis when it came to the Sabbath. Whilst their passion for watching sport remained constant, approaches towards their religion and their rest day varied considerably. Reflecting and influencing wider trends towards religious apathy within Jewish society, Jews interested in sport came to increasingly view Saturday as a day for indulging their passion, not for traditional Sabbath rest and spiritual enrichment.

Jewish clubs

Similar sentiments were also present within a number of Jewish youth organisations. During the interwar years especially, youth clubs and groups catering for young second and third generation Jews were also adopting relaxed attitudes towards sport on the Sabbath. Communal and religious leaders increasingly voiced concerns that the Jewish youth movement, founded to aid Anglicisation, was now effectively contributing to the erosion of Jewish identity. Not only did prioritising sport on the Sabbath catalyse the evident growth in ignorance of the laws and customs of the rest day; it was also argued that the obsession with sport that these organisations demonstrated well into the interwar years – an obsession so important in the Anglicisation project – was also affecting the growing religious apathy of wider Jewish society.

Whilst these organisations tried to avoid Sabbath desecration where possible, it was generally the case that the youth movement did not view the promotion of religion as a core objective. Though club leaders wanted to see 'some level of religiosity', they did not want their members to be 'too Jewish'. Some of the Jewish clubs were evidently more religious in tone and atmosphere than others; Stepney and Oxford and St George's, for instance, both held regular Sabbath services and promoted prayer and religious education. However, in a reflection of the centrality of Anglicisation to their work, the majority consciously minimised the religious content of their programmes.[62] Club leaders did work hard to ensure that sporting activities would not impede Sabbath observance, as evidenced by the creation of the Jewish Athletic Association. Yet this was driven mainly by sporting considerations and a desire to facilitate physical recreation, not as a way of promoting Sabbath adherence.[63]

It was common for some Jewish youth organisations to organise sport on the Jewish Sabbath for their members. For instance, the Myrdle Jewish Girls' Club was reported in the *Jewish Chronicle* in 1914 as regularly organising hockey for its members on Saturdays. One club leader commented that her girls were 'none the worse Jews for indulging in healthy and outdoor sport' on the Sabbath.[64] Likewise, the Jewish Lads' Brigade often took a lax attitude towards the Sabbath in the pre-World War One period. The programme for the Sabbath on their 1899 summer camp noted that after the Brigade Chaplain had 'read the service ... the whole day was given up to sport'.[65] In 1911 it was reported that the Liverpool JLB were organising cricket games on the Sabbath, a sport which 'has been indulged in on the Sabbath for years past without raising objections from any quarter'.[66]

Evidently, these examples reflect the fact that ideas of acculturation and Anglicisation were central to the Jewish youth movement during the pre-1914 period. At this time, Anglicisation was considered the most urgent need, resulting in the prioritisation of sport as a means of assimilation and the marginalisation of religious education. Despite the general acceptance of this before the First World War, however, there is some evidence that there was growing concern over the effect of promoting sport on the 'Jewishness' of club members. Much of this criticism came from within the youth movement itself. For example, the Reverend R.F. Stern, a co-founder of the Stepney Jewish Lads' Club, claimed in 1907 that the club's sporting programme was an impediment to religious education and the general spirituality of members. He argued that there was 'nothing specifically Jewish in athletics', claiming that the promotion of sport amongst the youngest of the population was harmful to the future of Anglo-Jewry overall.[67] Stern's comments were reflected later that year at the Jewish Literary Congress, where one speaker 'complained that too much attention was paid by the managers of boys' clubs to ... athletic exercises, to the disadvantage of Jewish culture'.[68]

Some of the club managers were also concerned over the spiritual effect of the clear sporting focus of the youth movement. In 1904, Simon Myers, manager at the Stepney Jewish Lads' Club, wrote to the *Jewish Chronicle* commenting that 'the pursuit of physical culture is being pushed in a manner too one-sided'. He continued:

> I am second to none in enthusiasm for the glories of the football and cricket field for our lads, but I think a halt should be called among the

managers of our clubs, so that something may be done for the
religious side of the work ... I am painfully aware that there is a
rooted objection among club managers to any kind of real religious
work being promulgated in the lads' clubs, but none of them dares to
deny that a large majority of the lads seldom see the inside of a place
of worship and seldom utter a word of prayer from one week to
another.[69]

Particularly concerning for some critics was the effect that sport
had on attitudes towards Sabbath observance. It was felt that, by
encouraging young Jews to develop a 'sporting' attitude, more
would see Saturday as a day of leisure and recreation, rather than
prayer and spiritual development. In 1914, Leonard Stern
condemned the Brady Street Club in an article in the *Jewish
Chronicle*. Stern noted that 'East London is not exactly a nursery of
religion' and that the 'whole question of religion in the Jewish clubs
stinks in my nostrils'. He attacked Brady Street for their role in the
growing religious apathy of the younger population, making particular reference to the fact that Brady was 'all on the side of the more
athletic form of Sabbatarianism'.[70]

Whilst there was some concern over the effect of sport on
religious observance before 1914, anxiety and pressure for change
grew considerably during the interwar years. Against the background of a general decline in religious attitudes in Jewish and
non-Jewish society at this time, Jewish communal leaders became
fearful over the future religious and ethnic identity of the
community. Up and down the country, religious and lay elites were
becoming increasingly distressed at what they saw as a 'lack of
religious spirit, religious apathy and disintegration amongst Jewish
youth' – something which they attributed to the success of
programmes of acculturation and assimilation. With regard to
Anglicisation, many within the Jewish elites in the 1920s felt that
'the whole thing had gone too far'. They now stressed that effort
was needed in order to stem the growing religious apostasy of the
population.[71]

During this period, the Jewish youth clubs faced condemnation
for failing to do more to protect and promote the 'Jewishness' of
their members. In 1927, Basil Henriques claimed that it was 'an
appallingly grave matter' that 'most of the clubs ... have failed
boldly to face the religious question'. Whilst he conceded that
Anglicisation was important during the pre-1914 period, when

immigration seemed to pose a threat to the community, this was no longer the case in the 1920s. He argued that 'the problem today is to keep the Jews Jews ... and to Judaise those who have become Anglicised ... Without guidance from their club manager-friends, the adolescents are being allowed to wander from the field'.[72] Mirroring this sentiment, the *Jewish Chronicle* began a campaign at this time to 'revivify the religious institutions of Anglo-Jewry' to work against the 'threat posed by ignorance and irreligion'. Central to this debate was the Jewish youth movement who had 'assisted ... assimilation' but had 'neglected the Jewish values that would give moral ballast to their [the members'] lives'.[73]

Sport was increasingly targeted for criticism. In the eyes of some, it was a factor in growing 'spiritual' apathy and acted as a block to a greater focus on religious education. Many within the communal and religious leadership believed that sport's usefulness to the community had ceased and that the continuing emphasis on physical recreation was detrimental to the spiritual well-being of the population. A 1930 conference convened by the Association for Jewish Youth on the theme of 'The Club and the Religious Problem' complained that 'sport' within the youth movement had been 'stressed unduly'. The 'main conclusion and consensus of opinion' reached was that a 'religious influence must be brought to bear on the clubs'.[74]

Throughout the 1930s efforts were made to bring a greater religious emphasis into Jewish club life and to improve Sabbath adherence – a key aspect of Jewishness which they felt had been marginalised. Communal leaders felt that the youth movement should spearhead attempts to 're-Judaise' the religiously indifferent immigrant youth. Suggestions were made, throughout the interwar period, for a 'strong religious bias' to be introduced into the various Jewish clubs.[75] In 1935, for example, all AJY clubs agreed to Sabbath services in conjunction with the United Synagogue to combat the fact that 'the majority of club members were growing up completely out of touch with religion and with a growing disregard for Jewish customs and traditions'.[76]

Despite this and similar initiatives, sport was not gradually marginalised in favour of greater religious education and activities. In reality, the various youth clubs and JLB groups retained a strong sporting focus throughout the 1920s and 1930s. Archival evidence from this period suggests that 'most organisations privileged sports, athleticism – all aspects of Britishness – and saw Jewish identity as essential, but arguably secondary'. Reflecting 'philosophical and generational differences' between the communal elites and the members of the youth movement, sport continued to be prioritised over religious education generally, and Sabbath observance more specifically.[77]

This was especially true with regard to the Jewish Lads' Brigade. During the interwar years 'JLB activities were not marked out by their religious atmosphere and their religious content was minimal' and sport was regularly, and without concern, organised on the Jewish Sabbath. Summer camps for Southern and Northern JLB battalions throughout the 1930s regularly gave the Sabbath over to organised sport and games. One account of the 1931 London JLB camp, for instance, noted that 'all kinds of games were played' on the Sabbath, with the Brigade Chaplain, Dr Morris Ginsberg, being a particularly enthusiastic participant. Clearly, not all religious authorities took issue with the promotion of healthy physical recreation on the rest day.[78]

Within the club movement, a similarly tolerant attitude towards Sabbath sport was also in evidence during the interwar years. In 1930, Basil Henriques – a vocal exponent of the need to protect young Jews' spiritual identity – claimed that 'with regards to Saturdays, we have just got to face facts – that the boys work in the morning and that they ... play cricket and football in the afternoon'. Whether they indulged in sport inside or outside of the youth club on the Sabbath, Henriques was generally supportive, seeing sport as a much more preferable alternative to 'lounging about and gambling'. Even at a time when there was growing concern over the apparent 'irreligion' of the younger generation, the belief still existed that sport had an important 'prophylactic' function. For Henriques, the appearance of Anglo-Jewry externally still took precedence over the internal dynamics and debates of the community.[79]

In the provincial clubs, an even more relaxed attitude towards physical recreation on the rest day was evident. In Manchester, where the Grove House Jewish Lads' Club and the Manchester JLB existed side by side, no real consistent concern for maintaining the Sabbath was perceptible throughout the interwar years.[80] Club leaders and managers regularly ignored the Sabbath and prioritised sporting activities over religious observance. The 1919 Grove

House annual report, for example, noted that opening hours had been extended to the Sabbath and that 'cricket, football and basketball games are organised on Saturday afternoon'.[81] Club teams regularly trained on the Sabbath whilst club leaders, who expressed no real anxiety over religious observance in their institution, readily entered teams into non-Jewish Saturday leagues and tournaments.[82] Ironically, one of the biggest hurdles encountered with organising these teams was not the local community, but the members themselves – many of whom often missed training or matches to watch professional football.[83]

The club further contradicted Sabbath law when they began charging an admission fee for football spectators coming to club grounds. As the Grove House football section became increasingly successful during the late 1920s, the decision was taken to begin asking those growing numbers who watched club teams on the Sabbath to pay for their entrance to the Elizabeth Street ground. For more observant members of Manchester Jewry, however, the idea of charging an admission fee took Grove House's desecration of the Sabbath a step too far. A letter to the *Jewish Chronicle* in 1931 from a Jewish resident of Hightown, Manchester (an area of settlement which had seen the arrival of more prosperous artisan and middle-class Jewish immigrants) complained

> If we will but study the activities of this club, we will find that although it consists entirely of Jewish youth … nothing is done to strengthen the spirit of Judaism in its members. The Sabbath is publicly and without the least shame desecrated by them. Football matches between them and rival teams are always played on Saturday afternoons. This desecration has been carried a step further by an admission fee being charged although most of the club's supporters are Jews.[84]

The response of the club to this criticism gives an interesting insight into the attitudes of club managers towards Jewish religious observance and the Jewish Sabbath. It is noted in club minutes days after the letter's publication that managers decided to 'ignore' the criticisms over the Sabbath 'desecration'. This judgement contrasts sharply with the club's eagerness to work to placate the County Football Association after they raised concerns about advertising games and charging for admission on Sundays a year later (i.e. encouraging the desecration of the Christian Sabbath). Grove

House's eventual resolution to honour the Christian Sabbath and ignore anxiety over the Jewish rest day demonstrated the continual sporting focus of the club as an aid to integration for the city's Jews. When it came to a choice between Jewishness and sport, sport clearly won, but not at the risk of causing problems with the local non-Jewish sporting authorities.[85]

Sport had a notable impact on levels of Sabbath observance amongst British Jewish society from the late nineteenth century through to the Second World War. It is not the case to say that every Jew was indulging in sport on their rest day.[86] However, evidence suggests that for many Saturday was seen as a day of play, or watching others play, rather than for attendance at Synagogue or adherence to Sabbath laws and customs. Whilst many social, economic and cultural factors account for the general decline in Sabbath observance seen in the early part of the twentieth century, sport also clearly worked to undermine and modify attitudes amongst British Jews towards their rest day.

When seen in the wider context of changing attitudes towards religion, the trend for a sporting use of the Sabbath takes on greater significance. The interwar years were a time when concern over levels of religious observance and 'Jewishness' grew considerably. This was especially true with regard to the British-born children of immigrant Jews, many of whom were seen to be becoming decreasingly concerned with Jewish religion, customs and values. It is clear that sport was one activity which impacted on the cultural and religious attachment of these younger Jews to their community – something that was increasingly understood and feared by communal and religious leaders. Sport may have been affecting observance of the Sabbath, but it was also having the wider effect of undermining the preservation and promotion of Jewishness.

While sport came in for a great deal of criticism for exacerbating apathy towards the Sabbath, many Jewish individuals and organisations continued to prioritise sport over religious activities. Mirroring wider trends, it is clear that some youth leaders themselves saw physical recreation as a more acceptable use of Saturday than either attendance at Synagogue or adherence to Sabbath laws. Whilst religious and cultural differences over sport on the rest day existed across the population, those who worked with the youngest of the community still placed great value in the benefits of physical recreation. Despite communal criticisms, for some youth leaders, as well as many British-born second and third generation Jews, Saturday was a day reserved for sport, not Synagogue.

The new 'golden age' of Jewish professional boxing

Whilst interest in sport exerted an impact on religious observance, it also affected Jewish ethnicity in a wider sense. In the early twentieth century, Jewish sporting involvement hastened a growing social and cultural 'drift' of younger Jews away from their elders. At a time when the second generation were gradually abandoning Jewish identity and culture, sport was a key area where the fracturing of immigrant society took place. The sport with which this process was most associated, and which concerned communal leaders the greatest, was British professional boxing – a sport dominated by Jews from the late nineteenth century through to the Second World War.

Historiographical notions of Jewish ethnicity being undermined by a socio-cultural 'drift' were first expressed by Endelman in his volume on *Radical Assimilation*. He contends that modern Anglo-Jewish history as a whole is characterised by a 'drift', whereby allegiance and concern for 'traditional sympathies' were gradually eroded due to the effects of life in the West on Jewish immigrants. For Endelman, the 'fabric of communal solidarity' was gradually eroded as 'new interests and loyalties jostled for primacy with old associations and concerns'. Whilst the cohesion of British Jewry was affected by this process, it also led to a 'dilution of Jewish identity' as more Jews gradually assimilated into mainstream society and became British in language, religion, dress, culture, work practices and settlement patterns.[87]

Similar notions are evident elsewhere within the historical literature on British Jewry. In an examination of the interwar period, Cesarani concluded that communal cohesion and immigrant identity were both undermined with the progression of a generation. Whilst not a 'monolithic formation', the immigrant Jewish community largely shared a language (Yiddish), were united by interest in Jewish knowledge, religion, Old Country politics and community and lived in a small geographic area. In contrast, by the interwar years their children spoke English, were generally becoming more secularised (as seen previously), were gradually more apathetic towards communal politics and organisations and were increasingly socially and geographically mobile. In essence, Jewish immigrant identity had been seriously undermined as the children of immigrants grew closer to the majority culture.[88]

One area where the 'fracturing' between generations can be clearly seen is in the leisure choices of younger Jews. Whereas first generation immigrants spent their free time at their own clubs, prayer halls, Yiddish theatre or silent cinema, during the early twentieth century their offspring were gradually 'socialised' into the indigenous working class and began taking up British leisure pursuits.[89] As Williams has noted with regard to second generation Manchester Jewry, their 'influences were no longer the traditions of the Eastern European *shtetl*, but those of working class Manchester, the culture of the street corner, the neighbourhood café, the Monkey Parades [promenading in public], the cinema, the ice palace and the dance hall'.[90] During this period, the *Jewish Chronicle* also believed that the leisure choices of the young 'contributed to the emergence of a disaffected, sometimes disorderly, population of young Jews'. It reported that increasing Jewish interest in leisure and sport was leading to the creation of an 'estranged generation' and contributing to the 'erosion of control by the traditional communal agencies'.[91]

This estrangement was very apparent with regard to Jewish involvement in professional boxing; a sport which impacted significantly on the cohesion of the community and caused great anxiety amongst the British Jewish elites. From the 1890s through to the Second World War, Jewish participation in the British professional boxing scene was widespread. During this time, British Jewish pugilists such as Ted 'Kid' Lewis and Jack 'Kid' Berg experienced considerable national and international success, and many Jews of immigrant origin also went on to become successful promoters (Harry Jacobs, Victor Berliner, Jack Solomons), managers (Harry Levene) and trainers (Jack Goodwin). Watching and betting on the sport, often at Jewish owned and managed 'small-halls', was also prevalent at this time amongst the younger section of the community.

By the 1950s, Jewish participation and interest in the sport had waned due to a number of factors.[92] In a sporting sense, the impact of Jews had been significant and had drawn many plaudits from within the British boxing community.[93] Importantly, however, Jewish involvement also had a discernible social and cultural impact on the Jewish community and on Jewish ethnicity more generally.

Not only did interest in the sport contribute to the growing 'drift' of the second generation, but professional boxers themselves also epitomised the new British-born Jew whose character and leisure tastes more closely reflected those of the British working classes.

Boxing acted as a powerful divisive force and impacted negatively on the perpetuation of immigrant culture and ethnicity. Likewise, Jewish involvement in boxing undermined the cohesion of the community more generally and was a source of considerable anxiety for the Jewish communal elites and 'respectable' Jewry – ever fearful of the 'disreputability' of the sport and the impact that Jewish interest in it could have on the socio-cultural well-being of the community. Whilst interest in boxing deepened a growing 'split' within the British Jewish community, it also symbolised the 'drift' of the second generation and increased their apathy towards the culture and ethnicity of their parents. Through boxing, many second generation Jews escaped what they saw as the stuffy and overbearing culture and authority of their elders and began forming their own secularised, independent, British Jewish identities.

Boxing and 'drifting' Jews

Between the 1890s and the 1950s, many second generation Jewish immigrants in Britain became professional boxers. By the interwar years, Jews of both British and American origin had become the largest ethnic minority group represented in the sport.[94] Many of the factors underpinning this were not specific to the Jewish community, and reflected the move of many non-Jews into the professional ring as well. For instance, the vast majority of Jewish migrant families settled in predominantly urban, working-class and economically deprived areas of major cities such as London and Manchester. Whilst throughout its history prize-fighting had always benefited from the patronage of the 'respectable' middle and upper classes, traditionally the large majority of combatants had been drawn from the geographical areas, and socio-economic milieu, in which most Jews resided.[95]

Like their non-Jewish counterparts, many Jewish boxers entered prize-fighting after being involved in street fighting as adolescents. It was common for young boys who fought on the street to make the move into the 'small-hall', often encouraged by their peers, in order to test their skills in a sporting arena.[96] Many young Jews who were involved in street fighting followed this path. Alf Mansfield, a second generation immigrant Jew who adopted an Anglicised moniker on his boxing debut, claimed he was encouraged to take up the sport after performing well in fights with local non-Jewish gang leaders.[97] Likewise, two-time World Welterweight Champion (1915–16, 1917–19), Ted 'Kid' Lewis claimed he began his career after being caught fighting by a London policeman who told him to try his hand in the professional game.[98]

Jews were also attracted to the prize ring for the financial rewards that it could offer. Many took to the sport because 'there was money to be had – never a fortune, but good, quick money at apparently little physical cost nor too much discomfort'.[99] For instance, Sam Aarons (aka 'Kid' Furness) – a second generation Jew from Manchester – claimed he only became a professional boxer because he couldn't find work after leaving the army after the First World War.[100] Likewise, Moe Mizler, a successful boxer in London in the 1920s and 1930s, noted his decision to turn professional was driven by the need for money to support his market stall.[101]

Whatever their individual reasoning, the decision of scores of young Jews to become professional boxers represented a clear break from the first generation and a challenge to the preservation of immigrant culture and ethnicity. To many first generation Jews, the idea of boxing as employment was completely alien and in stark contrast to life in the *shtetl*. The idea of fighting itself was frowned upon and religious authorities denounced boxing as *goyishe midas* (mores of the heathen), seeing the sport as being at odds to traditional Jewish religion and culture.[102] As well as having a 'deep aversion to the uses of violence', a legacy of life during the pogroms, many immigrant Jews saw boxing as an 'un-Jewish' leisure activity – unsurprising considering the immigrant community came from countries which lacked anything resembling British sporting culture.[103] In a reflection of contemporary American Jewish society, where 'parents universally decried boxing as violent, dangerous, immoral and dominated by bums and thugs', immigrant Jewish parents in Britain were 'nearly always religiously and emotionally opposed to their sons taking part in boxing'.[104]

This mentality is evident with regard to the first generation parents of the most successful British Jewish boxers at this time. Many immigrant parents felt that their sons' decision to enter the ring was a clear rejection of their authority and of immigrant culture. When Ted 'Kid' Lewis embarked upon his professional career aged fifteen, his decision became a source of considerable friction between him and his Russo-Jewish immigrant father, Solomon Mendeloff. Lewis, born Gershon Mendeloff on 24 October 1894 in St-George's-in-the-East, London, was the only son of eight children, a fact which exacerbated his parents' anxiety over his move into the professional ring. Solomon, who had lost family members during the pogroms (violent anti-Jewish riots) and who had fled Russia to avoid bloodshed, was appalled by Gershon's decision to engage in physical violence for sport. Equally as concerning, however, was the fact that Gershon had chosen boxing over becoming an apprentice in his father's furniture workshop, thus rejecting the 'traditional' move into the family business.[105]

Similar sentiments are also evident in the life and career of Jack 'Kid' Berg. Berg was born Judah Bergman junior on 28 June 1909 to Russian Jewish immigrant parents in the East End of London. During his successful career he became Junior Welterweight World Champion (referred to now as the Light-Welterweight division) between 1930 and 1931 and also held the British Lightweight Championship from 1934 to 1936. As with his idol, Ted 'Kid' Lewis, Jack faced considerable parental opposition when he became a professional boxer aged only fourteen. His father, a devout Jew and a strict disciplinarian, struggled to control his often wayward and 'precocious' young son.[106] Whilst he was concerned by his son's rejection of 'traditional' immigrant religion and culture throughout his childhood, he was enraged when Judah junior began his career in the ring – something which sat uneasily with the religious and 'resistant to change' first generation immigrant.[107]

Berg's father felt shame at his son's decision to enter what in his view was a disreputable form of employment. Evidence suggests that 'obdurate' and 'dignified' Judah senior refused to 'bow down and accept the inevitable'. As well as vainly ridiculing his son's fighting pretensions ('You! A box-fighter? Never!'), he warned him of the obvious physical dangers associated with the sport and the effects that it could have on his boyish 'good looks'. For young Jack 'Kid' Berg, however, these appeals did not matter. He cared little for the authority, culture and ethnicity of the older generation and remained insistent that he would not be prevented from pursuing his career in the ring.[108]

The reaction seen in these two cases was mirrored elsewhere in both British and American Jewish immigrant society. Many first generation immigrant parents struggled to come to terms with their sons' decisions to abandon Jewish religion and culture in favour of professional boxing.[109] For second generation Jews like Lewis and Berg, life in Britain improved their self-confidence and made them less willing to enter what they viewed as the 'claustrophobic' culture and attitudes of their parents. Whilst 'traditional Jewish culture' held 'little significance for them', boxing – the 'more amenable sub-culture of the streets' – held considerable appeal. Jewish interest in professional boxing 'contributed to a parting of the ways with the older generation who were being left behind, if not always physically, then certainly emotionally'.[110]

Boxing contributed to a 'parting of the ways' in a more direct sense for some of the most successful Jewish boxers of the time. By modern standards, a career in professional boxing in the 1920s and 1930s did not bring considerable financial rewards. Yet for a small number of British Jewish boxers, success in the ring facilitated social mobility and helped them secure a physical departure from the area and social stratum of their birth. 'Kid' Lewis, for instance, spent several successful years boxing in America and Australia and owned homes in Britain and the United States by the end of his career.[111] Likewise, 'Kid' Berg used his boxing earnings in the early 1930s to move from his Whitechapel home to a 'smart house in the suburbs with maid, car, dogs and all that goes with prosperous suburbanites'. Whilst social and geographic mobility of this kind would have been rare amongst Jewish professional boxers, the sport clearly offered rich social, material and financial rewards to the successful few.[112]

The 'parting of the ways' was evident in spiritual terms as well. Many British Jewish pugilists were not religiously observant and exhibited no real interest in traditional Jewish culture. This did not mean, however, that that they completely discarded their Jewishness. Whilst many may have adopted Anglicised aliases upon their entry into the sport (to help them avoid the detection of their ever-sceptical parents), they also often chose to wear both a Union Jack and a *Magen David* on their boxing shorts with pride. This was a visible demonstration of their dual British Jewish identity.[113]

Though not necessarily accompanied with a strong identification with Jewish religion, customs or traditions, this symbolic expression of ethnic pride showed that some vestige of their Jewishness remained. Likewise, although second generation Jewish boxers had clearly undergone a social, cultural and religious 'drift', this did not mean that their successes in the ring were not celebrated by the community of their birth. 'Kid' Lewis and 'Kid' Berg may not have been Jewish in their religion or cultural outlook, yet they proudly saw themselves as English Jewish boxers and their exploits were keenly followed by the British Jewish community. During and after their careers in the ring, boxers like 'Kid' Berg and 'Kid' Lewis were revered as 'idols' of the 'Jewish East End'.[114]

Whilst many boxers did not feel any strong sense of religious or cultural Jewishness, they were comfortable with using their minority background as a means of self-promotion.[115] This is particularly evident with Jack 'Kid' Berg when he embarked on his American boxing career in the late 1920s. There he regularly played on his Jewish background to help promote himself and increase his appeal to Jewish fight fans. Such a tactic was increasingly common at this time in America and was strongly encouraged by American boxing promoters eager to introduce an 'ethnic angle' into their fights. Although individual Jewish, Irish, Italian and black boxers may not have felt any strong sense of ethnic pride when competing, American fight fans (especially in large immigrant cities such as New York and Chicago) were generally drawn more to fights between boxers of different backgrounds where racial pride was apparently at stake.[116]

Although Berg did not feel any real religious or cultural affinity to Judaism, he began to emphasise his 'Jewishness' to increase his 'box-office' potential. Soon after he arrived in America in 1928, he began to use his background as a second generation Jewish immigrant to help in the promotion of his fights. In 1929, Berg introduced a pre-fight routine whereby he would come to the ring wearing various Jewish religious garments – including a *tallit* (prayer shawl) and a *kippah* (skull cap) – and then undergo a lengthy ritual of removing the items and praying. As Berg's trainer in America later noted, his boxer was by no means religious or interested in Orthodox customs or traditions, the routine being a means of garnering the support of local Jewish fight fans.[117] It was a 'stunt meant to emphasise the partisan lines by which boxers could be labelled, hopefully resulting in greater interest in ticket sales'. In this task, it was clearly successful, as Berg's later fights in America evidenced.[118]

When placed in its historical context, there was nothing extraordinary about Berg utilising his ethnicity as a means of sporting promotion. Indeed, such practices are as old as the sport of prize-fighting itself. In the days of Daniel Mendoza, bouts between Christians and Jews or Jewish and Irish fighters were amongst the most well-known contests of the time. Such ethnic and religious battles 'generated tremendous excitement' which 'helped drive the spectatorship, gambling and public attention that in turn provided the sport its financial support'. As Berg did in America in the late 1920s and early 1930s, in the much earlier period 'Jewish, Irish and Black boxers adopted symbols, manners of dress and distinctive styles that highlighted their difference ... to increase their popularity'.[119]

Berg's decision to 'highlight' his 'difference' – whilst himself being detached from any real sense of cultural or religious Jewishness – demonstrates the confidence he felt in himself and in his secularised Jewish identity. More generally, Berg represented the new, secularised second generation Jew who had experienced significant 'socialisation' into the British working classes and entered eagerly into this group's leisure and sporting pursuits. Boxers like 'Kid' Lewis and 'Kid' Berg had clearly discarded immigrant culture and identity in exchange for a new form of Jewishness – a Jewishness based on their experiences as British-born second generation immigrants, rather than the culture and lifestyles of their parents.

Undermining 'communal solidarity'?

Whilst boxing was a cause of much anxiety for first generation parents, it was also a cause for concern amongst the Jewish establishment. Within British Jewish 'respectable' society at this time, boxing was seen to be an especially negative influence on younger Jews.[120] For instance, in 1923 Rabbi Israel Brodie (1895–1979) claimed that boxing was one factor hampering communal attempts to 'get hold of the younger generation and try to induce them to show more interest in Judaism'.[121] In the 1930s the *Jewish Chronicle* began to view Jewish involvement in the sport as reflecting the growing 'social problems' amongst young Jewry. Indeed, the idea of there being a 'social chasm which split Anglo-Jewry' was a theme which ran through much of the newspaper's sports and leisure coverage at this time.[122]

Evidently, the Jewish communal elites viewed those Jews who had made the move into the professional ring with great disapproval.

Unlike other minority boxers, Jewish prize-fighters in the modern period 'had to endure much by the way of condemnation from within their own community'. They 'were seen by "respectable" Jews as an embarrassment' and would not only draw negative attention on British Jewry, but also act as encouragement for younger Jews to take up a career in the ring and 'drift' further from their religion and culture.[123] The fact that many British Jewish professional boxers maintained links with criminal elements and 'were tarnished by alleged association with gambling and what was believed to be promotion of poor morals' also impacted on the opinion of 'respectable' Jews on the sport.[124]

Clear efforts were made to protect Jews from the negative influence of the professional ring. Whilst boxing within the youth movement aided and supported the wider initiatives of the established community, increasing Jewish interest in professional boxing symbolised the growing 'drift' and detachment of some within the second generation. The sport was particularly disliked by those who supported and ran the various youth organisations and by those who worked with young Jews. For example, when Basil Henriques opened the Oxford and St George's Jewish Lads' Club in 1914, he found great support from local school headmasters. They felt that his club could offer a positive alternative for young Jews in their spare time instead of the increasingly popular, and unsuitable, 'temptations' of the street – particularly the local Premierland boxing arena.[125]

Leaders of the youth movement also worked hard to protect impressionable young Jews from being drawn to the disreputable world of prize-fighting. In 1921, cigarette magnate Bernhard Baron (1850–1929) – a patron of the Oxford and St George's Jewish Lads' Club – strongly voiced his disapproval at plans to allow 'Kid' Lewis to attend a tournament between Jewish amateur boxers. In a letter to Basil Henriques, Baron noted

> I cannot express in strong enough language my disapproval of the arrangement to have professional boxers to box in the same ring as amateur boys. I can have absolutely nothing to do with a function of this kind which has my strongest disapproval. At the present time, when it is so difficult for boys to get work, the temptation to become professional boxers is very great and your tournament is merely encouragement to club boys to act in this way.[126]

Although the tournament committee minuted that Lewis' attendance would have lucrative financial implications, his invitation
was withdrawn only days later.[127]

A similar attitude was evident elsewhere within the Jewish youth
movement throughout the interwar years. Whilst generally
apathetic towards Jewish ethnicity, Jewish youth leaders across the
country were keen for their members not to go down the wrong
path and 'drift' closer to disreputable elements of British community
and culture. In 1925, the Grove House Jewish Lads' Club
Committee rejected an appeal by a manager to allow local
promoters to use the club for boxing promotions – an attempt on
his part to help the club's poor financial standing. The suggestion
was summarily thrown out by the Committee, which noted that it
did not want members exposed to the 'undesirable elements' associated with the sport and the lure of the professional game.[128] In
1935, the Stepney Jewish Lads' Club introduced a rule whereby 'no
professionals are to be admitted to the boxing class' in order to
protect their amateur club boxing team.[129]

As well as concerns over Jews being lured into the ring, the Jewish
establishment was also alarmed at the growing number of Jews
watching and gambling on boxing at this time. Throughout the
early twentieth century, a number of boxing halls and arenas were
opened by Jews of immigrant background keen to capitalise on
growing interest in the professional fight scene. Halls such as
Wonderland (open between 1894 and 1911), the Judæans Athletic
and Social Club (1902–14), Paragon Hall (1911), Premierland
(1912–31) and the Devonshire Club (1931–40) all opened in the
'Jewish' East End. In the period between the late 1890s and the late
1930s, they became a central part of the vibrant London boxing
scene.[130] Although open to all, Jews made up the bulk of these clubs'
patrons and it is clear that watching professional boxing was a
popular leisure pastime for Jews during the first half of the
twentieth century. In 1914, it was noted that the Judæans, located in
a stable loft on Cable Street, East London, regularly drew in excess
of 1,000 people for its promotions, with the vast majority of spectators being of 'the Jewish race'.[131] Similarly, in December 1928,
reports indicated that 80% of the regular visitors to Premierland, a
3,000 capacity arena housed in a disused factory on Back Church
Lane, Whitechapel, were of Jewish origin.[132]

The reality of thousands of Jews attending boxing halls such as these was seen to be further evidence of the growing 'split' within British Jewry. For the Jewish elites, boxing spectating was another indication of 'Jews not associating themselves with Jewish life' and drifting physically and culturally closer to mainstream society.[133] One article from the *Jewish Chronicle* in 1929 asked 'Is Anglo-Jewry Decadent?' and voiced concerns over the contribution of attending boxing to the waywardness of younger Jews. It stated 'in the East End today we find young men growing up almost with a loss of moral sense. They are adherents of the cheap boxing halls … [and] are joining, unfortunately, the hooligan element of the populace'.[134]

At first glance, it is clear why fears were raised about the effects of watching boxing on the 'moral sense' of the Jewish population. Contemporary reports sometimes painted a 'rough and ready' picture of these establishments – as the Judæans was labelled in 1909.[135] Crowd disturbances were relatively common and were most likely and most violent when matches were held between Jewish and Gentile fighters. Seemingly, whenever 'racial considera-tion … cropped up' at a Jewish hall, 'it was certain that whoever finally triumphed in the ring, the real battle would be fought out afterwards'.[136] When joined with reports that Jewish boxing halls were habitually overcrowded (patrons at the Judæans were always 'packed in like sardines around the ring'), that gambling prolifer-ated and that they were often frequented by members of the criminal underworld (Jewish gangster Edward Emmanuel was a regular at Wonderland), then it is no surprise that 'respectable' society – both Jewish and Gentile – viewed their existence with a great deal of concern.[137]

As was the case with British boxing more generally during this period, Jewish boxing halls were not as 'unmanageable' nor as 'dangerous' as believed.[138] 'Disorder' was not uncommon, but the enthusiasm and knowledge of Jewish fans, and the high quality of the boxing at Jewish halls, was widely acknowledged. One member of the self-appointed controlling body of British boxing, the National Sporting Club, claimed in 1914 that he had regularly taken fellow NSC members to the Judæans Club where 'they have one and all come away delighted and amazed at the skill and vigour with which the boys fight their battles'.[139] Likewise, five years earlier, a correspondent for *Boxing* praised the organisation and efficiency at Wonderland, where 'no-one who has ever visited the place can ever insinuate that he did not receive plentiful value for money. There is scarcely a dull moment, there is always a long programme and there are no waits between the items'.[140]

The enthusiasm of the British boxing community was not shared by the Jewish elites. Indeed, 'respectable' society regularly made their 'disgust of such premises well-known' and worked hard to 'stamp out' what they saw as 'Jewish misconduct'.[141] When Jewish promoter Harry Jacobs opened Paragon Hall in East London in 1911, for instance, the 'respectable inhabitants were loud in their complaint'. As well as informing the London County Council that they believed the Hall was holding 'the most disgusting operations they had ever seen', residents in the area complained of 'being unable to leave their doors open owing to the crowds in the vicinity of the halls where the performances were going on'.[142] In 1935, two disgruntled members of the Devonshire Club, opened in 1931 by Jewish promoter Jack Solomons, complained to the LCC that the Club had become a 'low gambling hell, drinking den and in fact a place where men and women congregate for immoral arrangements and meetings'.[143]

The greatest indignation was reserved for Premierland, by far the largest and most well known of all the 'Jewish' boxing venues.[144] Concerns were raised by local residents during the planning stages for the hall in 1911, focusing on the potentially negative effects the venue's opening would have on the local population. One correspondent to the LCC claimed that Premierland 'would attract into the neighbourhood an undesirable element that may prove very troublesome and raise much annoyance'. Concerns were also raised that local schoolchildren, the majority of them Jewish, would stay at home on the days that boxing was held out of fear for their own safety. Although not explicitly acknowledged, local residents would have been concerned that the same schoolchildren might be tempted into the arena to watch one of the four promotions held each week.[145]

Premierland opened as planned in 1912, but went on to gain a degree of notoriety within East End Jewish and Gentile society. Contemporary reports suggest that crowd violence, gambling and dangerous levels of overcrowding were all relatively commonplace. One regular Jewish visitor to the hall throughout the 1920s later noted: 'first of all the place was packed to the rafters. For sixpence you just stood on a football terrace, on steps. Some spectators were most ingenious, they climbed onto the top rafters and hung there'.[146]

Before long, the hall began to attract the attention of the authorities. During the 1920s, both the LCC and the Metropolitan Police were beginning to take the issues of gambling and crowd safety in the small-hall boxing environment more seriously.[147] Investigations into Premierland, however, were initiated as a direct result of correspondence from 'respectable' elements of British Jewish society. In 1928, Mr Cohen, from Bow, East London (a self-labelled 'well known person' in the East End), complained that Premierland was a 'hot-bed of vice, for in addition to the serious overcrowding the place is a miniature race-course'. As well as noting the prevalence of gambling in the arena, he added that 'in the event of a panic, stampede etc I am sure it will result in a great loss of life and serious injury ... [as] spectators ... are packed in like sardines'.[148]

Resultant enquiries found the management guilty of turning a blind eye to illegal gambling and allowing dangerous levels of overcrowding. The Police's belief that Jews were pre-disposed to gambling – and the widespread anti-Semitic idea that Jews were a 'panicky race' – made the problems at the arena seem more severe than at similar non-Jewish halls.[149] Investigations into Premierland and other London arenas resulted in a tightening of health and safety rules concerning the staging of boxing from 1930 onwards. Together with growing pressure from a Sabbatarian lobby, which led to a ban on Sunday boxing in 1935, these tighter rules resulted in the permanent closure of several small-halls across London – including Premierland in 1931.[150]

The closure of Premierland brought great satisfaction to 'respectable' society, but it also marked the start of the decline of Jewish boxing in Britain. For one, Jews who were interested in watching and gambling on boxing no longer had a large hall within walking distance of their East End homes. Likewise, Jewish boxers lost a 'home' arena where they were guaranteed a favourable reception and opportunities unavailable to them in venues outside of the East End. Although Jewish boxers remained prominent in the sport during the 1930s (mainly boxers who had begun their careers in the amateur ranks or before Premierland's closure in 1931), many complained that the absence of a Jewish hall had had a negative impact on their career progression.[151]

Whilst Jews remained visible in the early post-1945 period,

Jewish involvement in boxing would never reach its early twentieth-century peak.[152] After the closure of Premierland, Jewish interest in the sport was also undermined by wider social and economic changes during the 1940s and 1950s. Jewish social and geographic mobility, cultural change, the general decline of 'small-hall' boxing and the arrival of fresh immigrants into the sport combined to effectively spell the end of this 'golden age' of professional Jewish boxing. By the end of the 1960s, professional boxing – in both Britain and America – had gone from being a sport dominated by British Jews, to a sport dominated by other minorities.[153]

Despite Jewish boxing's post-World War Two decline, the sport had a powerful impact on the ethnicity of the community during the early twentieth century. On the one hand, Jewish involvement caused considerable friction between second generation Jews and their immigrant parents. Through boxing, young Jews like 'Kid' Lewis and 'Kid' Berg undermined the culture and authority of their familial elders. Jewish involvement aided social mobility and often led to a physical and emotional departure from the immigrant milieu. Professional boxing was a factor in the creation of secularised British Jewish identities; identities based on a perceptible sense of ethnic pride, but without any real interest in traditional Jewish religion or culture.

Jewish interest in the sport also widened a growing chasm between this generation and the Jewish establishment. At a time when the fracturing of British Jewry was being increasingly debated, direct and indirect involvement in boxing was an alarming indication of the growing physical, psychological and spiritual 'drift' of Jews away from their birth community. Although campaigns were launched against some Jewish boxers and small-halls, the lure of the sport – and indigenous leisure more generally – remained strong. Boxing provides a clear indication of the social and cultural 'fissuring' of British Jewry and acted as an arena where second generation Jews ignored the wishes of their elders and 'respectable' society.

In essence, professional boxing played an important role in both the destruction and reconstruction of Jewish ethnicity. Interest in the sport impacted on immigrant culture and also on communal cohesion – argued by some historians to be an important facet of minority ethnicity more generally. The sport also symbolised and catalysed the formation of new identities, with a secular outlook on Jewishness mainly in evidence. Effectively, Jewish boxers and Jewish boxing fans were the embodiment of the new British Jewish second generation – many of whom were more interested in indigenous leisure and sport than in preserving immigrant ethnicity.

Creating a 'new Jew'? Sport and Maccabi Great Britain, 1934–70

Although sport impacted significantly on Jewish ethnicity, some Jewish sporting organisations believed that they could strengthen religious and cultural identity. Within British Maccabi, the belief was prevalent that sport could help promote Jewishness amongst an increasingly secularised and integrated community. In its mission to create 'a new type of Jew and Jewess', however, the organisation was largely unsuccessful.[154] Although the movement improved opportunities for sport and socialising for its thousands of British members, it could not act as a 'unifying force' nor instigate an 'inner revolution' in terms of Jewish religion and culture.[155]

To understand the development of British Maccabi, it is important to examine the movement's wider roots and its close links to Zionism. In the late nineteenth and early twentieth century, the notion of political Zionism underwent a significant resurgence. At this time, advocates of Jewish nationalism became increasingly vociferous, and drew growing support, in their calls for the establishment of a Jewish nation-state.[156] Alongside promoting the idea of a new Jewish homeland, which Zionist leaders felt was needed due to the 'failure' of Jewish Emancipation, many leading Zionist thinkers were also increasingly vocal in their belief in the wider need for Jewish 'renewal' – arguing that Jews would need to be stronger, in body, mind and spirit, in order to ensure the success of the Zionist dream.[157]

One of the most powerful advocates for Jewish physical 'regeneration' was the Hungarian Jewish physician, social critic, author and Zionist leader, Max Nordau (1849–1923). In a series of books, articles and speeches in the 1890s and 1900s, Nordau outlined his view that *shtetl* and Diaspora life had led to a physical 'degeneration' of international Jewry. He argued that unless this was consciously and pro-actively rectified, the Zionist project would be rendered futile.[158] Nordau advocated physical recreation – but not necessarily sport – amongst Jews in order to establish a trend of 'muskal Judentum' (muscular Judaism) which would help to practically and ideologically support and facilitate the creation of a Jewish nation-state.[159]

There was a strong response to Nordau's appeals for 'muscular Judaism' amongst the worldwide Jewish community. By 1914 there were over one hundred Jewish sports clubs in existence.[160] At the 1921 Zionist Congress held at Karlsbad, Czechoslovakia, the Maccabi World Union was formed in order to administer and expand the largest section of all the various Zionist sports organisations. Although there were other factions of the Jewish nationalist sports movement (Hapoel, for instance, was both socialist and leftist in its support for Zionism), Maccabi was the largest. It attracted 150,000 members worldwide by 1934 and nearly 175,000 members by the start of the Second World War.[161]

Despite the growth of Zionist-influenced sport worldwide, there was little British interest in Maccabi for most of the early twentieth century. A small number of Zionist-oriented sports organisations – such as London and Glasgow Bar Cochba and Maccabi Association, London (MAL) – were founded by Jews of German and Austrian origin in the 1920s, yet there was little impetus within Britain for a much larger movement based around Nordau's calls for 'muscular Judaism'.[162] During the 1930s, however, interest in establishing a British arm of the Maccabi movement grew amongst high-profile British Zionists. This was especially true with regard to Lord Alfred Melchett (1868–1930), founder of Imperial Chemical Industries, and his only son, Lord Henry Melchett (1898–1949); both Honorary Presidents of the Maccabi World Union during the 1920s and 1930s. Both were keen for British Jewry and the Jews of the British Empire to increase their involvement in Maccabi – a movement which the latter felt had essentially 'British' aims, i.e. the promotion of team spirit, sportsmanship and discipline. Through his intervention, Maccabi clubs were founded in Australia, Canada and South Africa and in March 1934 the British Maccabi Association (BMA) was created.[163]

From this year through to the 1960s, the British arm of the Maccabi movement underwent a significant growth amongst British Jewry. During this period, over thirty Maccabi clubs were founded across the country in both large and small Jewish settlements. By 1963, the movement had grown to over 6,000 members – easily dwarfing the number active within the contemporary Jewish youth club movement and the Jewish Lads' Brigade.[164] Although initially constituted to cater for over-eighteens – a group which had become increasingly critical of the Association for Jewish Youth for failing to do more for older Jews interested in sport – Maccabi gradually increased the number of junior members from the 1940s onwards.[165]

From its foundation in 1934 through to the 1960s, British Maccabi leaders espoused the notion that their organisation could play a role in combating Jewish physical, social and spiritual 'decay' – the focus of debates prevalent within early twentieth-century British Jewry. On the one hand, leaders argued that they could expand on the opportunities for physical recreation and thus further improve the strength and well-being of their largely British-born membership. As well as this, however, it was also believed that Maccabi could act as a vehicle for reinforcing communal cohesion, through promoting Zionism, and reinvigorating Jewish culture and religion, by means of a broad non-sporting programme of 'spiritual' activities and education. British Maccabi, in effect, believed it could create a 'new Jew' – in body, mind and spirit – and work against the weakening of Jewish identity occurring at this time.

Maccabi's aims were largely unrealised, however. Although Maccabi was a sports organisation which claimed to be able to tackle non-sporting issues, the movement did not prevent the 'drift' of younger Jews away from their community, religion and culture. In short, British Maccabi did little to reverse trends which had been negatively impacting on British Jewry for much of the first half of the twentieth century.

'Muscular Judaism' and sport

Given the centrality of physical recreation to Maccabi in its international context, it is unsurprising that the main effort of the British arm of the movement was focused on sport. Despite the importance of 'muscular Judaism' to worldwide Maccabi and the wider political Zionist project, British Maccabi did not publicly promote sport as a means of aiding the creation of a Jewish homeland. Reflecting the wider reticence towards linking the organisation to Jewish nationalism – discussed below – Zionism was not consciously highlighted as a motive underpinning the British Maccabi sporting programmes. In contrast to Europe and America, sport was not promoted as a way of practically supporting and developing the dream of a Jewish nation nor as a means of physical preparation for *aliyah* (migration to Israel).[166]

A variety of other reasons were proffered for Maccabi's concentration on sport. In a 1935 press release concerning the foundation of the organisation, it was claimed that Maccabi would imbue 'an eagerness for invigorating physical recreation' and '[create] a desire for emulation of the achievement of leading athletes in the various realms of international sport'.[167] National and local leaders also reasoned that sport was important as an aid to developing the physical health of the Jewish community. In 1951, Chief Rabbi Israel Brodie (at the time Vice-President of British Maccabi) claimed that 'Maccabi enriches Jewish life by providing opportunities for personal physical betterment'.[168] Pierre Gildesgame (1903–81), prominent administrator of British, European and World Maccabi from the 1930s onwards, argued that each Maccabi club should use sport to 'raise the standard of their [the members'] physical health and sporting performance'.[169]

Other similarities to the reasons behind the sporting programme of the British Jewish youth club movement can also be identified.[170] Many national and local Maccabi leaders, for example, espoused physical recreation for its wider effects on the mentality and character of its members. In 1937, the leaders of Maccabi Association, London (MAL), a club based in Bloomsbury, noted their club's promotion of sport was designed to create 'the highest qualities of discipline, morality and sportsmanship' and 'promote habits of punctuality, order and method'.[171] As one of the British movement's post-war leaders, Ken Gradon (1919–2002), commented, sport was important to the movement as it created 'team spirit and solidarity' which were both 'essential for the improvement of our social and communal structure'.[172]

As well as having important physical and psychological effects, sport was also believed to be a useful means of combating anti-Semitism. As the very first sentence of the original *Maccabi Code*, published in 1936, notes, members should 'Follow the ideal of Judas Maccabeus by proving yourself physically & morally courageous & fearless, both on & off the playing field'. Showing sporting courage would show non-Jews that Jews were strong and willing to defend themselves against racism and discrimination.[173]

In the structure of its national and local sporting programme, Maccabi also closely paralleled the youth club movement.

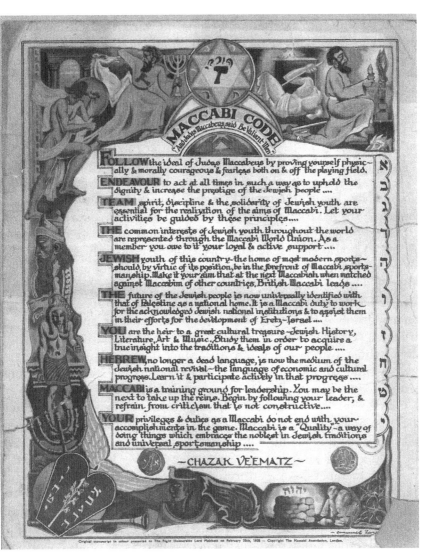

6 *The Maccabi Code*, 1936

Individual Maccabi clubs across the country dedicated the majority of their resources to providing regular sessions in as broad a range of sports as possible. In this respect, Newcastle Maccabi, founded in 1935, was typical – running sections in 'football, rugby, tennis, table tennis, badminton, swimming, cycling, physical training, wrestling and boxing'.[174] Likewise, at both a national and local level, competitions in various sports were organised on a regular basis. From 1936, Maccabi ran a national football competition, which split into Northern (1938) and Southern (1946) Leagues in the years immediately before and after the Second World War.[175]

British Maccabi was different to youth organisations founded by the British Jewish elites in that it could offer international competition against other Jews. From 1932 onwards, the tri-enniel Maccabiah Games was convened in Tel-Aviv by the Maccabi World Union. The 'Jewish Olympics' were designed to be an international showcase for Jewish physicality and sportsmanship, as well as being a means of strengthening the 'culture' and unity of the Jewish people.[176] National associations were invited to send representative teams to compete for the honour of both their country and the wider Jewish community.[177] In Britain, selection for the Maccabiah was labelled as the ultimate aim for every Maccabi member. Participation in the Jewish Olympics was used as an incentive to drive the very best Maccabi athletes to higher standards of performance, whilst British entry into the Maccabiah was also used as a propaganda opportunity to raise awareness of Maccabi within British Jewish society.[178]

One aspect of Maccabi ideology was to try and produce sportsmen and women of elite quality. The organisation's leadership believed that this would help raise the movement's profile and aid the wider aim of creating 'muscular Jews'. For some British Maccabi members, competition in the Maccabiah proved a useful stepping stone to further sporting success at the elite level. Tennis player Angela Buxton (1934–), winner of Wimbledon ladies' doubles in 1956, was a gold medallist at the 1953 Maccabiah, while 1960 Olympic Gold medallist fencer Allan Jay (1931–) won six golds in total at the 1950 and 1953 Jewish Olympics.[179] Elsewhere within British Maccabi, there were many other successful international Jewish athletes. MAL, for instance, was the base for Fred Oberlander (1911–96), an Austrian Jewish refugee and international champion wrestler, as well as Ben Helfgott (1930–), weightlifter and British Olympic weightlifting team captain in 1956.[180]

Although Maccabi leaders highlighted international success as a vindication of their organisation's sporting ideology, the movement's wider sporting achievements were also considerable. Only a small number of the British Maccabi members had the opportunity to take up sport at the highest level and sporting standards amongst the rank-and-file membership were generally very low – a fact frequently highlighted, and lamented, by members of the National Executive Committee.[181] However, Maccabi was a major provider of sport and sporting competition for the Jewish community during the period between 1934 and the 1960s. Contemporary observers remarked that Maccabi was 'most successful' in the sporting sphere, providing opportunities for a wide variety of physical recreations in small and large Jewish communities across Great Britain.[182]

Despite this, there were several factors which limited Maccabi's efforts in this sphere of their programme. Whilst sporting activities may have been widely offered, there was often no guarantee that individual Maccabi clubs could offer anything but rudimentary facilities, equipment or coaching. Financial constraints were a significant factor in this respect; especially in the years before the 1950s, when Maccabi began to receive larger amounts of international and domestic funding.[183] During the mid- to late 1930s, the BMA executive was run 'by officials in an entirely honorary capacity' and there were little or no financial resources available for the sporting programmes of affiliated clubs.[184] Problems with central funding for physical recreation continued well into the 1950s, with individual clubs left to provide whatever sport they could on an initial *ad hoc* basis, often with minimal finance.[185]

Linked in to financial constraints, Maccabi sport also suffered due to a clear disparity between larger London clubs and much smaller groups in Jewish provincial settlements. For example, MAL, founded in the 1920s by middle-class Jews of German and Austrian heritage, was the 'flagship' British Maccabi club and benefited from the generous and considerable funding of West End Jewry. In 1937, MAL opened a purpose built facility in the London Borough of Camden – called Compayne House – replete with comprehensive indoor and outdoor sporting facilities and professional sports instructors.[186] Membership of MAL ran into several thousand and in 1962 the facility was labelled 'an ideal youth centre' by Lord Aberdare (1919–2005), Conservative peer.[187]

In contrast, sporting provision in the provinces and in small London clubs could often be extremely rudimentary – as highlighted by the British Maccabi sports director in 1948.[188] Whilst Glasgow Maccabi – which started life as Glasgow Bar Cochba in 1929 – enjoyed a great deal of communal and financial support in the post-World War Two period, during its early days it worked on a shoestring budget. In contrast to MAL, Glasgow's first premises were based in the canteen of a local tailoring factory where 'the members had to clear away the canteen equipment before they could commence their gymnastics. After they had finished their sessions, they had to put the room back in order for the following day'.[189]

The members themselves could often prove a limiting factor on the movement's sporting programme. Over time, members began to see the club more as an opportunity for socialising with friends than for playing sport – facilities for which were becoming much more widely available, especially in the post-World War Two era.[190] Even during the movement's earliest period, many Maccabi members saw attendance at their local club as an important source of entertainment and a way of keeping in touch with fellow local Jews.[191] After the opening of Compayne House in 1937, MAL leaders voiced concerns that 'many members had joined simply in order to frequent a pleasant social club and had absolutely no intention of joining the numerous activities on offer'.[192] Likewise, similar anxieties were reported elsewhere during the 1940s.[193] In 1945, the national Maccabi sports director noted that a visit to Brixton Maccabi 'to give a demonstration of sporting activities' was unsuccessful as 'not more than 12 members from Brixton turned up, none of whom showed any interest in the events of the evening and [who] seemed anxious for the termination of the function so that they could dance to the radiogram'.[194]

A similar picture was evident in the provinces in the 1940s and 1950s. Increasing numbers were becoming ignorant of the wider Maccabi ideology and engaging with the organisation on their own terms – not for wider 'Jewish' sporting goals, but purely for their own enjoyment. In 1947, the Chairman of Newcastle Maccabi implored members to become more deeply involved in the sporting activities on offer and admonished the growing number who joined

the club for its social functions: 'it is the unanimous decision of the
Maccabi Council that there is no intention whatsoever of allowing
the club to be run as a Palais-de-Dance and the Council fervently
stress that the members without exception, belong to and take an
active interest in one or more sections'.[195] Interviews with members
of Leicester Maccabi in the 1940s and 1950s show that most joined
the club to meet up with friends, not to play sport.[196]

Whilst Maccabi sporting ideology became less prominent in the
post-war period, the organisation still played an important social
and cultural role. In the 1970s, Maccabi was criticised for allowing
members to ignore physical recreation and 'become primarily interested in the social life' of the movement.[197] However, the movement
was still positively regarded by members as a means of creating
some form of community and unity – especially important in
smaller provincial Jewish settlements. As one Leicester Maccabi
member commented, 'Maccabi was hugely important in keeping the
Jewish youth together'. In Leicester and elsewhere, Maccabi could
foster a significant feeling of ethnic cohesion in communities where
the local Jewish population was both small and geographically
widespread.[198]

This sense of community was even more important in areas which
had seen considerable Jewish social and geographic mobility. This is
what happened in Glasgow in the 1930s and 1940s, as increasingly
affluent second and third generation Jewish immigrants left the East
End and moved to the suburbs.[199] Mirroring this trend, Glasgow
Maccabi moved from the Gorbals to the Giffnock area in the 1960s,
where membership grew significantly and sporting and cultural
sections were very well attended. In Glasgow, local Jews viewed
Maccabi as an important source of communal cohesion at a time
when the Jewish population was becoming increasingly divided by
class, geography and identity.[200]

Zionism

In the post-World War Two period, Maccabi was viewed as playing
an important role in creating a sense of community – especially in
provincial Jewish communities. Such a role had been envisaged for
the movement during its earliest days. Yet the founders of the British
Maccabi movement did not necessarily aim to create a renewed
sense of Jewish unity simply through allowing the movement to
become a social centre. In a reflection of its European roots, it was

hoped that Jewish nationalism could be promoted – independent of sport – within British Maccabi as a way of drawing members together and helping create a sense of solidarity amongst the wider population.

Western and British Zionist leaders believed that Jewish nationalism would act as a means of creating cohesion and strengthening religious and cultural identity. In Britain, it was felt that support for Zionism as a whole could do 'an incalculable service to Judaism by retaining within the fold ... [Jews] whose bonds with the Jewish faith could no longer be maintained on religious grounds and had in practice been sundered'.[201] It was argued that if large numbers of Jews subscribed to the notion of political Zionism then the growing cultural and social separation of modern Jewish society could effectively be combated. One of the original Zionist goals was 'unifying Jews in support of the national home in Palestine and radically changing the modern Jewish condition'. In effect, support for a Jewish homeland could be a 'basis for local and international Jewish solidarity and sociability'.[202]

Leaders of the international and British Maccabi movement also subscribed to this idea. They believed that Jewish nationalism could be promoted amongst increasingly assimilated and secular Jews as a means of creating communal and ethnic cohesion. The original *Maccabi Code* in Britain, for instance, claimed that 'The future of the Jewish people is now universally identified with that of Palestine as a national home' and added 'It is a Maccabi duty to work for the acknowledged Jewish national institutions & to assist them in their efforts for the development of Eretz-Israel'.[203] In effect, it was hoped that the British variant of Maccabi would 'bring the Zionist enthusiasm of Eastern and Central European Jewry to Great Britain and shake up the inertia and complacency of Anglo-Jewry'.[204]

In Continental European and Israeli Maccabi clubs, strong links with the Zionist movement and its objectives were maintained. Although many Zionist-oriented sports organisations were founded during the early twentieth century, Maccabi was generally seen as the 'unofficial sports organisation of the whole Zionist movement'.[205] Whilst European Maccabi organisations displayed varying degrees of ideological and practical support for Jewish nationalism, the conviction was generally strong that the Zionist aims and goals were a central driving force of the movement's wider programme and ideology.[206]

In contrast, Jewish nationalism was not viewed by British Maccabi as a 'unifying' force. Although in the modern context British Maccabi maintains strong links to Israel, from its foundation well into the 1960s interest in the notion of a Jewish homeland was generally on the margins of the organisation.[207] In the 1970s, Ken Gradon commented that 'at no time did Maccabi adopt or preach a political Zionist doctrine'.[208] Within British Maccabi 'there was no concerted effort to implement a Zionist programme'. In effect, Maccabi in Britain 'was not the rallying cry for ... Jewish nationalism as it was in Europe' and could not be used effectively as a way of combating growing social and cultural detachment of younger sections of the community.[209]

Several factors can be highlighted to explain this. Most significantly, the national leadership of the British Maccabi Association from the 1930s through to the 1950s did not want the movement to openly espouse Jewish nationalism. Some leaders adopted this attitude because they did not want Maccabi to develop a 'political' nature and enter into the highly charged British debates concerning Palestine during the 1930s and 1940s. Some also felt that being seen to be politically active would have gone against the grain of the largely apolitical nature of British sport.[210] Pierre Gildesgame commented in 1976 that British Maccabi was not, and had not been, Zionist and that he believed that an outwardly pro-Zionist stance could act as discouragement for large numbers of potential members.[211]

This reticence resulted in no strong line on promoting Jewish nationalism being developed until well into the 1950s. During its first years in existence, British Maccabi's links to political Zionism in its European context were not mentioned in press releases or interviews with Maccabi leaders.[212] During the 1940s, a time of obvious significance for Jewish nationalism, there was a marked ambivalence towards the emerging Jewish nation-state. In fact, the creation of Israel in 1948 generally passed by without any significant acknowledgement or celebration at the national or local level. Evidence from National Executive meetings throughout the 1940s and early 1950s suggests there was a clear reticence from British Maccabi leaders to outwardly support the newly created Jewish homeland – even in the face of pressure from the Maccabi World Union.[213]

There are also indications that the rank-and-file membership was also ambivalent towards Jewish nationalism. Although there were some well-supported Zionist-influenced activities and campaigning, many members were unmoved by the idea of a Jewish nation-state.[214] On the recommendation of British Maccabi President Selig Brodetsky in 1947, efforts were made to begin a national programme of 'Zionist education' in all Maccabi clubs on one evening a week. The response was generally lukewarm and by 1948 – a pivotal year in political Zionism – many of the sessions had been abandoned due to lack of support.[215]

Undoubtedly, the emergence of a plethora of other Zionist youth organisations within Britain from the 1930s onwards undermined Zionism within Maccabi. At this time, young British Jews 'wishing to express an interest in Israel through membership of a Zionist youth group' were faced with a 'difficult, often bewildering choice'. By the late 1940s, there were nearly a dozen Zionist youth groups active within Britain – all of which took a much more publicly pro-Zionist stance than Maccabi.[216] Largest amongst these was Habonim (the builders), an organisation closely based on the Scout movement, which was founded in 1929 by Wellesley Aron (1901–88), a renowned Zionist campaigner and youth worker.[217] By 1939, Habonim had grown to over 4,000 members – twice as many as the contemporary membership of the Jewish Lads' Brigade.[218]

In Habonim – and smaller youth organisations such as Beter (founded 1938), Young Poale Zion (workers of Zion) (1938), Hashomer Hatzair (Young Guard) (1939) and B'nai Akiva (Sons of Rabbi Akiva) (1939) – Zionism was a much more central element than within Maccabi.[219] All had regular sessions and initiatives concerning Zionist education and Jewish history and culture, and many actively promoted the use of Hebrew. Whilst they did not ignore sport, their focus on physical recreation was generally marginal. In comparison to these organisations, Maccabi would have held relatively little appeal for young Jews interested in learning more about, or actively supporting, political Zionism.[220]

There are also wider issues to consider as to why Maccabi failed to promote Zionism more vigorously for its 'unifying' effects. For example, many Western Zionist youth organisations were 'wedded to their national contexts' and 'displayed characteristics of acculturation to Diaspora existence that were, or would later become, emblematic of Zionist youth in general'.[221] In effect, whilst there were more staunchly pro-Zionist British youth organisations in existence at the same time, Maccabi was not unusual in a wider context in displaying some reticence towards the promotion of Jewish nationalism – especially within a Diaspora where the perceived 'need' for a Jewish homeland was less pressing than in Continental European Jewry.[222]

The wider communal 'split' over Zionism within early twentieth-century British Jewry is also reflected within Maccabi. At this time, no clear consensus over political Zionism existed within the Jewish population. Many 'assimilationists' were staunchly anti-Zionist and Jewish nationalism was a significant 'cause of ... friction' within the community. In essence, the indecision concerning Zionism within British Maccabi reflected wider Jewish society, where a small minority were openly for and against a Jewish homeland and the vast majority 'remained persistently non-partisan'.[223]

Creating an 'inner revolution'?

When it was established, BMA leaders were vocal in their belief that their organisation would not focus solely on the physical rejuvenation of its membership. Many of those involved with the foundation of the British arm of the movement stated that they felt Maccabi could play a pivotal role in the spiritual and cultural renewal of British Jewry. In 1936, the first President of the BMA, Lord Melchett, declared that the Association would help instigate an 'inner revolution ... among the younger people and in a new generation'.[224] A year earlier, one press release declared that British Maccabi would help establish a 'link between Jewish spiritual and physical culture'.[225] As Pierre Gildesgame noted in 1976, the early motivation was to 'develop within Jewish youth, of both sexes, an understanding for the spiritual values of the Jewish faith and a better appreciation of the Jewish cultural and national heritage'.[226]

BMA leaders argued that such a programme was needed because of the 'spiritual' ineffectiveness of youth organisations patronised by the Jewish establishment. Throughout the 1920s and 1930s, youth organisations under the aegis of the JAA and the AJY were vocally condemned by sections of the community for their 'neglect' of Jewish culture and religion in favour of sport. Maccabi leaders entered this debate, arguing that Maccabi presented an alternative which would take its responsibility for the spiritual health of its membership much more seriously. In 1934, the first BMA Chairman, Dr Lawrence Jacobs, criticised what he saw as a 'vague and unregulated urge for participation in sport on the part of the young Jew' which had been promoted by the Jewish youth movement.[227] One year later, Jacobs' successor, Colonel J.H. Levey, claimed that Maccabi was 'a movement of tomorrow and totally different in character from other Jewish bodies ... [because] the Maccabi had not sacrificed spiritual and cultural values to a sole devotion to sport'.[228]

So how would British Maccabi achieve this 'inner revolution'? Maccabi leaders argued that the 'introduction of a cultural and educational programme' would take place which would be designed to 'foster within the ranks of our youth the principles of good citizenship as well as a kinship with their fellow Jews'.[229] The constitution of Maccabi Association, London claimed that efforts would be made to 'stimulate ... a deep interest in all that is best in Jewish culture, literature, ideals and history' through a regular cultural education programme.[230] National leaders hoped that Maccabi clubs would emulate MAL and begin holding regular lectures, debates, essay contests and other activities related to religious education, as well as demonstrating a more observant attitude in terms of opening hours, religious services and Kosher food. All this, they argued, would help to provide the link between physical and spiritual culture which had been missing within Jewish youth organisations.[231]

Despite this initial enthusiasm, Maccabi's efforts in cultural and religious matters failed. During the period from the 1930s to the 1960s, the organisation was seen to be generally 'religiously undemanding' and was said to have 'neglected the spiritual side of Judaism'.[232] Maccabi experienced significant 'difficulties' in its promotion of cultural and religious activities and the average member at this time was 'largely unmoved' by the non-sporting programme.[233]

Within the movement itself, there was a clear awareness from the early 1950s onwards that efforts in spiritual matters had been unsuccessful. In 1950, the National Executive Committee complained of the generally 'haphazard' approach taken within many clubs towards 'cultural activities'.[234] Eight years later, Pierre Gildesgame commented that 'cultural activities have been appallingly neglected' and said that he wanted 'to see clubs pursuing a policy of Youth Education, true to Maccabi's aims and objects and not just providing a means of escape and badly planned entertainment'.[235]

A number of reasons account for Maccabi's failure in the cultural and religious sphere. A lack of direction and consensus from the national leadership was most significant. Although the idea of propagating an 'inner revolution' by means of religious and cultural education was prominent during its early years, no national programme was developed to help drive change across the whole Maccabi movement. In addition, the National Executive did not provide a clear and strong lead when faced with important religious issues – as seen with the lengthy and protracted debate over Saturday sport during the 1940s. In 1943, the issue of whether or not Maccabi clubs should be organising sporting activities on the Sabbath arose within the National Executive Committee. Some within the national leadership argued that Saturday sport should be allowed as this was pivotal in Maccabi's primary mission of increasing interest in sport amongst the membership. Others believed that the movement had a duty to appear publicly observant on religious matters, claiming that 'Saturday ... should be treated as a day of rest' and, as such, with no Maccabi sport played. The result of the lengthy debate over several months was a confused compromise which was largely unsatisfactory to both camps within the movement's leadership. In a letter circulated across the movement, Pierre Gildesgame stated that clubs would be implored not to arrange sport on a Saturday, but it was noted that 'the Executive Committee propose to take no action if Saturday sport did take place'.[236]

Without a clear lead from above on cultural and religious matters, individual clubs followed whatever course on 'spiritual' matters that they saw fit. As it transpired, many chose simply to ignore non-sporting activities altogether. One of the largest provincial clubs, Manchester Maccabi, consistently ignored pleas from the National Executive during the 1940s to be more religiously observant and expand its cultural education programme. In 1967, the club was threatened with disaffiliation due to their leaders' complete reluctance to organise any non-sporting activities.[237] Likewise, in 1954 Birmingham Maccabi was criticised for its decision to cease all activities apart from rugby, cricket and football. In 1959 the club was thrown out of British Maccabi as it was 'now functioning purely as a rugby club'.[238]

These examples demonstrate another significant hurdle with regard to cultural and religious activities – the apathy prevalent within the rank-and-file membership towards anything but sport and socialising.[239] During much of Maccabi's early history, the average member displayed a significant lack of interest in non-sporting activities.[240] In 1947, for example, the Chairman of Newcastle Maccabi pleaded with members to take a more active role in cultural activities – most of which were generally 'sparsely attended'.[241] Evidence from members of Leicester Maccabi during the 1940s and 1950s also shows cultural activities were generally not eagerly anticipated. Marilyn Aarons, for instance, noted that 'we used to have cultural programmes on a Sunday evening which terrified me in case I had to say anything. I later found out that the boy who organised these evenings was just as scared in case no one said anything'.[242]

Between the mid-1930s and the 1960s, the British Maccabi movement was unsuccessful in its mission to create a 'new Jew'. Whilst the organisation's early leadership may have believed that the movement could act as a bulwark against the erosion of Jewish ethnicity, it did little to reverse growing Jewish disunity and secular-isation.[243] In effect, the early advocates of British Maccabi were naïve in their belief that a sports movement rooted in a different Jewish context could be imported to strengthen British Jewish identity.

This is not to say that the organisation is of little historical signif-icance. Although there were evidently some problems in this aspect of its work, Maccabi was still a major provider of sport for a signif-icant proportion of the British Jewish population. In a limited way, British Maccabi contributed to a national and international growth of 'muscular Judaism' and a wider Jewish physical 'renaissance'. The growth of the movement and its large geographic base should be seen as another indication of the growing appetite for sport amongst British-born sections of British Jewry – a trend which was so often at the cost of spiritual and cultural 'Jewishness'.

It is away from sport where the clearest failings of the organisa-tion can be identified. Although the movement provided an important sense of community during the early post-war period, it was envisaged at British Maccabi's foundation that it would play a much more active role in creating cohesion amongst the population. The belief was that Zionism – the ideology underpinning Maccabi in its international context – could be used to help unite the membership and create a much-needed sense of Jewish solidarity. However, due to the apathy of both leaders and members, and the lack of consensus over Jewish nationalism more generally within British Jewish society, Zionism was not positioned as centrally within the movement as it was elsewhere. The 'unifying' effect of Maccabi was limited to creating a desire for sport and socialising, rather than through developing a wider consensus over support for a Jewish homeland.

British Maccabi could do little to begin an 'inner revolution' amongst an increasingly secularised community. The movement was initially characterised as a defender of Jewish identity and a force for the renewal of interest in Jewish religion and culture. However, indications are that this element of its programme lacked direction, focus and support at all levels of the movement and, consequently, Maccabi did not instigate a spiritual 'renewal' amongst its members.

In short, Maccabi in the British environment did not strengthen or protect Jewish identity to anywhere near the extent predicted. Unsurprisingly, given its evident prioritisation of physical recreation, achievements were generally limited to within the sporting sphere. Although it initially claimed to be able to create 'a new type of Jew and Jewess', British Maccabi was unrealistic in its belief that it could positively impact on the changing identity of British Jewry.

Conclusions: sport and Jewish ethnicity

Jewish interest in British sport had a significant impact on the ethnicity and identity of the British Jewish population. During the period from the late Victorian era through to the 1960s, Jewish direct and indirect involvement in physical recreation played an important role in the undermining of Jewish immigrant identity and culture and in the construction of new secularised forms of British Jewishness. Whilst sport exacerbated the socio-cultural 'drift' of the second and third generation, and helped Jews move physically, culturally and spiritually closer to mainstream society, it also provided an avenue in which Jews could redefine themselves in the eyes of their familial and communal elders, as well as their Jewish and Gentile peers.

Within the trend for growing secularity amongst the Jewish population during the early twentieth century, sport was a significant factor in the decreasing concern for religion amongst the young generation. More specifically, sport also impacted negatively on observance of the Jewish Sabbath – a key aspect of Jewish religious identity. Jewish involvement and interest in sport seemingly undermined both adherence and respect for the rest day. Whilst their parents and religious leaders may have exhibited concern at these Jews' apparent religious laxity, it seems that many Jews increasingly believed that Saturday was a day for play, rather than rest or prayer. Not every British Jew was desecrating the Sabbath in favour of sport. Yet many were increasingly found in the sports stadium or on the sports field, rather than in Synagogue, on a Saturday.

Jewish involvement in sport also impacted on the community's ethnicity in a wider sense. With an examination of professional boxing, it becomes clear that physical recreation proved to be another factor in the decreasing unity and solidarity of the community. Against the wishes, beliefs and culture of their elders, a significant number of second generation Jews took to the professional boxing ring. High-profile boxers such as 'Kid' Lewis and 'Kid' Berg, and the evident interest in watching and gambling on the 'unrespectable' sport of boxing, demonstrated a wider detachment and 'drift' of the younger immigrant generation away from the immigrant community and the Jewish establishment. Through boxing, we can see both the formation and expression of secularised, British Jewish identities.

Jewish sporting organisations themselves could seemingly do little to stem this religious and cultural 'drift', as shown by the early history of Maccabi in Britain up to the 1960s. In its attempt to create a 'new type of Jew' through uniting sport, Zionism and Judaism, Maccabi was markedly unsuccessful. Although this can be partly explained by reticence over Jewish nationalism and cultural and spiritual education at all levels of the movement, the clear prioritisation of sport within Maccabi rendered wider efforts at promoting Jewish ethnicity ineffectual. In short, Maccabi achieved success in the sporting and social spheres only, doing little to affect powerful social and cultural trends already in motion within younger sections of British Jewry.

Scholars working to expand our understanding of the complex nature of Jewish ethnic identity during modern times should more comprehensively examine the sporting interests of the population. This is because an analysis of sport's role in the erosion and redefinition of 'Jewishness' within the second and third generation immigrant community illustrates that physical recreation exerted a powerful effect on the way that many Jews formed their own identities. Research into sport also reveals much about the tension which existed over religion and culture between the younger Jews and their familial and communal elders. In essence, sport was not just a simple recreational activity for a significant section of the Jewish community of Britain during this period. Interest in sport went to the core of changes occurring in individual and collective Jewish ethnicity and was a major tenet of the social, spiritual and cultural constitution of 'British Jewishness' between the 1890s and the 1960s.

Notes

1 Panayi, *An Immigration History*, pp. 136, 140–141, 144.
2 Ibid. pp. 136, 141.
3 Endelman, *Radical Assimilation*, pp. 3–7.
4 Ibid. p. 203.
5 Gurock, *Judaism's Encounter*, p. 11. Gurock refers to the 'corrosive spirit of sports' with regard to Jewish ethnicity and details how, from the Middle Ages onwards, Jewish interest in physical recreation had contributed to the erosion and reconstruction of Jewishness.
6 Levine, *Ellis Island*, pp. 25, 38.
7 Ibid. p. 176; Endelman, *The Jews of Britain*, pp. 205–206.
8 Livshin, 'Acculturation of Immigrant Jewish Children', pp. 90–93.
9 D. Cesarani, 'A Funny Thing Happened on the Way to the Suburbs: Social Change in Anglo-Jewry Between the Wars, 1914–1945', *Jewish Culture and History*, 1, 1, 1998, pp. 13, 16.
10 Leonard Stern, quoted in Tananbaum, '"Ironing Out"', p. 66.
11 P. Panayi, *Immigration, Ethnicity and Racism in Britain, 1815–1945* (Manchester, 1994), p. 90.
12 Panayi, for instance, claims that 'faith has remained central in the collective and individual identities of virtually all migrant communities in Britain'. Panayi, *An Immigration History*, p. 145.
13 See, for instance, B. Homa, *Orthodoxy in Anglo-Jewry: 1880–1940* (London, 1969). One commentator claimed in 1964 that 'a basic fact of religious life in Anglo-Jewry is that the great bulk of the community has only the slightest concern with Judaism'. N. Cohen, 'Trends in Anglo-Jewish Religious Life', in J. Gould and S. Esh (eds), *Jewish Life in Modern Britain* (London, 1964), p. 41. Writing seventeen years later, Immanuel Jakobovits claimed that 70% of the community was 'largely indifferent' to religion. See I. Jakobovits, 'An Analysis of

Religious Versus Secularist Trends in Anglo-Jewry', in Lipman and
Lipman, *Jewish Life in Britain*, p. 32. Although there has been a post-
war revival in Britain in Ultra-Orthodoxy, mainstream Orthodox
religious practice declined considerably from the 1970s onwards.
Endelman, *The Jews of Britain*, pp. 248–251.
14 Panayi, *An Immigration History*, p. 155.
15 See, for instance, E. Smith, 'Jews and Politics in the East End of
London, 1918–1939', in Cesarani, *The Making of Modern Anglo-
Jewry*, p. 144.
16 D. Cesarani, 'The East London of Simon Blumenfeld's *Jew Boy*',
London Journal, 13, 1, 1987, pp. 47–49.
17 J. Green, *A Social History of the Jewish East End in London, 1914–
1939: A Study of Life, Labour and Liturgy* (Lampeter, 1991), p. 330;
Gartner, *The Jewish Immigrant*, p. 194.
18 For instance, Henrietta Adler claimed in 1934 that declining levels of
Sabbath observance were most evident amongst second generation
immigrants. H. Adler, 'Jewish Life and Labour in East London', in H.
Llewellyn Smith (ed.), *The New Survey of London Life and Labour*,
Volume VI, *Survey of Social Conditions, Part II: The Western Area*
(London, 1934), p. 278.
19 Not least the need for immigrant Jews to work on Saturdays to make
ends meet. Ibid. p. 278. Green has also commented that technological
changes, such as the invention of the electric light and the wireless,
eroded the sanctity of the Sabbath. Green, *Social History*, p. 330.
20 Lowerson has shown that nineteenth-century Christian religious
leaders saw sport as a hindrance to observance of the Christian
Sabbath and that there was much 'secularisation arising from social
habits'. J. Lowerson, *Sport and the English Middle Classes 1870–
1914* (Manchester, 1993), pp. 268–277.
21 Several historians have incorrectly argued that Jewish participation in
sport was affected by strict observance of the Jewish Sabbath.
McKibbin, for instance, claims that the reason why professional
boxing became so popular amongst Anglo-Jewry during the early
twentieth century was that 'observant Jews' could not play football
on the Sabbath and looked to alternative sports on alternative days of
the week. R. McKibbin, *Classes and Cultures: England, 1918–1951*
(Oxford, 2000), p. 366. Likewise, Shipley has similarly claimed that
Jewish success in boxing can be explained 'because the Jewish
Sabbath ruled out the alternative sport, football, for it was chiefly
played on Saturday before sundown'. Shipley, 'Boxing', p. 99.
22 See Endelman, *Radical Assimilation*, pp. 176–177.
23 As Englander has noted, the Jewish elites of the late Victorian period
often mirrored their Christian peers in terms of approach to religious

matters – their social, communal and political lives being characterised by strict observance, but their attitudes in private being
governed more by an 'inconsistent Victorian religiosity'. Quoted in
Langton, *Claude Montefiore*, p. 66.

24 Ibid.; E. Green, 'Montagu, Samuel, first Baron Swaythling
   (1832–1911)', *Oxford Dictionary of National Biography* (Oxford,
   2004).
25 *Jewish Chronicle*, 4 November 1898.
26 Harris was later an outspoken advocate for pacifism amongst the
   Anglo-Jewish community during the First World War. See E. Wilcock,
   'The Reverend John Harris: Issues in Anglo-Jewish Pacifism,
   1914–1918', *Jewish Historical Studies*, 30, 1987/88.
27 *Jewish Chronicle*, 28 February 1902.
28 B. Lammers, 'The Birth of the East Ender: Neighbourhood and Local
   Identity in Interwar East London', *Journal of Social History*, 39, 2,
   Winter 2005, p. 338.
29 Cesarani, 'A Funny Thing', pp. 13–17.
30 W. Goldman, *East End My Cradle: Portrait of an Environment*
   (London, 1988), p. 32. Interestingly, Goldman notes that his father
   had a less than observant attitude to the Sabbath as well, preferring a
   lie-in on Saturdays to attending Synagogue.
31 MJM J100, Interview with Abraham Goldstone.
32 Collins, 'Jews', p. 146.
33 *Jewish Chronicle*, 22 June 1990. On Morris' career at Swindon more
   generally, see D. Mattick, *100 Greats: Swindon Town Football Club*
   (Stroud, 2002), pp. 78–79.
34 MJM J43, Interview with Martin Bobker.
35 MJM J89, Interview with Joe Garman.
36 Green, *Social History*, p. 331. Spectating at sporting events grew in
   other Jewish communities in Europe and the USA. See, for instance,
   Levine, *Ellis Island*; M. John, 'Anti-Semitism in Austrian Sports
   between the Wars', in Brenner and Reuvani, *Emancipation Through
   Muscles*, p. 131.
37 Collins, 'Jews', p. 146.
38 MJM J309, Interview with Sydney Lea.
39 Quoted in Endelman, *Radical Assimilation*, p. 176.
40 Quoted in Lazarus, *A Club*, p. 38.
41 Green, *Social History*, p. 99.
42 Endelman, *The Jews of Britain*, p. 197.
43 Green, *Social History*, p. 331.
44 A number of histories of the club have been published. For the period
   from the club's inception in 1882 through to 1946, G.W. Simmons,
   History of Tottenham Hotspur Football Club 1882–1946 (London,

1947) is an invaluable resource. Later volumes on the club's history include J. Holland, *Spurs: A History of Tottenham Hotspur Football Club* (London, 1956) and R.L. Finn, *The Official History of Tottenham Hotspur Football Club, 1882–1972* (London, 1972).

45 In his autobiography of his life in the East End during the interwar period, Joe Jacobs (Communist Party activist and prominent anti-Fascist campaigner in London) claimed that a 'large number of Jewish football fans' of the time were Tottenham supporters. He recounts that during the early 1930s he and several friends 'would go to the pub when we had finished work [on Saturday morning] and then on to see Tottenham play when they were at home'. J. Jacobs, *Out of the Ghetto: My Youth in the East End, Communism and Fascism, 1913-1939* (London, 1991), p. 87. See also, *Jewish Chronicle*, 15 March 1996.

46 *Manchester Guardian*, 16 October 1935. The match was a source of much controversy at the time, with many fearing that the presence of a Nazi German national team at a London ground with a large Jewish fanbase could be a potential flashpoint. A relatively strong campaign against the match emerged, with support from Jewish groups, trade unions, factory groups and football organisations, whilst concerns were also raised that there could be potential clashes between Nazi supporters and anti-Fascist groups. The match passed off peacefully, being seen by historians as something of a propaganda coup for Germany, and indicative of the policy of 'sporting appeasement' which the British Government chose to follow throughout the 1930s. See Beck, *Scoring for Britain*, chapter 7: 'The Greatest Ever Triumph of the "Keep Politics Out of Sport' Brigade"? England versus Germany, 1935', pp. 173–213; B. Stoddart, 'Sport, Cultural Relations and International Relations: England versus Germany, 1935', *Soccer and Society*, 7, 1, 2006, pp. 29–50; P. Spencer, 'A Discussion of Appeasement and Sport as Seen in the *Manchester Guardian* and *The Times*', *Australian Society for Sports History Bulletin*, 2, 1996, pp. 3–19; R. Holt, 'The Foreign Office and the Football Association: British Sport and Appeasement, 1935–1938', in P. Arnaud and J. Riordan (eds), *Sport and International Politics: The Impact of Fascism and Communism on Sport* (London, 1998).

47 *Daily Express*, 22 October 1934.

48 J. Efron, '"When is a Yid not a Jew?" The Strange Case of Supporter Identity at Tottenham Hotspur', in Brenner and Reuvani, *Emancipation Through Muscles*, pp. 235–256.

49 Ibid. p. 236. On the geographical relocation of a large portion of London Jewry during this time, see H. Brotz, 'The Outlines of Jewish Society in London', in M. Freedman (ed.), *A Minority in Britain:*

Social Status of the Anglo-Jewish Community (London, 1955).
50 *Jewish Chronicle*, 15 March 1995.
51 C. Korr, *West Ham United: The Making of a Football Club* (Chicago, 1986), p. 210.
52 *Jewish Chronicle*, 15 March 1995. This is somewhat ironic considering that, in the modern context, White Hart Lane is seen to be one of the most poorly serviced grounds in terms of public transport.
53 Efron, '"When is a Yid"', p. 236; *Jewish Chronicle*, 2 August 1963. In 2004 Arsenal fanzine *Arsenal World* reported that 'many Jewish Arsenal fans' had raised objections to their new ground at Ashburton Grove being named after a well-known United Arab Emirates-based airline. See *Arsenal World*, 28 December 2006.
54 *Jewish Chronicle*, 16 November 1934.
55 Clavane, *Promised Land*, pp. 76–81; *Jewish Chronicle*, 22 August 1963; MJM 2008/23/18, 'My Sporting Life – David Cohen', p. 1. Cohen recounts that his love for Manchester United developed during his adolescence, when he would often rotate attending United and Manchester City games each Saturday.
56 See MJM J43, Interview with Martin Bobker; J89, Interview with Joe Garman; J309, Interview with Sydney Lea.
57 MJM J309, Interview with Sydney Lea.
58 Ibid.
59 *Jewish Chronicle*, 2 November 1934.
60 Interview with Leonard Dee, 21 June 2011.
61 Ibid. 15 March 1995.
62 Tananbaum, '"Ironing Out"', pp. 64, 69.
63 Bunt, *Jewish Youth Work*, p. 168.
64 *Jewish Chronicle*, 9 September 1914.
65 Kadish, *'A Good Jew'*, p. 98.
66 *Jewish Chronicle*, 4 August 1911.
67 *Jewish World*, 22 February 1907.
68 Ibid. 28 June 1907.
69 *Jewish Chronicle*, 7 October 1904.
70 Quoted in Tananbaum, '"Ironing Out"', p. 66.
71 Livshin, 'Acculturation of Immigrant Jewish Children', p. 90. Livshin highlights the example of the Manchester Jews' School whose curriculum was overhauled at this time in an effort to introduce a stronger religious element and combat trends for growing religious apathy. Fears abounded amongst Anglo-Jewry that more should be done to protect religious and spiritual identity.
72 *Jewish Graphic*, 25 February 1927.
73 D. Cesarani, *The 'Jewish Chronicle' and Anglo-Jewry, 1841–1991* (Cambridge, 1996), p. 137.

74 *Jewish World*, 17 April 1930.
75 Smith, 'Jews and Politics', p. 144.
76 *East London Advertiser*, 26 January 1935.
77 Tananbaum, '"Ironing Out"', p. 65.
78 Kadish, *'A Good Jew'*, p. 103.
79 UoSSC M172/AJ250/15, Basil Henriques, 'An address on the "Club and the Religious Problem"', 4 April 1930, p. 12.
80 Kadish has noted that the 'religious element' of Grove House was particularly marginal. Kadish, *'A Good Jew'*, p. 103.
81 Quoted Ibid. p. 99.
82 MCA M130/3, Grove House Lads' Club Managers' and Subscribers' Minutes, 6 January 1919, 7 June 1920, 2 October 1934, 30 May 1939.
83 Ibid. Minutes, 6 September 1920. The club's minutes from 6 September 1920 demonstrate this problem aptly. It was noted that the captain of one of the club's cricket teams had been 'suspended sine die from the club for having wilfully absented himself from a cricket match in order to watch a professional football match'. The Secretary also noted that 'due to the early commencement of professional football' and the attendance of members at local games, the cricket section had folded and club teams had been withdrawn from local competition.
84 *Jewish Chronicle*, 9 January 1931.
85 MCA M130/3, Minutes, 12 January 1931, 6 July 1932, 6 February 1933.
86 For example, Jewish sports writer and author, Anthony Clavane, claimed that despite being a keen footballer, he was not allowed to break the Sabbath in his highly observant household to indulge in his passion on the rest day. Clavane, *Promised Land*, p. 76.
87 Endelman, *Radical Assimilation*, pp. 1–3.
88 Cesarani, 'A Funny Thing', p. 6.
89 Ibid. pp. 13–16. As Smith has noted, however, it was not the case that second generation Jews were completely assimilated into the English working classes. She argues that whilst most Jews were 'divorced from Jewish tradition and as a consequence are removed from the Jewish masses, they could not assimilate themselves with the English working class because they did not possess a common tradition'. Smith, 'Jews and Politics', p. 142.
90 B. Williams, *Manchester Jewry, A Pictorial History: 1788–1988* (Manchester, 1988), p. 81.
91 Cesarani, *The Jewish Chronicle*, p. 145.
92 Shipley, 'Boxing', pp. 103–104. Social mobility has been pinpointed as a significant factor in the decline in American Jewish boxing after

the Second World War. S. Riess, 'Tough Jews: The Jewish American Boxing Experience, 1890–1950', in Riess, *Sports and the American Jew*, p. 103.

93 In 1914, *Boxing* remarked that Jews had done a 'special service' to the sport and that 'it is actually since the arrival of the Hebrew professional boxer that the ring has made its big stride in social esteem'. *Boxing*, 12 September 1914. Likewise, in 1935, an official from the British Board of Boxing Control claimed that 'there is no doubt in my mind that were it not for the influence of Jewish boxers, the game, so beloved of sportsmen the world over and in England, would scarcely be where it stands today'. Quoted in *Jewish Chronicle*, 22 March 1935.

94 R. Ungar and M. Berkowitz, 'From Daniel Mendoza to Amir Khan: Minority Boxers in Britain', in Berkowitz and Ungar, *Fighting Back?*, p. 6.

95 Holt, *Sport and the British*, p. 20.

96 Shipley, 'Boxing', p. 83.

97 *Boxing*, 26 September 1914.

98 Lewis, *Ted 'Kid' Lewis*, p. 11.

99 J. Harding with J. Berg, *Jack 'Kid' Berg: The Whitechapel Windmill* (London, 1987), p. 26.

100 MJM J1, Interview with Sam Aarons.

101 *East London Advertiser*, 3 November 1934.

102 Harding, *Jack 'Kid' Berg*, p. 24.

103 Green, *Social History*, p. 309; Cesarani, 'A Funny Thing', p. 16.

104 Green, *Social History*, p. 309; Riess, 'Tough Jews', p. 65. This is not to say that first generation Jews in Britain were completely averse to physical confrontation. See, for instance, the example of Ralph Finn's first generation immigrant grandfather, Zaida, who, whilst completely socially, culturally and religiously opposed to sport and boxing, was not afraid of defending himself physically when either he or his family were in danger. R. Finn, *No Tears in Aldgate* (Bath, 1973), pp. 50–53.

105 Over time, however, the money 'Kid' Lewis earned from his increasingly successful exploits in the ring eased the tension caused by his rejection of his parent's authority and culture. See Lewis, *Ted 'Kid' Lewis*, pp. 5, 20–21.

106 As a child, young Judah was unruly and uncontrollable. Much of his early childhood, when not at school, was spent on the streets surrounding his first home at Cable Street and his second family home in Fieldgate Mansions on Romford Street. By the time he was in his early teens he was regularly staying out all night four to five times a week and taking regular trips 'up West' to enjoy the dance-halls and cinemas of the capital's West End. Harding, *Jack 'Kid' Berg*, pp. 17–20.

107 Ibid. p. 31.

108 Ibid. p. 38.

109 Levine recounts the stories of several prominent American Jewish boxers of the early twentieth century, such as Louis Wallach, Abe Attell and Benny Leonard, whose decisions to enter the prize ring caused considerable friction between them and their elders who felt that 'boxing went against Jewish tradition'. Levine, *Ellis Island*, pp. 151–152.

110 Harding, *Jack 'Kid' Berg*, p. 33.

111 Lewis, *Ted 'Kid' Lewis*, p. 102.

112 Harding, *Jack 'Kid' Berg*, p. 200.

113 M. Berkowitz, 'Jewish Blood-Sport: Between Bad Behaviour and Respectability', in Berkowitz and Ungar, *Fighting Back?*, pp. 70–71.

114 M. Taylor, 'Round the London Ring: Boxing, Class and Community in Interwar London', *London Journal*, 34, 2, 2009, p. 148. There were significant outpourings of Jewish support for these two boxers when they each returned from successful spells boxing in America. Lewis, *Ted 'Kid' Lewis*, p. 137; Harding, *Jack 'Kid' Berg*, pp. 161–163.

115 Such was the market and commercial value of being a boxer of immigrant background at this time, especially a Jewish boxer, that some fighters even claimed immigrant roots falsely. Take for instance the non-Jewish American Heavyweight boxer Max Baer, who 'claimed Jewish origins as a means of attracting a Jewish following' during the 1930s. Berkowitz, 'Jewish Blood-Sport', p. 70.

116 A. Bodner, *When Boxing was a Jewish Sport* (London, 1997), p. 67.

117 Riess, 'Tough Jews', p. 96.

118 Berkowitz, 'Jewish Blood-Sport', p. 70. When Berg undertook the sixth defence of his Junior Welterweight title in 1930 against black boxer Kid Chocolate, it was noted that whilst Berg 'was an Englishman' he had gained significant support from Jewish fight fans across the country, with over ten thousand 'Hebrew rooters' from inner-city New York travelling and paying to watch the contest. *Boxing, Racing and Football*, 13 August 1930.

119 A. Chill, 'The Performance and Marketing of Minority Identity in Late Georgian Boxing', in Berkowitz and Ungar, *Fighting Back?*, p. 34.

120 This contrasted with other minority groups, such as the Irish, whose elites applauded the efforts of their professional boxers. As Green has noted, 'unlike the situation in other poor minority groups ... there was considerable ambivalence in the Jewish community towards pugilism'. Green, *Social History*, p. 308.

121 Quoted in Alderman, *Modern British Jewry*, p. 306.

122 Cesarani, *The Jewish Chronicle*, pp. 144–145.

123 Harding, *Jack 'Kid' Berg*, p. 25.

124 Berkowitz, 'Jewish Blood-Sport', pp. 76–77. Berkowitz claims that both 'Kid' Berg and 'Kid' Lewis had clear links to the criminal underworld, and with the world of gambling, both during and after time in the professional ring. He alleges that the 'criminality' of Jewish boxers is one factor in why relatively little academic research has ever been done on their careers.

125 UoSSC MS132/AJ195/7, R. Henriques, 'Unpublished typescript of a biographical journal of Basil Henriques' [c.1970], p. 247.

126 UoSSC MS132/AJ220/3/5, Letter to Basil Henriques from Bernhard Baron, 11 July 1921.

127 Ibid. 'Report of a meeting of managers of competing clubs and members of the Hutch Boxing Committee', 18 July 1921. The report noted that one member of the committee claimed 'although they would lose financially in dropping Kid Lewis, he felt quite certain that they would gain in prestige and that all present were quite convinced they were doing the right thing.'

128 MCA M130/3, Grove House Lads' Club Managers' and Subscribers' Minutes, 7 December 1925.

129 UoSSC MS172/AJ250/1, Stepney Jewish Lads' Club Minute Book, 10 September 1935.

130 R. Samuel (ed.), *East End Underworld: Chapters in the Life of Arthur Harding* (London, 1981), pp. 25–26, 315; Shipley, 'Boxing', p. 93; Lewis, *Ted 'Kid' Lewis*, p. 15; Harding, *Jack 'Kid' Berg*, p. 44. See also Taylor, 'Round the London Ring', pp. 144–147.

131 *Boxing*, 28 November 1914.

132 The National Archives, Kew, Surrey (hereafter NA), MEPO/2/2215, Minutes, 8 December 1928.

133 Cesarani, 'The East London', p. 48.

134 *Jewish Chronicle*, 30 August 1929.

135 *Boxing*, 16 October 1909.

136 Goldman, *East End*, p. 74. The biography of 'Kid' Lewis recounts one such fight between him and a young non-Jewish boxer at Premierland in 1912. Violence that began during the match continued after Lewis' opponent had been awarded a controversial victory and there 'then ensued a typical Premierland "free-for-all" with fist fights around the ring and bottles flying'. Lewis, *Ted 'Kid' Lewis*, p. 22.

137 *Boxing*, 18 December 1909; Samuel, *East End Underworld*, p. 182.

138 Taylor has argued that whilst 'drunkenness', gambling and general high spirits were always in evidence amongst boxing crowds, the widespread belief in the sport being characterised by crowd 'disorder' and violence has been somewhat overstated. Despite a rowdy

minority, most fight fans behaved with 'civility and good order'. Taylor, 'Round the London Ring', p. 152.

139 *Boxing*, 28 November 1914.

140 Ibid. 18 September 1909.

141 Berkowitz, 'Jewish Blood-Sport', p. 76.

142 Correspondence to London County Council quoted in Lewis, *Ted 'Kid' Lewis*, p. 7.

143 Quoted in Taylor, 'Round the London Ring', p. 151.

144 With both the Judæans and Wonderland closing in the period before and during the Great War, the post-war years saw the rise of Premierland as the principal 'Jewish' boxing hall. Weeks after Wonderland's destruction by fire in somewhat mysterious circumstances in 1911, Harry Jacobs took on the lease of a warehouse owned by Fairclough's butchers on Back Church Lane, Whitechapel 'for the purpose of holding boxing competitions and showing cinema pictures'. Premierland opened in January 1912 and between that date and its closure in the winter of 1930/31, it came to be regarded as one of Britain's principal boxing arenas alongside the Albert Hall and the Ring in Blackfriars. Interestingly, Premierland also became something of a political and social focal point for the Jewish community, with protest meetings, political debates and Jewish union meetings regularly being held there during the First World War and 1920s. See *Jewish Chronicle*, 27 October 1916, 5 November 1920; Harding, *Jack 'Kid' Berg*, p. 44; Lewis, *Ted 'Kid' Lewis*, p. 19; LMA GLC/AR/BR/07/410, Letter from Henry Smith to Superintending Architect, London County Council, 13 July 1911.

145 LMA GLC/AR/BR/07/410, Letter to London County Council, 8 September 1911.

146 Harding, *Jack 'Kid' Berg*, p. 46.

147 Taylor, 'Round the London Ring', p. 153.

148 NA MEPO/2/2215, Letter from Mr S. Cohen to Commissioner of Police, 8 December 1928.

149 Ibid. Police Report 'H' Division, 27 December 1928; W.H. Campbell, 'Premises used for Boxing Exhibitions', 9 January 1929.

150 Taylor, 'Round the London Ring', pp. 153–154; *Boxing, Racing and Football*, 7 January 1931.

151 Hyman Barnett 'Harry' Mizler, the most successful Jewish boxer of the mid-1930s, was said to have suffered during his early career because the closure of the various Jewish halls put him at a disadvantage to the previous generation of Jewish boxers. Harry, who was born in 1913 and was British Lightweight Champion in 1934, later claimed he suffered because there was no hall or arena where he could fight in front of large numbers of partisan Jewish fans or fight against

fellow Jewish boxers on a weekly basis. *Boxing News*, 3 January 1952, 10 January 1952.

152 There were a small number of Jewish boxers who achieved national and international success in the post-World World Two period. Lew Lazar, for instance, challenged for the British and European Welterweight and Middleweight titles during the 1950s, whilst his brother Harry was also a relatively successful middleweight. *Jewish Chronicle*, 14 May 2010. Jewish involvement in the business and promotion of the sport continued well into the 1960s and beyond, however. Jack Solomons became a well-known international promoter during the 1960s, staging famous fights with boxers such as Sugar Ray Robinson and Cassius Clay. Siegman, *Jewish Sports Legends*, pp. 59–60.

153 Green, *Social History*, p. 310; McKibbin, *Classes and Cultures*, p. 367; Shipley, 'Boxing', pp. 103–104. Siegman, *Jewish Sports Legends*, pp. 59–60.

154 *East London Advertiser*, 23 February 1935.

155 *Jewish Chronicle*, 28 February 1936.

156 For a comprehensive history of political Zionism at the end of the nineteenth century and beginning of the twentieth century, see W. Laqueur, *The History of Zionism* (London, 2003), pp. 84–136.

157 Ibid. pp. 162–171. Leading exponents of the notion of 'practical Zionism', which encompassed these wider views on Zionism, were Ahad Ha'am (1856–1927) and Martin Buber (1868–1965). Ha'am, in particular, was critical of what he saw as Theodor Herzl's promotion of a purely political form of Zionism. He believed that Jewish nationalism should be more than just a drive towards the foundation of a Jewish nation-state and called for a 'deeper attachment to national life' and a concentration on 'Jewish culture, of its language and literature, of education and the diffusion of Jewish knowledge'. Laqueur, *The History*, p. 163.

158 T. Presner, *Muscular Judaism: The Jewish Body and the Politics of Regeneration* (Abingdon and New York, 2007), pp. 1–3.

159 G. Mosse, 'Max Nordau, Liberalism and the New Jew', *Journal of Contemporary History*, 27, 4, 1992, pp. 567–570. Mosse notes that Nordau did not feel that sport was as important as gymnastics for the Zionist cause, as the former 'was not specifically designed to perfect the human body'. He also condemned football as 'rough and devoid of spiritual substance'.

160 European Maccabi has recently begun to attract the attention of various scholars interested in Jewish sport. See, for instance, A. Helman, 'Zionism, Politics, Hedonism: Sports in Inter-War Tel Aviv', in Kugelmass, *Jews, Sports and the Rites of Citizenship*; D. Blecking,

'Jews and Sports in Poland before the Second World War', in Mendelsohn, *Jews and the Sporting Life*, pp. 17–36; J. Jacobs, 'The Politics of Jewish Sports Movements in Interwar Poland', in Brenner and Reuvani, *Emancipation Through Muscles*.

161 On the history of the Maccabi World Union, see A. Hanak, 'The Historical Background of the Creation of the Maccabi World Union' in U. Simri, *Physical Education and Sport in the Jewish History and Culture* (Netanya, Israel, 1973), pp. 149–152.

162 M. Rosen, 'The Maccabi Movement in Great Britain in 1934–1948' (MA dissertation, University College, London, 2001), p. 6.

163 Ibid. p. 6; *Jewish Chronicle*, 8 June 1934. The arrival of large numbers of refugee Jews who had been involved in Maccabi clubs in Europe, and the relocation of the Maccabi World Union headquarters from Berlin to London in 1935, again in order to flee Hitler, also gave British Maccabi significant impetus during its foundation and early years.

164 LMA 4286/03/01/005, Minutes of the Maccabi National Executive Committee, 18 October 1964; Kadish, *'A Good Jew'*, p. 121.

165 Bunt, *Jewish Youth Work*, pp. 174–175.

166 Levine, *Ellis Island*, pp. 264–265 notes that interest in sport in American Maccabi clubs, especially after 1948, was inextricably linked to creating strong Jews to help in the physical and structural development of Israel. Likewise, Helman, 'Zionism', p. 99 demonstrates that Maccabi clubs in Palestine in the 1930s felt strongly that 'sport was ... curing the Jewish body, educating the young generation into national discipline and preparing it for any national calling'.

167 *East London Advertiser*, 23 February 1935.

168 Tyne and Wear Archive Services, Newcastle upon Tyne (hereafter TWAS), S/MAC/6, *Souvenir Programme for the Opening of Maccabi House*, Windsor Crescent, Newcastle (Newcastle, 1951), p. 13.

169 LMA 4286/03/07/010, Pierre Gildesgame, *Maccabi: Past and Present* (Leicester, 1976). On Gildesgame more generally, see Siegman, *Jewish Sports Legends*, p. 226; *Jewish Chronicle*, 13 March 1981.

170 For the motives behind the Anglo-Jewish youth movement's sporting programme, see Chapter 1.

171 LMA 4286/03/07/014, Maccabi Association, London, *Commemorative Brochure for the Opening of Maccabi House* (London, 1937), p. 3.

172 LMA 4286/03/07/020, Ken Gradon, *What is Maccabi?* (London, 1976), p. 8. Gradon was born in 1919 in Germany and was originally called Kurt Gradenwitz, before escaping to Britain as a refugee in the 1930s. He played a crucial administrative role in British and European Maccabi in the post-World War Two period. See, Siegman, *Jewish Sports Legends*, p. 229.

173 TWAS S/MAC/2, *The Maccabi Code* (London, 1936). See below, Chapter 3, for a broader discussion on Maccabi's attitude towards combating anti-Semitism.

174 TWAS S/MAC/1, 'Constitution of the Newcastle-Upon-Tyne Maccabi Association' (1935), p. 2.

175 D. Dee, '"Your religion is football!" Soccer and the Jewish Community in London, 1900–1970' (MA dissertation, De Montfort University, 2007), pp. 49–51.

176 Jewish Agency for Israel, 'The Story of Sport in Israel', chapter 6: 'Rule Britannia! The British Influence and the Maccabiah Games'. Found at www.jewishagency.org/JewishAgency/English/Jewish+Education/Comp elling+Content/Eye+on+Israel/Sport+in+Israel/Rule+Britannia+The+Brit ish+Influence+and+the+Maccabiah+Games.html (accessed 23 March 2010).

177 On the Maccabiah, see Y. Galily, 'The Contribution of the Maccabiah Games to the Development of Sport in the State of Israel', *Sport in Society*, 12, 8, 2009, pp. 1,028–1,037; M. Sashon and B. Schrodt, 'The Maccabi Sports Movement and the Establishment of the Maccabiah Games, 1932', *Sport History Review*, 16, 1, 1985, pp. 67–90; G. Eisen, 'The Maccabiah Games: A History of the Jewish Olympics' (Ph.D. thesis, University of Maryland, 1979).

178 See, for instance, *Jewish Chronicle*, 1 March 1935, 1 September 1935; LMA 4286/03/07/010, Gildesgame, *Maccabi: Past and Present*, p. 6.

179 J. Hoffman, *Ten Great Maccabians: A History of Maccabi for Young People* (London, 1981), p. 13; Siegman, *Jewish Sports Legends*, pp. 71, 174.

180 On Helfgott – a Holocaust survivor – see J. Finklestone, *Ben Helfgott: From Victim to Champion* (London, 2002). Provincial Maccabi clubs also produced several sportsmen who went on to achieve significant success. See, for example, former Glasgow Maccabi members Monty McMillan, an international table tennis player in the 1950s, or Brian Coussin, who later played professional football in the Israeli League. *Jewish Echo*, 19 October 1990.

181 See for instance, LMA 4286/03/01/003, NEC Minutes, 18 December 1955, 5 May 1954.

182 Bunt, *Jewish Youth Work*, p. 177.

183 Financial assistance from the Maccabi World Union increased steadily in the post-war period, whereas it wasn't until the foundation of the 'Sportsmen's Century Club' in 1959 that significant British finance was forthcoming. The club's members, largely English Jewish philanthropists and businessmen, made annual donations to the British Maccabi Association, and other Jewish charities, from this year onwards. In 1967, the club donated over £8,000 to the BMA. See

LMA 4286/03/10/001, Sportsmen's Century Club minutes.

184 See for instance, TWAS S/MAC/2, Letter from British Maccabi Organisations of Jewish Sports Organisations to Newcastle Maccabi, 19 October 1935.

185 LMA 4286/03/01/003, NEC Minutes, 5 May 1954.

186 LMA 4286/03/07/014, MAL, *Commemorative Brochure*, p. 8.

187 *Jewish Chronicle*, 30 November 1962.

188 LMA 4286/03/01/002, NEC Minutes, 11 October 1948.

189 Scottish Jewish Archives Centre, Glasgow (hereafter SJAC), Glasgow Maccabi Archives, *Souvenir Brochure to Celebrate the Opening of the New Gymnasium at May Terrace, Glasgow* (Glasgow, 1968), p. 9.

190 See, for instance, T. Mason and R. Holt, *Sport in Britain: 1945–2000* (Oxford, 2000), pp. 148–152 which notes that post-war public provision for sport vastly increased from the 1950s onwards.

191 Bunt, *Jewish Youth Work*, p. 177.

192 Rosen, 'The Maccabi Movement', p. 8.

193 For example, see LMA 4286/03/01/001, NEC Minutes, 13 December 1943 which noted that South London Maccabi, founded in Tooting in 1935, was fast becoming nothing but a 'glorified palais-de-dance'.

194 Ibid. NEC Minutes, 2 May 1945.

195 TWAS S/MAC/3/2, *Maccabi News*, 4, 1947, p. 8.

196 R. Adam, *Jewish Voices: Memories of Leicester in the 1940s and 1950s* (Leicester, 2009), pp. 66–74.

197 Bunt, *Jewish Youth Work*, p. 177.

198 Adam, *Jewish Voices*, p. 66.

199 B. Braber, *Jews in Glasgow, 1879–1939: Immigration and Integration* (London, 2007), chapter 7: 'Change and Continuity'.

200 SJAC, Glasgow Maccabi Archives, L. Davidson, 'Potted History of Glasgow Maccabi' (1990), pp. 1–3.

201 P. Goodman, *Zionism in England: 1899–1949* (London, 1949), pp. 47, 58.

202 M. Berkowitz, *Western Jewry and the Zionist Project: 1914–1933* (Cambridge, 1997), p. 196.

203 TWAS S/MAC/2, *The Maccabi Code*.

204 Rosen, 'The Maccabi Movement', p. 8.

205 Helman, 'Zionism', p. 101; Jacobs, 'The Politics of Jewish Sports', pp. 93–94.

206 Helman, 'Zionism', p. 99.

207 The current, official Maccabi GB website claims 'We aim to deliver a broad range of Sporting, Educational and Social events for the whole of the Jewish community with the ethos of Jewish continuity and the centrality of Israel as our primary motivation'. www.maccabigb.org/about.html (accessed 24 March 2010).

208 LMA 4286/03/07/020, Gradon, *What is Maccabi?*, p. 8.
209 Rosen, 'The Maccabi Movement', p. 11.
210 LMA 4286/03/07/020, Gradon, *What is Maccabi?*, p. 9. Gradon noted that he was against outwardly espousing or supporting political Zionism because 'teenagers, who constitute the majority of the movement, should not be allowed to become involved in any political controversy'. See also LMA 4286/03/01/002, Minutes of the Maccabi National Executive Committee, 21 March 1950 where one leader noted his belief that the organisation was a 'non-political youth movement' and should not enter into 'dangerous' political debates.
211 LMA 4286/03/07/010, Gildesgame, *Maccabi*.
212 See for instance, *Jewish Chronicle*, 9 August 1935; *East London Advertiser*, 23 February 1935.
213 See, for example, LMA 4286/03/01/002, NEC Minutes, 10 June 1947 when it was noted that the Maccabi World Union had pressurised British Maccabi to force all members to purchase the shekel and financially support the idea of Jewish nationalism. After weeks of deliberations and calls against this within the NEC, the Committee reluctantly gave in to MWU demands and made shekel purchase obligatory for members. It noted, pointedly, however, that 'while it is recognised that the shekel grants rights of franchise and participation in Congress elections, Maccabi Union has no intention of exercising these rights'.
214 Rosen, 'The Maccabi Movement', p. 15; *Jewish Echo*, 4 October 1939. Glasgow Maccabi, for instance, had very active Zionist sections throughout the 1930s.
215 LMA 4286/03/01/002, NEC Minutes, 15 July 1947, 15 December 1947, 11 October 1948.
216 Bunt, *Jewish Youth Work*, p. 178.
217 On Aron more generally, see H. Silman-Cheong, *Wellesley Aron: A Rebel with a Cause* (London, 1992).
218 On Habonim, see Bunt, *Jewish Youth Work*, pp. 103–108.
219 On the history of Poale Zion in England, see G. Shimoni, 'Poale Zion: A Zionist Transplant in Britain, 1905–1945', *Studies in Contemporary Jewry*, 2, 1986, pp. 227–261.
220 On Zionist youth organisations, see Kadish, *'A Good Jew'*, pp. 120–122.
221 Berkowitz, *Western Jewry*, pp. 148, 160.
222 Rosen, 'The Maccabi Movement', p. 13.
223 S. Cohen, *English Zionists and British Jews: The Communal Politics of Anglo-Jewry, 1895–1920* (Princeton, 1982), pp. 13, 317.
224 *Jewish Chronicle*, 28 February 1936.

225 Ibid. 21 May 1935.
226 LMA 4286/03/07/010, Gildesgame, *Maccabi: Past and Present*, p. 1.
227 *Jewish Chronicle*, 10 August 1934.
228 Ibid. 9 August 1935.
229 LMA 4286/03/07/020, Gradon, *What is Maccabi?*, p. 2.
230 LMA 4286/03/07/014, MAL, *Commemorative Brochure*, p. 3.
231 Rosen, 'The Maccabi Movement', pp. 8–10.
232 Ibid. pp. 11, 17.
233 Bunt, *Jewish Youth Work*, pp. 175–176.
234 LMA 4286/03/01/002, NEC Minutes, 21 March 1950.
235 LMA 4286/03/01/003, NEC Minutes, 12 October 1958. Outside observers of British Maccabi also criticised it for its lack of non-sporting content. In 1963, a report from the Ministry of Education concerning an application for an education grant noted that Maccabi's request would be unsuccessful. This was partly due to low national membership numbers, but the report also suggested that the fact there was a 'marked lack of cultural activity' had severely hindered the application. See LMA 4286/03/01/005, NEC Minutes, 7 April 1963.
236 LMA 4286/03/01/001, NEC Minutes, 20 December 1943, 14 February 1944, 15 July 1947, 25 November 1947. The Saturday sport debate continued during the rest of the 1940s and was never properly resolved. Indeed, many clubs simply ignored the directive from the NEC and continued to play Saturday sport throughout the whole decade.
237 LMA 4286/03/01/005, NEC Minutes, 21 March 1967.
238 LMA 4286/03/01/002, NEC Minutes, 10 October 1954, 5 May 1959.
239 This was not the case with all British Maccabi clubs. Glasgow Maccabi, for instance, developed a thriving cultural and religious education programme from the 1950s onwards. When the club moved premises to the Giffnock suburbs from the Gorbals area of inner city Glasgow in 1968, it prided itself on its observant attitude towards religious matters and its well-attended lectures, debates and discussions on cultural and spiritual matters. See SJAC, Glasgow Maccabi Archives, Davidson, 'Potted History', pp. 1–3.
240 This was not just a problem limited to British Maccabi. Helman claims that cultural programmes were often ignored by members of Maccabi clubs in Palestine during the 1930s as well. Maccabi Tel-Aviv, for example, became more reminiscent of a simple social club at this time, with regular music and 'singing and dancing well into scan-dalous hours of the night'. Helman, 'Zionism', p. 101.
241 TWAS S/MAC/3/2, *Maccabi News*, 4, 1947.
242 Adam, *Jewish Voices*, p. 72.

243 This contrasts somewhat with Maccabi in the modern context, which is seemingly playing an important role in preserving Jewish identity. In April 2011, a survey of Maccabi GB members found that 60% felt that their involvement with the organisation had played an 'important' or 'extremely important' role in shaping their Jewish identity; 40% said membership made them more likely to keep Jewish customs; and 50% said it increased their chances of marrying within the community. *Jewish Chronicle*, 11 April 2011.

3

Anti-Semitism

Introduction

Within the academic literature concerned with British Jewish history, there is a notable split with regard to anti-Semitism. Historians of the Whig school have generally argued that discrimination of Jews was a marginal phenomenon within British society. Whig scholars often stress British Jewry's 'good fortune, its freedom from mob violence and state discrimination [and] its uneventful acculturation and integration', whilst downplaying social, political and economic anti-Semitism.[1] The historical writing produced by these so-called 'historical apologetics' often inferred that hostility towards Jews was both uncommon and 'un-British'.[2]

New school historians of British Jewry have worked to 'undermine the upbeat, filiopietistic reading of Anglo-Jewish history' associated with Whig scholars.[3] Their research has shown that hostility towards Jews in Britain has been prevalent since medieval times, when the small Jewish community were subjected to a form of religious anti-Jewishness, facing allegations of ritual murder and 'blood libels'.[4] Significant research has been conducted on anti-Semitism in a more modern context. For instance, both Holmes' seminal *Anti-Semitism in British Society* and Lebzelter's *Political Anti-Semitism in England* were published in the 1970s. Although taking different approaches and forming contrasting conclusions on the nature of British anti-Semitism, these two academic works demonstrated that 'anti-Semitic tension was present in Britain and the expression of hostile attitudes towards Jews was not uncommon' from the late nineteenth century through to 1939.[5] Others have shown that anti-Semitic hostility was also prominent during the Second World War and its immediate aftermath.[6] Recent research has also illustrated that anti-Semitism in the 'contemporary period' since the 1960s was 'somewhat intense in expression and has acquired a distinctive political character'.[7]

The body of scholarship on British anti-Semitism has generally focused its attention on 'organised' and 'social' forms of hostility.[8] The former encompasses the political forms of racism propagated by groups hostile towards the Jewish community such as the British Union of Fascists or the Britons. The latter deals with everyday hostility towards Jews and the so-called 'anti-Semitism of exclusion' which saw Jews discriminated against in their employment, housing and work, and in their attempts to join various private leisure and social clubs.[9] Both modes of anti-Semitism have been prominent throughout the period between the 1890s and the 1960s – illustrating that hostility towards Jews has taken on many forms and has occurred in many different social, cultural, political and economic milieus during modern British Jewish history.[10]

Outside of Britain, some attention has been paid to the relationship between 'organised' and 'social' forms of anti-Semitism and sport. For instance, it has been shown that Central European Jews involved in sport in the interwar period faced anti-Semitism from non-Jewish political groups and student fraternities.[11] Similarly, much research has been conducted on the link between 'social' anti-Semitism and sport in its international context. In his research on American Jewish country clubs in the 1920s, Levine demonstrates that discrimination towards German Jews was prevalent within the American middle-class sporting and social club environment.[12] Likewise, Eisen has shown that discrimination towards Jewish sportsmen was prominent within student duelling fraternities and gymnastics societies in Central and Eastern Europe during the late nineteenth and early twentieth century. Such was the strength of this anti-Semitism, Jews were forced to create 'parallel institutions' to enable them to engage in sport free of discrimination.[13]

Within the literature on British anti-Semitism, there is a limited focus on the links between sport and various forms of discrimination against Jews. For instance, Lebzelter briefly discusses the relationship between middle-class anti-Semitism and sport within her examination of 'social discrimination' against Jews during the interwar period.[14] Within recent research conducted on the links between anti-Semitism and British Fascism during the 1930s, some attention has been given to the role of sport within the ideology espoused by the British Union of Fascists. Significantly, these discussions have often concentrated more on the broader relationship between the BUF and physical recreation, rather than focusing wholly on the element of their anti-Semitic programme and propaganda espoused regarding sport.[15]

This chapter will provide a much more comprehensive analysis of the links between anti-Semitism and sport in a British context. It will illustrate that some of the most powerful expressions of anti-Jewish sentiment were located within the sphere of British sport. Not only were Jews attacked by right-wing organisations for being 'foreign' in their sporting outlook and demeanour, they were also summarily excluded from the middle-class sporting environment due to their ethnicity. Sport was not just a setting in which Jews experienced hostility, it was also a site where they felt they could actively respond to anti-Semitism both within sport and in wider society.

Anti-Semitism was much more prevalent within the milieu of British sport than the extant historiography suggests. Jews involved in British sport encountered a strong exclusionary form of discrimination, whilst also being subjected to hostility and bigotry from many different sources due to their alleged racial 'difference'. On the one hand, physical recreation provided a vehicle for perceptions of Jews as 'outsiders' to be both reinforced and conveyed. Yet it was also true that Jewish sporting participation worked against anti-Semitism inside and outside of the sporting world. In short, a historical investigation of British sport sheds new light on the way that Jews were subjected to racism by the wider community and the manner in which Jews dealt with the anti-Semitism that they faced.

The British Union of Fascists and the 'sporting' Jew, 1935–39

Since the late Victorian era, there has been a clear trend for 'organised group hostility' towards the Jewish community.[16] Whilst anti-Jewish violence was not uncommon, the majority of these organisations expressed their anti-Semitic ideology in the form of written and verbal propaganda. Within the anti-Semitic ideology of one of the largest and most well-known groups hostile to the Jewish community, the British Union of Fascists, sport came to assume a prominent position. From 1935 through to 1939, the BUF's two main publications, *The Blackshirt* and *Action*, contained numerous anti-Semitic references to the supposed negative effect of Jewish involvement in British sport.

These sporting expressions of BUF ideology were designed to reinforce ideas of hidden Jewish 'power' and alleged Jewish racial, social and cultural difference – labelled 'the two clearest features of modern British anti-Semitism' since the end of the nineteenth century.[17] However, by trying to create the spectre of a Jewish 'other' within the realm of British physical recreation, the BUF sought to establish the idea that Jews were a threat to the nation's sporting and cultural character and well-being – a danger, which the BUF claimed, they were best placed to combat. In effect, the BUF's sporting anti-Semitism was used as a propaganda tool to create popular and political support for the organisation.

Organised forms of anti-Semitism have been evident within Britain since the 1900s.[18] During the Great War, several British right-wing writers and organisations also demonstrated considerable hostility towards German Jews, whilst in the interwar years anti-Semitism became a central component of the ideology and propaganda of several British Fascist groups.[19] Although 'there is no necessary or natural correlation' between British Fascism and anti-Jewish sentiment, it is evident that many right-wing organisations in existence during the interwar years incorporated anti-Semitism into their verbal and written propaganda.[20] The Britons, for example, formed in 1918, became known for publishing 'virulent anti-Semitic propaganda' which propagated notions of Jewish influence and cultural aloofness.[21] Similarly, the Imperial Fascist League, founded in 1928, espoused a 'doctrine of racial anti-Semitism' and campaigned for the expulsion of Jews from British shores.[22] Some right-wing groups, such as the British Fascisti, only became outwardly anti-Semitic many years after their foundation, whilst others, such as the Nordic League and the Right Club, were 'intensely pro-Hitlerite and anti-Jewish' throughout their entire existence.[23]

Anti-Semitism also came to eventually assume a prominent position in the ideology of the only Fascist 'organisation with any pretension to significance' at this time.[24] In 1932, estranged former Labour MP, Oswald Mosley, formed the British Union of Fascists after the failure of his New Party in the 1931 General Election. It has been argued that Mosley was 'not at first regarded as unfriendly to Jewish interests', although by the mid-1930s he had become well known for his sharply anti-Semitic views.[25] Up until the BUF were banned by Government order in 1940, the organisation espoused an openly anti-Semitic party line in which 'Jews were portrayed as undermining and dominating Britain in their own interest'. During the mid- to late 1930s, the party zealously pursued the Jewish 'issue' as a means of political progress.[26]

Reflecting the large body of writing on the BUF, multiple scholarly viewpoints on the origins, nature and extent of the organisation's anti-Semitism have been developed.[27] Whilst some historians allege that the BUF's anti-Semitism was due to political opportunism, the beliefs of individual leaders or a response to Jewish 'anti-Fascist' activity, others claims that the hostility had much deeper roots.[28] Holmes, for example, claims that the BUF's anti-Jewish ideology emerged out of the dire domestic socio-economic atmosphere of the late 1920s and early 1930s and tapped into an 'anti-Semitic folk memory' which had existed since the British Brothers' League agitation in the early 1900s.[29] Cheyette claims that both Mosley and his organisation drew from existing 'discourses' of anti-Semitism prevalent in wider society and culture.[30]

Whatever its cause or character, the BUF's anti-Semitism ran along two distinct, but not wholly unrelated, lines; both of which reflected long-standing notions propagated by organisations hostile to the Jewish community. Firstly, the BUF sought to promote the idea of a Jewish 'Hidden Hand' and advance the myth that the Jewish community had a disproportionate amount of influence at the highest echelons of politics, business and finance. This idea of 'Jewish power' was a 'major obsessive theme' of Mosley's speeches during the mid-1930s, reflecting beliefs in the existence of an 'overpowering Jewish internationalism' which had its roots in the late nineteenth century.[31] Secondly, the BUF attempted to demonstrate through their propaganda that Jews were racially 'distinct' from the British. It was argued that Jews lacked the ability, desire or characteristics necessary to fully integrate and become active and contributing citizens to both British society and the British Empire. The presence of Jewish aliens on British shores was claimed to be undermining social, cultural and political stability, development and cohesion – with Jews being viewed as an 'anti-national element' which could never 'add a valuable contribution to British life'.[32]

Whilst the majority of BUF propaganda focused on the Jewish

impact on British politics, business, economics and culture, sport was also an arena of British life regularly addressed by party publications. In a reflection of the party's obsession with sporting ideology and the public school ethos surrounding masculinity, sport formed a prominent strand of the party's anti-Semitism.[33] By highlighting areas where Jewish power and authority seemed disproportionately strong in the sporting world, and using sporting 'examples' of Jewish otherness and supposed racial difference, the BUF worked to further define Jews as a social, physical and cultural 'other' – an outsider group which the BUF, as the self-labelled epitome of Britishness and sportsmanship, were willing to oppose.[34]

The main vehicles for the BUF's anti-Semitic sporting ideology were the party's two major publications, *The Blackshirt* and *Action*, which together reportedly had a readership of 48,000 in the mid- to late 1930s.[35] Within these newspapers, two themes dominated the BUF's racist discussions surrounding Jews and sport. Firstly, they maintained that Jewish 'control' of the administration, finance and management of British sport was having a harmful effect on British participation. BUF propaganda argued that the Jewish 'Hidden Hand' in politics, economics and business stretched into the world of British sport. Secondly, they also regularly argued that Jews lacked a sporting attitude and had no true understanding of the ethos pervading British sport. It was maintained that this was further evidence of the inherent racial difference and distinct alien and 'foreign' outlook of the British Jewish community. Through their propaganda, the BUF manipulated well-established right-wing mythology to project the notion of Jewish sporting 'difference' in a bid to further strengthen their wider anti-Semitic programme.

The 'Hidden Hand' in British sport

The anti-Semitic notion of an international Jewish 'Hidden Hand' is long-established. Whilst 'the persistent myth of a world-wide Jewish conspiracy' is the 'theme that figures most prominently in anti-Semitic propaganda' of the interwar period, a 'fear' of Jewish 'power' became increasingly prevalent in the late nineteenth century.[36] In the years between the Russian Revolution and the start of the Second World War, however, 'conspiratorial anti-Semitism' gained some popular support, with the idea of an international Jewish scheme to dominate global politics, finance and business being propagated by extreme right-wing groups.[37]

By the 1920s, the idea of a Jewish 'Hidden Hand' had gained a noticeable level of support at many levels of British society. Yet whilst the general British public gave the suggestion of a Jewish conspiracy little or no credence, 'concern over Jewish power in society ... did not disappear in inter-war Britain'. Numerous Fascist and right-wing groups, including the BUF, perpetuated the idea that Jewish influence was disproportionately strong in many areas of life in Britain. A minority believed that Jewish influence – in politics and finance especially – would be used for ethnic rather than national interests and would only prove damaging to Britain in the long-term.[38]

Within the anti-Semitic propaganda of the BUF, the 'theme of Jewish power' figured prominently. At the party's September 1934 rally at Belle Vue, Manchester, Mosley 'launched into an indictment of Jewish influence' and bemoaned the power held by 'Jewish money'. He stated that 'What they call today the will of the people is nothing but the organised corruption of the Press, cinema and Parliament, which is called democracy but which is ruled by alien finance'.[39] This notion of a 'Hidden Hand' was a recurring theme in the party's propaganda right up to the Government action taken against them in June 1940. On several occasions, BUF leaders tried to position themselves in the public psyche as the defenders of Britain against this apparent Jewish 'conspiracy'. This primarily involved promoting the idea that the BUF would fight against British Jews who were allegedly 'highly organised for sectional rather than national interests'.[40]

In BUF propaganda, sport came to play a significant role in instilling the idea that Jewish influence was exerting a negative effect across British society. By propagating the notion that Jewish power extended to the world of sport – that so sacred a British institution – the BUF hoped to demonstrate to its supporters that the Jewish conspiracy threatened Britain's cultural, as well as political and economic, well-being. Given the pervading belief during the early twentieth century in the apolitical, amateur, public school ethos of British sport, this notion was all the more powerful.[41]

One of the first examples of the BUF utilising sport to reinforce the idea of a Jewish 'Hidden Hand' came in 1935. In December of that year, an international football match between England and Germany was held at White Hart Lane, ground of Tottenham Hotspur FC – a club which had a significant Jewish fanbase. In the lead up to the match, party publications claimed that Jewish Tottenham fans were 'dictating' to the FA that the game should be cancelled. *The Blackshirt* reported that the TUC, labelled by the BUF as the 'pawns of Jewry', were being forced by the Jewish elites to exert pressure on Government ministers to prohibit the game.[42] One week after the match, renowned anti-Semite and BUF organiser, A.K. Chesterton, celebrated the failure of the Jewish elites in their attempts to stop the game and undermine relations between the two nations. Chesterton went on to note that 'as they controlled and cornered everything else in Britain, the Jews naturally saw no reason why they should not control and corner British sport as well'.[43]

Alongside notions of Jewish sporting 'power' on a national level, the BUF also contended that Jewish influence extended to the vast network of small, local sporting and athletic clubs. They argued that Jewish power on a local level was leading to 'British' athletes being effectively excluded from participation or hampered in their training. In 1936 the party's Manchester correspondent, Jack Kinsey, reported he had 'found sport practically barred to him' due to the influence of Jews in local athletic clubs. Even more offensive for the BUF, who believed strongly in the public school ideology surrounding physical recreation, was that not only were Jews barring non-Jewish participation, but they were also taking the contemptible line of mixing sport with politics. Kinsey claimed that Jews had taken over his local club for use by the Communist Party's British Workers' Sports Federation and that he had been asked to leave the club because he had told them he was unwilling to support the 'Red' cause. He went on to claim:

> This is but one instance in the career of but one sportsman. Throughout the country, such things are a daily occurrence. Sports clubs, even when not controlled by Jews, are permeated with brothers of their race and sycophantic 'Reds' and the lot of British sportsmen, already made difficult by the indifference of the Government, is made doubly so by the influence of the Jew.[44]

The BUF were also vociferous in their claim that horse-racing was suffering at the hands of 'alien tricksters'. In 1938, *Action* claimed that the business of the sport, from the ownership of the horses down to the trackside betting, was dominated by members of the Jewish community. These 'aliens', *Action* argued, had little interest in the sporting contest on show and were driven by purely financial motivations. The correspondent claimed that Jews were a parasite within the sport and that 'whenever large sums of money change hands with any frequency – there, battening like carrion on the pickings that may be found, are the most degraded specimens of an alien race'. The article called on the horse-racing authorities to 'protect' the sport from further Jewish interference:

> If the pastime is going to be again worthy of its proud title 'The Sport of Kings' those responsible for its welfare should take immediate steps to wipe out the rottenness attracting to its name ... The stewards of the Jockey Club have full authority to 'warn off' any owner, trainer or jockey who contravenes their rules. Let this be extended to eliminate the bad odour that aliens and crooks have brought into a great sport.[45]

However, most of the BUF's propaganda concerning a sporting 'Hidden Hand' was reserved for professional boxing. As Jewish involvement in the sport was both nationally and internationally prominent at this time, it proved a natural target for propaganda designed to strengthen the notion of Jewish sporting 'influence'. Boxing was also targeted because of the special relevance the sport attained within the BUF. The party's organisers held boxing in extremely high esteem ('it was boxing which was exalted as a sport above all others') and actively promoted the sport amongst BUF members. Regular columns were printed in *Action* concerning boxing technique, whilst multiple local and national competitions were held to help increase interest in the sport amongst BUF supporters.[46]

Promoting boxing obviously had a 'practical relevance' within the party (especially when faced with physical attacks from anti-Fascists). But it was also believed to be one way of showing the 'innate masculinity' of the party and demonstrating the 'physical superiority' of the Anglo-Saxon race to the wider community. Mosley himself had been a schoolboy boxing champion and the BUF is said to have also attracted well-known supporters from within the professional world such as Joe Beckett (a former British Heavyweight champion), Len Harvey (former British Heavy-, Light-Heavy- and Middleweight champion) and Jewish boxer Ted 'Kid' Lewis. For the BUF, 'more than any other, the sport was seen as a means of asserting the superiority of British manhood'.[47]

The fact that British boxing had many successful Jewish prize-fighters within its ranks was a cause for concern for BUF leaders. The way they worked to undermine this clear contradiction of their own ideology was to claim that professional boxing was controlled by a Jewish 'racket' and therefore just another aspect of the international 'Hidden Hand' then supposedly in existence. On the one hand, party publications focused on Jewish involvement in the business of the sport, claiming that 'alien' managers and promoters were abusing the sport and ignoring its core values simply for financial gain. In 1936 *Action* claimed that 'the fistic art has most certainly ceased to exist as a reasonable sport and, except for the amateurs, it has developed into a rather unhealthy racket'. The article went on to suggest that real control of the sport lay not in the hands of the British Boxing Board of Control but with 'Jewish rack-eteers'. They 'scandalously underpay young or unknown fighters' who are 'ruined both physically and morally by these leeches who spin wonderful stories of success to follow if the lad will only put himself in their hands'.[48]

Regular *Action* columnists also contributed articles about the negative effect of Jewish influence on the sport. In an article entitled 'Jewish Boxing Racket', Clement Bruning tapped into anti-Semitic stereotypes and suggested that 'for the sport he cares little, but for the money he cares a great deal. First class professional boxing involves large sums of money and is naturally controlled almost entirely by Jews'. The article also claimed that Jewish influence extended into the international administration of the sport – something which apparently explained why the German boxer Max Schmeling found it difficult to challenge for world titles in the late 1930s. This kind of 'un-sporting' action, Bruning contended, would only offend the principles of the sportsmanlike Briton, who would be deeply insulted by the Jewish use of sport for political gain. He argued 'whatever British people think of National Socialism, anti-Semitism is bound to grow through this Jewish attempt to turn this fine sport, a product of Britain, into a Yiddish medium for revenge against Germany'.[49]

Particular Jewish businessmen involved in boxing also came in for attention from the BUF's anti-Semitic publications. Jack Solomons, the well-known Jewish boxing promoter and manager from the 1930s through to the 1970s, was attacked by *The Blackshirt* in 1937 for the 'victimisation of boxers' at his

Devonshire Club in East London. The criticism focused on the instance of taking 'seconds money', where the club provided trainers to stand in the boxer's corner during the fight, and said that Solomons was taking extortionate amounts from his boxers' pay packets.[50] Although this was a regular practice at the time, it seems that the BUF believed that Jewish promoters were the worst culprits of this deduction from an already underpaid boxer's earnings. The conclusion of the newspaper was that the evidence suggested that Jewish 'businessmen' were ruining the sport for their own financial gain:

> Up to the beginning of the present century, boxing was one of the finest sports in the world. The purses were small but the men were big. This country was then the world's boxing centre ... once the Jewish promoter enters the world of sport it ceases to be a world of sport and becomes a world of business. Often it becomes a world of discreditable business.[51]

By 1939, the BUF's attacks on Jewish involvement in boxing had become even more vociferous and were voiced in an increasingly aggressive tone. In January, *Action* published an article entitled 'Alien Stranglehold on Boxing: A Sport No Longer' reportedly written by a 'prominent boxer who for obvious reasons must remain anonymous'. The correspondent claimed Jewish promoters and agents were exploiting 'British youth' for 'easy money' by dealing in 'male flesh and blood'. It was noted that, compared to the lowest non-skilled workers, boxers were extremely underpaid. The explanation given for this was the 'deductions' forcibly taken from their wages by exploitative Jews – the 'lice of the ring' – and the article hinted that those wanting to stand up for their own interests would struggle to succeed against the Jewish element ruling the sport. This was because 'crooked promoters and managers work hand in hand in the evil business. If a boxer has the courage to refuse to pay the illegal deductions they ask for he finds himself without engagements, not at one or two halls but up and down the country'. The BUF claimed that the simple answer to this problem was for the 'racketeer ... Jew' to be 'removed from control of the sport'.[52]

The notion of a sporting 'Hidden Hand' was also propagated by prominent former BUF personalities during wartime. Although the organisation was banned in 1940, some of its previous leaders continued to promote the idea that Jewish power and influence had command over British physical recreation. William Joyce, who was propaganda director for the BUF between 1934 and 1937, moved to Germany in 1939 and adopted the personality of Lord Haw Haw for English-language Nazi war broadcasts. He was eventually hanged in January 1946 for treason.[53] In one radio message in December 1939, Joyce described the Jewish Lads' Brigade as the 'greatest of Jewish sports organisations' and suggested that it was 'in control of British sport'.[54] Likewise, in 1942, another message attacked the Maccabi Association, London and its Chairman, Pierre Gildesgame, for their influence on British sport and noted that the club and Gildesgame himself had been placed on Gestapo black-lists.[55]

The 'unsporting' Jew

As well as emphasising the notion of a 'Hidden Hand', BUF sporting propaganda also promoted the idea that Jews were foreign and could never be integrated into the British mainstream. The BUF contended that Jewish sportsmen lacked any awareness of fair play and sportsmanship – without which, Jews would always remain as outsiders in British society. In a similar vein to their discussions of Jewish sporting 'power', the party's notion of 'unsporting' Jews also arose out of the wider anti-Semitic ideology espoused by the organisation. At the Albert Hall rally in October 1934, Mosley launched an anti-Semitic tirade about the effects of 'little Jews' who represented an undermining influence to the nation's cultural and racial well-being. Mosley attacked the rank-and-file Jewish citizen for their apparent intrinsic dissimilarity to British people and for destabilising the British racial stock. These 'little people who can hardly speak English at all' appalled Mosley because, in his eyes, they had no appreciation or respect of the wider culture and society.[56]

Over subsequent years, the party tried to reinforce the idea that 'Jews were mentally and morally different' to the British. The BUF repeatedly contrasted the Jewish community's foreignness and 'oriental' origins to the British 'Nordic' stock, which had produced pioneers and 'Empire builders' throughout modern history. In the BUF's analysis, 'Jews were not only seen as an eternally foreign and inferior element whose religion, ethics and instincts were anathema to Europeans, but an innate aggressiveness was attributed to them which allegedly distinguished them as a singular peril threatening the very existence of the nation'.[57] The BUF's tactics of highlighting the foreignness of the British Jewish community was their attempt to make their own radical political programme and ideology seem to be more acceptable and palatable.[58]

The party also used sport to pursue their line of argument concerning supposed Jewish racial and cultural 'difference'. As with the 'Hidden Hand' concept, the party utilised sport as a propaganda vehicle to promote the notion that Jews were an 'alien' element within British society and that their presence undermined the preservation of British character and culture. The BUF wanted to advance the view that 'Jews were alien because of their alleged failure to value games and sports in the same manner as the local population'. It was argued that without a sporting mentality similar to the non-Jewish population, Jews would continue to represent a danger to British racial, social and cultural integrity and cohesion.[59]

This particular argument was of special significance to the organisation as it went to the core of its political ideology. The party promoted a 'militaristic masculinity' that had its roots firmly in the sphere of nineteenth-century private education. Physical, moral and psychological well-being were promoted as the cornerstones of BUF philosophy and 'the BUF's politics ... [were] the ethos of public school masculinity as a political programme'.[60] The portrayal of Jews as 'un-British' and 'un-sporting' not only tied into wider notions of Jewish difference, but also contrasted sharply with the self-image promoted by the BUF. In effect, by claiming that Jews were 'alien' in their sporting outlook, the inference was that the BUF were innately and proudly British in their attitude to physical recreation and their wider approach to politics.

One of the first and most comprehensive attacks on the Jewish sporting mentality appeared in *Action* in March 1936. In an article focusing on the growing Jewish support for Tottenham Hotspur FC, A.G. Findlay linked increasing instances of heckling and 'barracking' from the White Hart Lane crowd to Jewish supporters. Findlay argued that crowd unrest was 'part of a logical sequel to the permeation of the sport of Nordic peoples by races foreign to them who are incapable of understanding the psychology of the Northerners of Europe'. He also believed that this showed that the Jewish mindset lay at odds to the mental character of the British, as Jewish sports fans 'cannot understand the meaning of a "good loser"' because 'their mentality is exactly the same in business as in sport – to win at any price and to hell with the other fellow'.[61]

For the BUF, this was further evidence that Jews' inherent racial differences meant that they could never fully assimilate into British society. Because Jews could not apparently appreciate sport in the British 'way', support was allegedly given to the anti-Semitic argument that their 'difference' would prove a block to full integration. As the 'Hebrew' race struggled to appreciate the core values of British sport, they could not, according to Findlay, hope to be accepted by the British mainstream:

> In the first case, we look upon our games as something to enjoy, to keep bodily fit and treat them just as games. In the other way they are treated partly as business with the 'heads I win, tails you lose' motto. It does not matter how much time and money we 'Britishers' spend in trying to make other people adopt our mentality to athletics or games of any description, we cannot alter their racial characteristics.[62]

The BUF claimed it was further vindicated in these views when the Jewish community itself questioned the behaviour of Jewish football fans. In 1937, *The Blackshirt* reprinted a letter from the *Jewish Chronicle* from an Anglicised Jew concerning Jewish Tottenham fans. Mr Henry, from north-west London, noted that 'hundreds of people' around him at a recent game were of Jewish origin and complained that 'abusive language, freely mixed with phrases in Yiddish and all uttered in raucous voices in the presence of so many people, can only tend to create the impression that these dreadful specimens are representative of Jewry'. The correspondent from *The Blackshirt* simply commented that the 'loud mouthed creatures' referred to in the letter were 'typical flowers of Judah's youth'.[63]

Jewish sporting 'difference' was most evident when 'aliens' tried to introduce a political angle into sporting events. In 1938, *Action* reported that a German police football team had been invited to play a team from the Brighton and Hove police force. Whereas, when the British team visited Germany the year before they were 'given a reception indicative of the German desire for friendship with Britain', on the occasion of the return fixture the German side met with animosity from a crowd of protestors – *Action* noting that 'these visiting sportsmen were grossly insulted by a shouting, gesticulating Jewish crowd which greeted the visitors with the "Red Flag" and cries of "Get back to Germany"'. This unsportsmanlike reception underlined the lack of Jewish comprehension of the 'sporting attitude' of the British and provided additional evidence of

the racial otherness of the Jewish community: 'This is not the first
time that aliens in Britain have attempted to drag their political and
racial questions into the sporting arena; by doing so they are
increasing the animosity which all true sportsmen must feel towards
their kind'.[64]

Alongside football, the other sport most often pinpointed for
showing the clear lack of a sportsmanlike attitude amongst the Jewish
community was golf. In 1937, it was reported that German golf
courses had introduced a ban on non-Aryans playing at courses
frequented by golfers of Aryan stock. *Action* claimed that courses with
Jewish golfers in Britain 'will turn longing eyes to those fortunate
German courses which can legally ban Jews'. Seemingly, the lack of
sportsmanship and fair play demonstrated by the vast majority of
Jewish exponents of the game was a cause for growing resentment:

> Thousands of British golfers who are not anti-Semitic for any reason,
> become rapidly so when they play on courses where Jews in front of
> them hold them up and will not let them through; where Jews behind
> them drive into them without apology; and where Jews on adjoining
> fairways pull and slice into them without apology and where Jews are
> loud and offensive in the club houses.[65]

The BUF's answer to this problem was simple – use the secret
machinery of the golf clubs to block Jewish participation.[66] In 1939,
Action reported on the 'blackballing' of 'wealthy Jews' in Scottish
golf in a celebratory tone, claiming that the 'summary rejection of
Jewish applications to well-known golfing circles' was widespread,
even when the Jewish golfers in question were 'impeccable' in both
'business and private life'. As well as rejoicing in this blow against
Jewish financial 'muscle', the article claimed that Jewish golfers
were hardly 'sporting' in their lifestyles or demeanour and were
therefore unworthy of the reward of golf-club membership. It was
claimed that 'first-class golfing circles' in London were 'plagued by
flashy [Jewish] sportsmen and their friends who monopolise the
clubhouse and ostentatiously parade their wealth, causing much
heart-burning among other members'. Not only were Jews in
complete ignorance of the spirit and etiquette of golf on the course,
therefore, but the BUF claimed that their actions off it were hardly
similar to that of a 'respectable' British golf enthusiast.[67]

Although the British Union of Fascists experienced little electoral success, and existed mainly on the margins of the British political mainstream, it is important not to understate the effect that the party's presence had on the Jewish community. Whilst many historians of British Fascism have tended to understate the impact of organised anti-Semitism on Jewish society, it would be incorrect to believe that campaigns mounted by groups such as the BUF did not exert a negative effect. As Kushner has noted, whilst Mosley may have remained a political outsider figure, his organisation and ideology were at least partly responsible for creating anti-Jewish violence and a physical and psychological 'fear' of attack amongst the Jewish working classes during the 1930s. The kind of 'extremist anti-Semitism' promoted by the BUF was an 'innovative' and 'reinforcing factor in hostility to Jews' during the majority of this decade.[68]

Likewise, it is also important not to underestimate the influence that BUF propaganda and campaigning had on reinforcing popular anti-Semitism. For example, one poll conducted in November 1939 claimed that 17% of those interviewed believed Jewish influence had played a role in drawing the world closer to military conflict. Given their political and popular failure, the BUF's actions alone cannot account for nearly one in five people holding anti-Semitic views concerning the reasons for going to war. However, their anti-Semitic propaganda, in a limited way, 'helped to maintain the fear of Jewish influence' that was already evident within Britain.[69] Likewise, the party's anti-Semitic campaign also both reflected and reinforced 'a ubiquitous racist view of the supposed flaws and characteristics of Jewish people that existed in contemporary popular culture'.[70]

The emphasis that the BUF placed on sport within its propaganda consolidated various long-standing anti-Semitic beliefs and myths. The overall aim of the party's sporting anti-Semitism was to strengthen racist beliefs regarding the 'Hidden Hand' conspiracy and the alleged racial distinctiveness and lack of assimilatory potential of the Jewish community. By using 'examples' of Jewish sporting dominance or iniquitous behaviour, the party aimed to instil the idea that the Jewish community's deleterious effect on British society spread beyond the spheres most commonly associated with Jewish influence and activity. The supposedly negative Jewish effect evident within politics, business and popular culture, the BUF argued, was also prevalent within British sport – an area of life which impacted more immediately and frequently on the average Briton and where Jewish influence and lack of fair play was even more offensive to British sensibilities.

Put succinctly, sport was used by the BUF as one way of helping to define the Jewish community as an 'other' – an 'alien' element – within British society. By using sport as a means of reinforcing and promoting popular Jewish stereotypes and mythology, the party sought to place the Jewish community in physical, moral and psychological opposition to the masculine, fair and 'sporting' Fascist. Jewish involvement and influence in physical recreation also provided a point of reference against which the BUF could establish themselves in a positive light. By using sport to 'degrade and marginalise Jews' the BUF aimed to show 'themselves as Britons by demonstrating their conformity with the specifically English manifestation of the sporting ethos and its associated notions of morality, masculinity and Britishness'.[71]

'There is no discrimination here, but the Committee never elects Jews': anti-Semitism and golf

Sport was also an arena for social, non-organised expressions of anti-Semitism from the 1890s onwards. Several scholars of British Jewry have used the term 'anti-Semitism of exclusion' to highlight a trend for discrimination of Jews in their everyday lives which existed alongside organised, right-wing/Fascist expressions of racism.[72] It has been argued that British Jews faced considerable 'economic and social discrimination' in the early part of the twentieth century which negatively affected their opportunities and experiences with regard to employment, housing, education, travel and access to services and leisure.[73]

The wider social and occupational discrimination of Jews was not limited to this time period – having been prominent in various forms throughout modern British Jewish history.[74] However, this type of non-organised anti-Semitism intensified in the period after the end of the First World War, as larger numbers of Jews moved out of the immigrant milieu and came into greater contact with the Gentile population. 'Increasing Jewish mobility' in the period after 1918 meant that 'contact with the non-Jewish world could no longer be avoided', with the result being that these Jews met increasing levels of 'hostility' from the wider community.[75]

Whilst Jews faced discrimination from the indigenous working classes, it has been argued that 'the most serious anti-Semitism was located amongst the lower middle-classes'.[76] The reaction of this section of British society to what they saw as a Jewish 'invasion' was 'defamation', 'whispering', 'sniggering' and occupational, educational and social discrimination in a variety of different environments.[77] As Endelman has noted, 'whilst this kind of racism was not systematic ... it was common enough that few Jews could have avoided it altogether or been unaware of its existence'.[78]

Jews entering into the middle classes also faced considerable discrimination in their leisure choices. This was especially true when they attempted to enter the inherently exclusive milieu of British 'clubland', which closely 'represented the hierarchical structure of society and bourgeois class-consciousness'.[79] One typical example can be seen with regard to a large motoring club in Middlesbrough, which in 1933 was found to have introduced a quota for Jewish members.[80] Jews faced similar situations across the country in other social and leisure clubs where 'usually there was no rationale behind such a policy except for an intuitive dislike of people who might have achieved wealth and social status but still carried the stigma of being different'.[81]

This form of 'anti-Semitism of exclusion' was especially visible with regard to middle-class sports clubs.[82] During the period from the 1890s through to the 1960s, there are numerous examples of Jews being openly or secretly discriminated against and finding their entrance into tennis, badminton and squash organisations blocked due to anti-Semitic membership policies.[83] In a reflection of similar trends in America, the middle-class British sporting environment responded to an 'invasion' of outsiders with discriminatory membership policies to limit Jewish involvement.[84]

Anti-Semitism against Jewish sportsmen and women was also prevalent in British golf – labelled as '*the* elite game for the urban ... middle classes'.[85] Jewish interest in the sport emerged during the late nineteenth century as an increasing number of courses were opened in suburban areas, making the sport much more accessible for Jews mainly living in urban areas at this time.[86] By the 1900s, an increasing number of adverts for golf holidays, courses and equipment began to be printed in the *Jewish Chronicle*, which in 1912 declared that there were an 'ever-increasing' number of golfers amongst the Jewish community.[87] During this decade, a number of English Jews, such as Albert Goldsmid and Edward Sassoon, became prominent in golfing circles.[88] Jews also began to experience some success at the elite level of the sport. In 1908, E.A. Lassen, a merchant and Old Rugbeian born in Bradford in 1876, won the coveted British Amateur Championship at Royal Sandwich.[89]

Whilst some acculturated and socially mobile 'native' British Jews were readily accepted by the golfing community, many Jewish golfers from lower down the social scale and hailing from the Russian and Eastern European migration faced considerable anti-Semitism.[90] Though the sport has traditionally had an exclusive attitude towards participation (female and artisan golfers both experienced prejudice at various points in the sport's history), one of the 'most powerful' strands of discrimination within golf was directed towards Jews.[91] In a reflection of similar trends in the United States and Australia, Jewish golfers in Britain faced considerable hostility from the golfing press, golfing establishment and individual clubs from the late Victorian era through to the 1960s.[92] Golfing anti-Semitism was not only prevalent over a considerable period of time and geographically widespread (affecting every sizeable Jewish community in Great Britain), but it originated from both individuals and organisations involved in the sport.[93]

Whilst the 'anti-Semitism of exclusion' faced by many Jews in their social and occupational lives extended into their sporting choices, golf also allowed a way to respond to racism through sporting means. Unwilling to allow anti-Semitism to prevent their enjoyment of the sport and access to the social and business opportunities it also offered, Jewish golfers strove to create their own 'parallel institutions' – clubs and courses which, symbolically, remained open to all non-Jewish golfers, regardless of race or creed.[94] By opening their own clubs and pursuing an 'integrationist' membership policy, Jews protected their sporting interests against a non-organised form of anti-Semitism that seriously affected their social and sporting lives. Effectively, however, the discrimination against Jewish golfers led to the separate development of Jewish golf and the creation of 'Jewish apartheid' in the sport.[95]

'Flashy' Jews? Anti-Semitism in British golf

As early as the 1890s, Jews interested in joining local golf clubs encountered considerable anti-Semitism. In a May 1894 issue of *Golf* (a weekly journal which was absorbed into *Golf Illustrated* when that newspaper began publishing in 1899) a letter was published from a regular correspondent entitled 'The Exclusion of Jews from Golf Clubs'. 'Fair Play' asked: 'Sir, I am sure it would be interesting to know what the golfing fraternity thinks of a Manchester Golf Club that excludes all Jews from membership'. The author believed that this seemed an affront to efforts by local Jewish philanthropists to help the non-Jewish population of the city. He noted his surprise at the discrimination against Jewish golfers when 'the trustees of a Jew (the late David Lewis [a leading retail pioneer in the late nineteenth century]) have last week presented £70,000 to the Manchester Southern Hospital'. No further discussion of the letter was published in the newspaper.[96]

Similar accounts of discrimination against Jewish golfers emerged elsewhere in the golfing press during the pre-1914 period. In February 1911, a letter concerning the 'qualification for membership of a golf club' was published in *Golf Illustrated*. Detailing one Jewish golfer's attempts to become a member of a 'club not nearly so high in the golfing firmament', it was written by a regular correspondent to the newspaper named 'Truth'. He noted that

> I am told what this club was. He [*Truth's* Jewish friend] was asked to withdraw his name and for no other reason, so far as he can gather, save that the candidate was of the Jewish persuasion. I have no doubt that the nominee did not lose socially by his failure to join such a club. Christianity supplies plenty of bounders. And these Christian men, whilst thanking themselves that they are as not as other men, probably forgot that if there had been no Jews there would be no Christians.[97]

Despite the publication of this letter, *Golf Illustrated* often itself demonstrated a 'casually virulent' form of anti-Semitism towards Jewish golfers in the period before the First World War.[98] At a time when increasing numbers of Jews were being drawn to the sport, the newspaper began to publish a series of cartoons and fictional stories depicting Jewish players as foreign, 'flashy' and unsporting. The first cartoon was printed in 1910 and touched on notions of Jewish 'mistrust' by depicting two Jewish golfers named 'Ikey Junior' and 'Ikey Senior' talking in broken English.[99] The last cartoon was published in October 1912, a large imposing front-cover image of a swarthy, rotund Jewish golfer wearing a fur-lined coat and a large piece of jewellery around his neck. The golfer's clubs were dwarfed by the man's frame, insinuating, together with the passive nature of his face and his pound-sign emblazoned cap, a lack of sporting interest on his part and tapping into popular mythology about Jewish money 'obsession' and 'ostentatious' behaviour.[100]

These cartoons were aimed at underlining the physical and psychological difference of the stereotypical Jewish immigrant golfer; a 'sportsman' whose appearance and personal conception of British sport were distinctly 'foreign' and at odds with the British enthusiast. The visual message of the cartoons was reinforced on several occasions by sporadic written pieces about fictional Jewish golfers. These short written sketches depicted the Jewish golfing approach as being overly competitive and alluded to ideas about a Jewish 'win-at-all-costs' mentality which supposedly characterised their dealings in the fields of business and trade.[101]

Such articles were designed to emphasise the notion that the Jewish sporting attitude was completely 'alien' to the prevailing British sporting ethos of the time. For example, in 1910 an article

Ikey, Junr.: "Fader, I von two balls. Here, I make you a present of von.'
Ikey, Senr. (after careful scrutiny): "Vat's der madder vid it?"

7 *Golf Illustrated* cartoon, 1910

entitled 'A Keen Match' was published, depicting a game between two Jewish golfers who spoke in broken English named Isaacs and Levy:

> They were looking for a ball in the rough:
> ISAACS (suddenly finding one): Vat pall are you playing Levy?
> LEVY: Vat is dat?
> ISAACS: A Colonel.
> LEVY: Dat is so! It is a Colonel I blay!
> ISAACS (affecting closer scrutiny of the ball): Sorry ole shap, put I see dis is a Shallenger!
> LEVY: Ah, of course, I remember now – I but down a Shallenger at de last dee, tidn't I poy?!
> CADDY: Yus.
> LEVY: Now den Isaacs!
> ISAACS (again looking at the ball): But I mistake. Dis is a Craigbank, so I keep him.
> PLAYER (hurrying up from the other side of the hedge): Excuse me, Sir, but I think that is my ball. I pulled horribly from the seventh. It's a Kite with a purple mark – yes, that's it! Thanks very much!
> LEVY: Dat done you one Isaacs!
> ISAACS (looking at his watch): As ofer fife minutes 'ave gone since you bekun de 'unt I claim de 'ole. Cheer up old poy!
> LEVY (to his caddy): When he get in de rough, shust leaf 'im alone and time him to de segund. 'Ere is my cold vatch – you ear poy?
> CADDY: Yus.[102]

Later in the same month, *Golf Illustrated* also published a short article about a fictional Jewish golfer named 'Isaacstein', who regularly cheated when playing by using different length clubs to measure penalty shots for himself and his playing partner.[103]

Sentiments such as these were not confined just to the golfing press. In 1924, the *Daily Mirror* ran an article entitled 'The Winning Hazard', documenting a fictional match play game between two golfers named 'Abrahams' and 'Cohen' which the latter had won by tricking his opponent into forfeiting the match. Ironically, this 'example' of unsporting Jewish behaviour was published on the same day as reports of the victory of the English Jewish sprinter, 'the old Cantab' Harold Abrahams, in the 1924 Olympic Games 100 metres.[104]

Whilst this form of anti-Semitism towards Jewish golfers disappeared in the period following the First World War, discrimination

PRESENTLY.

Solomon : "Lend you a tousan' pounds ! Yes, put vare is der security ?,"
Golfer : "Well, I've a box of old golf balls here."
Solomon : "Ma tear fellow, vy did'nt you say so pefore ?" (writes cheque).

8 *Golf Illustrated* cartoon, 1910

against Jews by golf clubs became much more prevalent. This has much to do with the changing socio-economic profile of British Jewry at this time. During the interwar years, greater numbers of second and third generation Jews left the original urban areas of immigrant settlement behind and experienced considerable 'residential and economic mobility'.[105] Similarly, in the period following the Second World War, Anglo-Jewry became much more dispersed across Britain. From the late 1940s, 'suburbanisation … accelerated' as a result of evacuation, destruction caused by the war, the expansion of secondary and tertiary education and a general increase in affluence. As is reflected with other Western Jewish populations, between 1945 and the mid-1960s Anglo-Jewry became increasingly 'middle-class in character'.[106]

Many within the growing Jewish middle classes went on to become interested in golf – a sport closely connected to this social class within Britain. However, as these Jews moved closer in physical, social, cultural, economic and sporting terms to their non-Jewish peers, they experienced a considerable level of hostility. Part of this broader trend for 'social' discrimination is evident within golf. From the 1920s through to the 1960s, many socially mobile Jews faced considerable racism from golf clubs, especially when seeking membership of these organisations. Not all clubs discriminated against Jews.[107] Likewise, not all Jewish golfers would have been on the receiving end of a rejected membership application driven by underlying anti-Semitism. However, the vast majority found where they played, and who they played with, limited by racial hostility driven by crude stereotypes and irrational beliefs surrounding Jewish players.

On occasion, discrimination against Jewish golfers could be openly and freely admitted to by clubs seeking to prevent Jewish golfers from becoming members of their institutions. In 1960, the *Jewish Chronicle* undertook an 'exhaustive investigation' into anti-Semitism in the sport, which looked at racism in golf on a national level. The newspaper published its findings in a series of special reports which demonstrated that Jewish golfers across Britain were experiencing considerable discrimination when attempting to join private clubs. One Jewish golfer claimed that after being informed of vacancies for membership at Hampstead Golf Club and subsequently applying, he was openly told 'There is no discrimination here, but the Committee never elects Jews'.[108]

Even in clubs where Jews 'figured prominently', it was sometimes the case that anti-Semitic membership policies were openly introduced. This is what reportedly occurred in one club in Yorkshire, which was founded by local businessmen, including several 'prominent Jews', in the early twentieth century and attracted a number of Jewish members. In 1915, the club's committee informed current Jewish members 'not to nominate any more members of their faith'. After a backlash by the Jewish members the resolution was eventually withdrawn and a number of Jews were invited to take up positions in office at the club as a result.[109]

Whilst it was rare that clubs would admit to anti-Semitic attitudes, there were several occasions where Jewish golfers were openly refused membership because of their faith. In 1960, the *Hendon Times* interviewed a German Jewish golfer who had reportedly been refused membership by a number of local golf clubs because of his religion. The golfer, who claimed he had failed in applications to ten different clubs over a three year period, noted that 'one Secretary had the audacity to agree with me that if I had been a German Gentile I would have been admitted'.[110]

Although openly anti-Semitic membership policies were evident, most golf clubs used much more concealed means of discrimination against Jews. One of the most common selection methods used by 'private' institutions was the 'blackball' system. In self-perpetuating private institutions, such as the Freemasons, guilds and private sports clubs, such systems were used to ensure that prospective members were 'acceptable' to the majority. The 'blackball' was believed to be a vital means in ensuring that the ethos and exclusivity of the club was maintained. Obviously, as votes of this kind were secret, they often proved a significant hurdle for Jewish golfers seeking membership of clubs to overcome, as the prejudice of a minority could effectively prevent the will of the majority being carried out.

There are numerous examples where Jewish golfers suffered from the 'blackball' system, even when the clubs they were applying to already had a number of Jewish members. In 1948, it was noted that two Jewish golfers applied for membership of one golf club on Merseyside and were subsequently blackballed, despite the fact that the club already had a small number of Jewish members.[111] Similarly, in the 1950s, Michael Leek, an ex-officer in the British army during World War Two, sought membership at a club in Worcestershire, where his father and uncles were long-standing members and financial donors. Despite his evident suitability, Michael's application was rejected due to a single 'blackball', for no other apparent reason than his religious background:

> When I came out of the army, he [Michael's father Eric] wanted me to join North Worcester, so I went up and was interviewed by them. In those days, clubs used to operate a secret blackball system. I was blackballed. Just come out of the army, I was a fine, upstanding, public school lieutenant in the army and I was blackballed. Why? Because I was Jewish, although he [Eric Leek] had been in the club for years. He kicked up a hell of a fuss about it and eventually they found out who it was who blackballed me and he was asked to resign from the club and eventually I became a member.[112]

Formal quota systems for non-Jewish members were not uncommon. On occasion, such quotas were freely admitted to, but for the large part they were kept secret from potential Jewish members. In 1960, the *Hendon Times* discovered that anti-Semitic membership policies were relatively widespread at a number of golf clubs in the north London area. At the Finchley Golf Club, it was claimed that there was an 'unwritten rule' that only a few Jews could be admitted. When questioned by the reporter, the Hendon Golf Club freely acknowledged a quota system was in place for Jewish golfers: 'we do accept them, but only in certain numbers'.[113]

Further evidence of quota systems being used with regard to Jewish golfers emerged at a conference concerning 'Anti-Semitism and Racial Incitement' held in March 1960. One speaker, the Bishop of Southwark, Dr Mervin Stockwood (1913–95), claimed that he had received evidence to indicate that quota systems were in use at a number of clubs in and around Greater London. He recounted a letter he had received from Mr Moss Kaye, a Jewish golfer from Edgware, who claimed he had approached the Bushey Hall Golf Club in Hertfordshire after seeing a notice in the club asking for new members, but was told 'sorry, we have a quota for Jews and it is full'.[114] Similar sentiments towards female Jewish golfers were also uncovered at Hendon Golf Club and Highgate Golf Club in north London. On applying to one golf club, a female Jewish golfer was 'told by the Secretary that if Jews were accepted there would be no room for ordinary people'.[115]

For many Jewish golfers, a wall of silence was sometimes encountered from the institutions they applied to. For instance, one Jewish golfer applying to the Mill Hill Golf Club in north London faced this situation in the late 1950s. After meeting the club's committee on two separate occasions and then speaking to the club captain on the matter, the golfer heard no more concerning his application. Despite writing to the club twice in the following months, he received no reply. Similar situations occurred when the golfer applied to clubs in the Rickmansworth, Highgate and Pinner areas.[116]

This is reflected in provincial Jewish communities. In the 1930s, Sydney Lea was encouraged by his two non-Jewish friends to apply for membership at the Heaton Park Golf Club, Manchester. Despite Sydney's reservations – aware of the situation facing Jewish golfers around the country, he said 'they won't have me, I'm Jewish' – he applied and was seconded by his two friends. Several months went by without hearing from the club, until a chance meeting with the captain:

So the Captain came along and we were all stood there talking, the three of us, the two Whittaker brothers, and he called them. Tom Whittaker said 'What's this? You've not let Syd know, he's not had his card to join the club'. So he looked at me, this Captain, and said 'Why don't you join the Whitefield Club [a Jewish golf club founded in Manchester in 1932]?' I said 'Do you want a smack in the eye, coz you'll bloody well get it!' So Whittaker the younger one said 'Why ain't you let him know, what you telling him to join another club for? He wants to join here, we're friends'. So the Captain said 'Well, I've not heard from the Committee', I said 'You know quite well what it is, it's because I'm Jewish, they wont take it'.

Sydney's two non-Jewish friends subsequently challenged the Committee on the matter and received no reply, eventually choosing to surrender their membership in protest of the treatment of their friend.[117]

Many clubs hid behind the defence that they were private institutions and could refuse any potential member if they felt them 'undesirable'. This view was supported by the golfing authorities of the time, as evidenced by correspondence between the Council of Christians and Jews and the English Golf Union in 1954. In that year the Council contacted the EGU to protest at reports of anti-Semitism in a club in Blackpool. The EGU was implored to do more to combat discrimination against Jewish applicants, yet it issued a reply stating: 'The Union does not assume any moral obligation of the sort you propose as this would involve intrusion into the domestic concerns of the private clubs, many of which are largely social institutions which conduct their affairs much along the lines of other social clubs'.[118] When challenged on the subject by the *Jewish Chronicle* in 1960, the captain of the EGU, W.G.L. Folkard, defended a club's right to ban Jews by noting 'a golf club is the extension of one's own home, the election of new members is a purely domestic matter'.[119]

There also seemed to be a degree of popular support for golf clubs following discriminatory membership policies. In the immediate aftermath of the *Hendon Times* investigation into local golfing anti-Semitism in 1960, the newspaper received correspondence noting support for the 'right' of private clubs in matters concerning membership. One letter asked, 'surely the members of a club have a right to exclude or to admit anyone they wish to, Jew or Gentile?' Another correspondent defended anti-Semitic discrimination in this way and claimed that Jews were sullying the spirit of the private club. Jews are wrong, he argued, to believe that they have a natural right to entry to these organisations: 'No one, regardless of his religion, can walk into a members' club and demand admission'.[120]

Due to the secrecy surrounding the application process it is difficult to directly assess the motivations underpinning this form of anti-Semitism. A basic racist fear of 'outsiders' is no doubt partly to blame, but there were some occasions where more specific 'reasons' for discrimination against Jews did emerge. In many instances, stereotypical and racist viewpoints of Jews informed the decisions of private golf clubs to block, or limit, Jewish members. Many of these beliefs were narrow-minded and the 'threat' that Jewish golfers posed to both the sporting and social element of golf was often irrationally overemphasised. Much focused on the idea that Jews were markedly different in their outlook, attitude and demeanour and clubs argued that they discriminated against Jews in order to prevent the nature of the sport being harmed both on and off the course.[121]

One argument put forward to defend anti-Semitism focused upon the 'clannishness' of Jewish people. It was argued that allowing one Jewish golfer in or letting current Jewish members freely elect more of their 'own kind' was potentially very dangerous for the club, which would soon be 'overrun' and changed out of all recognition. In 1923, the *Yorkshire Post* defended golf clubs in their locality against allegations of anti-Semitism in the *Jewish Chronicle*.[122] Whilst admitting that Jews had experienced difficulties in gaining membership at local clubs, the article felt it was 'absurd' to claim that this was because of anti-Semitism, before going on to say:

> Like other people, the Jew suffers from the defects of his virtues. One of these virtues is 'clannishness' or perhaps a more polite way to put it would be to say that he is intensely loyal to his own folk. When a Jew joins a golf club, he wants all his family and friends to share his pleasure. Consequently, one sees happy family parties wandering around the links, following the matches of their relatives – a delectable enough thing in itself, but when the persons composing this party have no idea of the established usage of the game, it is rather apt to be irritating to the serious minded British golfer ... It is for definite, distinct and practical reasons such as these that the Jews have not become popular in golf clubs.[123]

Jewish golfers themselves believed that it was a club's fear of being 'overrun' which accounted for the discrimination they experienced. Sol Bennett, playing on Merseyside in the 1940s and 1950s, believed that clubs would purposely limit Jewish numbers 'as they were frightened that we might take over'.[124] In Glasgow, Jewish golfers freely admitted that they believed local clubs were concerned they would be 'swamped' by Jews if they didn't practise anti-Semitic membership policies. One Jewish golfer in Glasgow in the post-World War Two period claimed that this was a 'big fear of non-Jews. There is a fear that once they see Jews in numbers, they are going to come in with an alien culture ... Non-Jewish clubs are frightened that the Jews will take over'.[125]

Some organisations argued that the number of Jews was limited in order to prevent their inherently 'foreign' nature from changing the atmosphere of the club. Such a belief is evidenced in the work of Geoffrey Cousins, who claimed that Jewish golfers had 'tastes' that were not conducive to a club's desire to keep costs and expense down. Additionally, he claimed that because 'the Jew is deeply interested in administration and finance' he would not be able to resist the urge to interfere in the business side of the club.[126] As Cousins suggested, the average club member often had pragmatic, yet still inherently racist, concerns about Jewish golfers. They feared that allowing Jews who were 'flashy' in their tastes and poor patrons of the bar to join their clubs in high numbers, would lead to higher membership fees to cover the shortfall. Evidence in this respect was uncovered by the *Jewish Chronicle* in 1960. Its investigations found that the 'fear' of higher subscriptions due to 'modest' Jewish drinking habits was common and helped to explain the passive anti-Semitism faced by Jewish golfers when applying for membership at private clubs.[127]

The other factor put forward to 'explain' discrimination harked back to *Golf Illustrated*'s anti-Semitic cartoons and stories surrounding the supposedly 'unsporting' nature of the Jewish golfer. Although rarely going into specific details, many clubs claimed that the 'unsatisfactory behaviour on the golf course' of Jewish golfers was another reason for their apprehension over admitting Jews more freely. Clubs feared that their reputation could be damaged by 'foreign' Jews who did not understand the finer nuances of etiquette surrounding the game. For instance, the 1923 *Yorkshire Post* article about anti-Semitism in local clubs claimed that as 'golf to the Jew is a new game … he has not yet acquired the appreciation of the game that comes instinctively to the ordinary Britisher'. The allegation was that whilst Jews might be able to play the game, they failed to approach it in the right spirit or in the correct 'sporting' manner.[128]

Despite this 'evidence', there was little truth in the suggestion that Jewish golfers were any less sporting in their play than the average non-Jewish golfer. Indeed, some sources claimed that Jewish golfers could display a remarkably better attitude than their Gentile counterparts. Jewish golfers were very hospitable toward guests and eager contributors to local charitable and philanthropic endeavours linked to their clubs.[129] According to the *Jewish Chronicle*, one professional golfer commented that 'his travels throughout numerous golf clubs had left him of the opinion that Jews were keener members than non-Jews and that they knew more about golfing etiquette'.[130]

Discrimination against Jewish golfers could occasionally come to the wider public's attention. For instance, in the late 1950s and early 1960s, anti-Semitism at one golf club in north London had a considerable political impact. In the aftermath of the 1957 local council elections, evidence was brought to the public's attention in the *Hendon Times* concerning 'discrimination of the most despicable kind' against Jews applying to Finchley Golf Club – claims that were made more controversial by the fact that the club had several Conservative councillors on its board and was partly funded out of local rates.[131]

Local voters protested strongly at the treatment of Jews by the club. Over the subsequent decade, the Liberal Party 'pursued' this matter and underwent a significant local revival – something which political commentators attributed to a shift in allegiance of the ward's Jewish population (which was reported as about 20% of the total) because of the actions of the golf club and its links to the Conservative Party. The incident was reported to have seriously affected Jewish voting patterns in the ward, as evidenced by one survey of local Jews which concluded that 66% had switched political allegiance due to the actions of Finchley Golf Club. It has even been suggested that the local Conservative MP, future Prime Minister Margaret Thatcher, adopted a consciously pro-Jewish stance after 1964 in order to protect her seat.[132]

'Parallel institutions': the Jewish response

Although the political controversy surrounding Finchley Golf Club did liberalise that organisation's membership policy, Jews elsewhere continued to struggle to join many private clubs.[133] As appeals to golfing authorities were ineffective – and because many Jewish golfers felt it 'bad form' to directly question a club's membership policy – Jews were forced to create their own touring societies and clubs. In doing this, Jewish golfers in Britain mirrored a 'process' followed by Jews elsewhere in Western society who had been excluded from social and sporting organisations.[134] In Central Europe it was common for Jews from the late nineteenth century onwards to form 'parallel institutions as a response to blatant discrimination and exclusionary policies' within non-Jewish organisations.[135]

Yet whilst the formation of Jewish golf clubs in Britain was catalysed by anti-Semitism, it was facilitated by economic advance. By the 1920s – a time when anti-Semitism in the sport was growing considerably – Jews descended from the refugee community were increasingly lower-middle or middle class. This not only enabled physical moves out of the original immigrant enclaves, but also created expendable income for leisure and sporting pursuits. This trend grew in the post-World War Two period, when more and more Jews were represented in the higher echelons of the socio-economic ladder.[136] Unlike other British minority groups, Jews had the economic profile to cover the considerable expense involved with creating golf clubs from scratch or purchasing going concerns.[137]

As well as the drive and the finances to create their own 'parallel institutions' in this sport, British Jewry also benefited from a strong sense of communal endeavour. For instance, the first Jewish golf club to open in Britain – Moor Allerton Golf Club – was built north of Leeds in 1923 with funds raised from the local Jewish community. Leaders of Leeds Jewry, as well as numerous prominent Jewish business leaders, were all represented amongst the 170 original shareholders.[138] The motivation of this group to create their own golf club was clearly driven by the anti-Semitism experienced by local Jewish golfers in the early twentieth century. In 1922, local cloth merchant Abraham Frais called a meeting to introduce the idea of forming a Jewish course. He was reported as saying that as many within the Community were 'being banned from golf courses' in the local area, there was a 'duty to the next generation to see that this matter was dealt with immediately'.[139] The club, which also had a thriving tennis section, had 150 playing members by 1937 – a figure which had expanded to 650 by the time of the 1958 AGM.[140]

The second Jewish golf club to open was the Whitefield Club, founded in north Manchester in October 1932. Like Moor Allerton, the course and clubhouse at Whitefield was built with the assistance of the wider Manchester Jewish community. The locally well-known German Jewish Cassel family, who had made their fortune through construction, were pivotal in bringing together a group of Jewish businessmen to raise money to secure the lease of the land for the course in June 1932. The first nine holes of the course were formally opened on 30 October 1932, with the other nine finished by June 1933.[141]

Like its counterpart in Yorkshire, the formation of Whitefield was firmly driven by anti-Semitism and the desire of a section of Manchester Jewry's golfing community to play their sport in a friendly atmosphere.[142] In 1936, the *Jewish Chronicle* printed an article entitled 'The Whitefield Club: Its Genesis and Progress', which noted:

> Some years ago many reputable and substantial members of the Jewish community found their applications for membership of certain clubs turned down – solely on account of their being Jews. Fortified rather than mortified by their experience, a number of these gentlemen met to discover ways and means of founding a golf club which Jews could join and be proud of, and in which the spirit of sportsmanship in the best sense would be paramount.[143]

In smaller provincial Jewish communities, it was often the case that Jewish golfing societies would be formed in order to help local Jews play together and avoid the anti-Semitism and persecution often faced when trying to join private clubs. In 1931, a golf section was formed at the Glasgow Jewish Institute and was followed by societies in Merseyside (1948), Birmingham (1949), Southport (1950), Sheffield (1951), Belfast (1951), Sussex (1952), the North-East (1953), Nottingham (1959) and Blackpool (1963). These groups, which could range from a dozen to over a hundred members, played as touring private societies at local clubs and local municipal courses. Society days, an important source of income for golf clubs, were open to Jewish organisations such as these because they could be hosted without any permanent attachment to the club being created. Competitions would be held both within and between individual Jewish societies on a regular basis, meaning that a network of Jewish golfers was built up across the country.[144]

Over time, some of the larger societies began to realise that this kind of arrangement was untenable in the long term. As many of these groups grew larger, the idea of raising funds to build or purchase their own clubs became more popular. The Glasgow Jewish Institute's golf section, for instance, grew so rapidly during its first five years that the need for privately controlled golfing facilities quickly became apparent. In 1956, the opportunity to purchase the Bonnyton Moor Golf Club, south of Glasgow, arose and a 'prodigious effort' was made within Glasgow Jewry to raise the necessary finance. On 19 May 1957, the Bonnyton Moor Golf Club was formally re-opened with Jewish owners, an occasion, recounted in the Glasgow *Jewish Echo*, which saw over seven hundred people in attendance with the clubhouse 'gaily bedecked for the occasion with Union Jacks and Blue and White flags'.[145]

Jewish golfing societies located elsewhere gradually became interested in the idea of buying or building their own clubs and having a permanent base. In 1953 the Merseyside Jewish Golfing Society collected together money in order to purchase a farm estate in Netherley. The result of this was that in May 1954 the first six holes of the Lee Park Golf Club were formally opened. The brochure outlining plans for the new course noted that 'the venture, when established, will provide for ourselves and our children a centre where we will be able to meet in an atmosphere entirely free from prejudice'. By 1959, club membership had grown to 428.[146]

Within a year of the Birmingham Jewish Golfing Society's foundation in 1949 over one hundred members had joined, including leading figures from Birmingham Jewry's religious, social and political elites. In September 1950, the idea of finding private facilities was first mooted and gained considerable support within the Society. In the space of one month over £10,000 was raised through the donations of members. In May 1955, with the financial support of members, sections of Birmingham Jewry and several bank loans and overdrafts, the Society purchased the derelict Shirley Park racecourse. The first nine holes of Shirley Golf Club were opened in

June 1958, with the homewards nine completed in November 1958.[147]

There were a variety of other means by which Jewish golfers could play the sport in a friendlier environment. It was also the case, especially in the London area, that small groups of Jewish golfers either created clubs on an equal basis with Gentile partners or purchased and took over pre-existing clubs. With the Potters Bar Golf Club in north London, it was reported that a group of Jewish and non-Jewish businessmen came together in 1923 to build the club in order to provide a friendly atmosphere in which Jewish golfers could play. Although Potters Bar was created on an equal basis between Jewish and non-Jewish members, the former soon made up the majority, due mainly to the anti-Semitism prevalent within many north London clubs. By the late 1930s over 85% of the membership was Jewish.[148]

Although not founded by Jews, a number of other clubs in the Greater London region became the home for large numbers of Jewish golfers in the post-World War Two period. Both the Hartsbourne Country Club in Hertfordshire and the Coombe Hill Golf Club, based in Kingston upon Thames, were not originally formed as Jewish clubs, but by the 1960s had effectively become so in that most of their members were Jewish golfers. Hartsbourne reportedly had a number of Jews as founder members, but it was not until the 1940s that it came to be regarded in wider golfing circles as a Jewish club. Coombe Hill, however, was purchased by a group of Jewish golfers in 1946 that had been refused admission to other golf clubs in the Surrey region and wanted to play together in a friendly environment free of anti-Semitism.[149]

By the 1960s, a large network of 'parallel institutions' was created by the Jewish golfing community in order to allow them to play the sport in an environment free of anti-Semitism. By 1964 there were eleven 'Jewish' clubs (either founded or purchased by groups of Jewish golfers) in existence across Great Britain, all of which were located within close proximity of the main Jewish communities and areas of Jewish secondary, suburban settlement. One conservative estimate, taking into account the membership of both clubs and societies, would put the number of Jewish golfers at somewhere between 4,000 and 4,500 in 1960. In order to assist with the administration of the large Jewish golfing network – and to arrange matches and competitions between the various organisations – the Association of Jewish Golf Clubs and Societies was formed in 1949.[150]

Despite the evident hostility shown towards Jewish golfers, all Jewish clubs noted that golfers of any colour, race or religion were free to join. In addition, even though these clubs had been built or purchased by Jews, primarily to allow Jews to play the sport, no mention of the word 'Jewish' was made in their name. The first Jewish club, Moor Allerton, pledged from its outset that 'although its foundation was due to intolerance, membership would be open to all, irrespective of religion'. Jewish clubs had a friendly reputation towards outsiders and visitors and it was applauded that 'Jewish clubs welcome visitors without introduction and only one has a definite rule requiring introduction by a member at all times'.[151] Similarly, Bonnyton Moor Golf Club was advertised as an 'open club … [with] no bar on the grounds of religion, race or colour'.[152]

The fact that Jewish clubs adopted this stance was a significant retort to the bigotry encountered by many Jewish golfers. However, it was also for practical and financial reasons, especially in clubs in the smaller provincial communities, that non-Jewish members were actively sought. The historian and former captain of Shirley Golf Club in Solihull, William Hiscox, noted that part of the enthusiasm of the original committee in seeking members outside of the Jewish faith was driven by practical considerations: 'The idea was to open the club to anyone … the Committee knew straight away that they needed new members and basically that they had to be non-Jewish because there weren't enough Jewish members at all to make it a viable project'. The club's current President, Michael Leek, commented that Birmingham Jewry's relatively small size meant that it was financially necessary to actively seek outside members from the outset.[153]

Most Jewish clubs proved successful at attracting non-Jewish members and visitors.[154] One report in the *Yorkshire Evening News* from 1931 claimed that Moor Allerton was 'one of the most popular of golfing resorts in the Leeds district' and that non-Jewish visitors to the club abounded, especially at weekends. The article claimed that, although the course was designed by a renowned architect, kept in excellent condition and easily accessible, it was the extremely hospitable atmosphere of the club that was Moor Allerton's main attraction to outsiders.[155] Lee Park in Liverpool was often referred to locally as the 'friendly club', due to the cordial welcome that visitors and guests received.[156] Similarly, Shirley Golf Club has prided itself throughout its history on the level of integration between Jewish and non-Jewish members, a notable number of whom joined the club during its very early days in existence.[157]

Many Jewish clubs attracted non-Jewish members in considerable numbers, testimony in part to their inclusive atmosphere but also indicative of the high quality facilities with which most Jewish clubs were blessed.[158] In 1937, the Potters Bar Golf Club claimed that 50 from a total of 400 members were non-Jewish, whereas by 1960 Coombe Hill Golf Club reportedly had 25% non-Jewish membership.[159] Numbers of non-Jews in provincial areas, where much smaller Jewish communities were found than in London, could often be much higher. By 1967, for instance, Shirley Golf Club in Solihull was 53% non-Jewish, a figure that rose to 65% by 1974.[160]

Despite significant levels of integration, Jewish clubs did not receive an entirely positive reception. In April 1937, for example, it was reported in the *Jewish Chronicle* that Potters Bar Golf Club had been the target of an attack by local vandals. As well as pouring acid on to the club's greens in the shape of a swastika, the intruders also painted anti-Semitic graffiti on the outside walls of the clubhouse.[161] Some within golfing circles criticised Jewish clubs for apparently catering for the 'flashy' tastes of their members. Because many Jewish clubs were created from scratch and were furnished with modern facilities, the clubs themselves and the members were viewed by some as overly 'opulent and ostentatious'.[162]

The opening of 'parallel institutions' for Jewish golfers liberalised the policies of some local clubs towards Jewish membership. This was not necessarily driven by a change in attitude. Rather, it was because clubs felt they had less chance of being 'taken over' by Jews with a Jewish club in the vicinity.[163] For example, one member of the Bonnyton Moor Golf Club noted that it had become markedly easier for a Jew to join a non-Jewish club after Bonnyton's opening in 1957. He remarked that 'now that there is a Jewish club, non-Jewish clubs are more ready to accept Jews'. He added that 'they know there's no danger of them being swamped ... Knowing that there is a Jewish club in the area, they are not worried'.[164]

Effectively, as one correspondent to the *Jewish Chronicle* in 1960 realised, what was created in British golf was a 'Jewish apartheid'.[165] Jews in Britain – as in America and Australia – had been forced to pursue a separate line of development due to wide-spread racial discrimination. Jewish golfers were not inherently 'different' or 'foreign' compared to their Gentile peers, yet an embedded form of anti-Semitism blocked them from freely playing golf in the manner they wanted. Whilst considerable numbers of non-Jews have joined Jewish clubs in recent years, anecdotal evidence suggests that some vestiges of the discriminatory attitude towards Jewish golfers still remain.[166]

The so-called 'Jewish apartheid' in the sport during large parts of the twentieth century received support from within the golfing community. When he published his history of the sport in 1975, entitled *Golf in Britain: A Social History from the Beginnings to the Present Day*, journalist and writer Geoffrey Cousins noted his belief that the creation of Jewish golf clubs was a 'logical and even desirable solution'. In a very thinly veiled anti-Semitic critique on 'Jews in Golf', Cousins remarked that 'some of the differences' between Jewish and non-Jewish golfers were 'beyond elimination'. He concluded that the formation of Jewish golf clubs and societies was a 'practical' step for people with 'flamboyant and luxurious tastes' and a 'different outlook on life, different ideas on running a club and modest drinking habits'.[167]

Some Jewish golfers were critical of the stance taken towards anti-Semitism in the sport. It was claimed that forming Jewish clubs signified a 'Ghetto' attitude amongst the community and calls were made for a more direct response to bigotry in the sport. According to one golfer who had experienced discrimination first hand, his fellow Jews were taking an overly apologetic course of action towards racism within the British golfing community. He remarked to the *Hendon Times* in 1960: 'I could join a predominantly Jewish club – there is one at Potters Bar – but why should I? The ghetto is a thing of the past. Most of my business is with Gentiles. I want to feel free to work and play with them on equal standing'.[168]

From the earliest days of their involvement in the sport, Jewish golfers faced a considerable level of racism from the British golfing community. Jews interested in this typically 'middle-class' sport faced a particularly powerful form of 'anti-Semitism of exclusion' and suffered racial hostility from clubs, the golfing press and the golfing authorities. Whilst the 'restrictive ... ethic' prevailing within middle-class sport in Britain may partly explain the exclusive attitude held by many golf clubs, it is clear that a 'veiled, but unmis-takeable ... anti-Semitism' has also been widespread within the sport.[169]

The case study of golf highlights a new aspect of life in 'middle' England where Jews were prevented from engaging more fully with the British majority due to discrimination and bigotry. The work of a number of scholars of British Jewry has shown us that many socially and economically mobile Jews faced a 'social' form of anti-Semitism which impacted significantly on their social, educational and occupational lives. An analysis of golf demonstrates that this kind of discrimination clearly extended to the world of sport – a sphere of life where sections of the non-Jewish community were vehemently racist in the face of an 'invasion' by a foreign, alien element.

Jewish golfers in Britain were not as different, 'alien' or 'foreign' as the golfing press, authorities and many clubs believed. There is a certain irony in the fact that the people who so many golf clubs were keen to bar were much more like their members than they seemingly appreciated. The truth was that Jews interested in golf were largely Anglicised, were socially, geographically and economically mobile and were 'sporting' both on and off the course. They were enthusi-astic about the game and the social, business and leisure opportunities which the sport presented. Many of them were, in essence, the perfect golf club 'material'.

Not only did the Jewish community clearly face anti-Semitism in the sporting arena, but they also used sport as means of responding to discrimination and racism. Jewish enthusiasts, often with the considerable support of their local communities, found ways and means to play golf in a friendlier environment. The resourcefulness shown by the Jewish golfing community in establishing 'parallel institutions' – which symbolically remained open to non-Jews – points to the communal spirit of the Jewish population and also demonstrates the evidently high regard in which Jews held their participation in this and other 'middle-class' sports. It is paradoxi-cal, however, that the 'Jewish apartheid' which existed in British golf meant that the wider golfing community could not benefit from the drive, finances, enthusiasm and sportsmanship of participants within this particular minority community. Anti-Semitism evident within golf effectively undermined the financial, moral, social and sporting fabric of the 'Royal and Ancient game'.

Kicking discrimination into touch? Sport as a response to anti-Semitism

Sport was not only an environment where Jews experienced anti-Semitism, but it was also a milieu in which pro-active responses to discrimination were formed. From the 1900s through to the 1960s, there are numerous examples from within the sporting world of Jews using sport to challenge racial hostility. Some sporting Jews used their participation as a retort to anti-Semitism within their chosen fields, but sporting participation was also viewed as a way in which to challenge racism in wider British society. For many British-born working- or lower-middle-class Jews, sport was seen as an effective means of disproving stereotypes and creating goodwill, whilst sporting success often provided a direct rejoinder to anti-Semitism.

With this in mind, sport gives a clear reflection of the varied ways in which British Jewry tackled anti-Semitism. Although an 'anti-anti-Semitic tradition' has been evident within the community since the 1880s, there has often been a distinction between the strategies espoused by the Jewish establishment and those of the mainstream of the community for confronting anti-Semitism.[170] With regard to the former, a generally non-confrontational approach was taken. Communal organisations such as the Board of Deputies often 'preferred behind the scenes diplomacy', whilst many lay leaders called for Jews to be 'restrained, and to give no cause for provocation' in the face of anti-Semitism.[171]

In contrast, 'non-official communal organisations' originating from the rank and file of the Jewish community often proved willing to tackle discrimination much more directly.[172] This 'alternative, grass-roots response to anti-Semitism' prominent from the 1900s onwards was generally much more assertive than that of the official communal bodies, stressing the need to protest vigorously and directly against those propagating racism towards the Jewish community.[173] The polarisation between the 'timidity' of official bodies and the 'vigour' of rank-and-file organisations is most apparent during the 1930s, when the Jewish community faced considerable anti-Semitism from Fascist and far-right groups.[174]

It is also possible to detect the wider split in attitudes and approaches towards anti-Semitism in the world of British sport. There are numerous examples of Jewish sporting responses to racism which reflect both the 'conservative, non-confrontational' position of the Jewish establishment and the more direct approach generally taken by sections of the wider Jewish community.[175] With regard to the former, it is possible to argue that attempts to use sport as a means of Anglicisation were an indirect effort on the part of the Jewish establishment to alleviate growing non-Jewish hostility towards Jewish immigration.[176]

This 'conservative' non-confrontational approach with regard to sport can also be seen with the Jewish Lads' Brigade. In 1936, the JLB decided to withdraw temporarily from the Prince of Wales' Boxing Shield competition for fear of creating racial tension through being 'overly successful'. Although the JLB declared their withdrawal was due to sporting reasons, the decision was 'governed too by other motives' – principally a desire to prevent anti-Semitism.[177] In May 1936, Commander of Manchester JLB, E.C.Q. Henriques, commented: '[we do] not go out for "pot-hunting" and indeed there was a danger in the Jewish clubs always being so successful, so much so that jealousy was perhaps created and non-Jewish clubs would not enter the competitions'.[178]

Many sporting responses to racism from this period mirror the more 'assertive attitude towards Jewish self-defence' prevalent amongst the rank and file of the community.[179] Within the sporting experiences of many second and third generation immigrant Jews, a tendency for a more direct response to anti-Semitism can be identified. Willingness was also demonstrated, on numerous occasions, to use sport to challenge prejudice against Jews in wider society. The wider trend for a more direct approach to anti-Semitism clearly stretched into the world of British sport – an increasingly important social and cultural milieu for British Jews, as well as an environment in which Jews and non-Jews met regularly.

An examination of the sporting response to anti-Semitism between the 1900s and the 1960s demonstrates that a generally assertive approach to combating anti-Semitism was in evidence. Sport provides further illustration that, in contrast to the passive, non-confrontational attitude of the Jewish establishment, Jews originating from and representing working-class Jewry used a more direct method of tackling prejudice. In short, many Jewish individuals and organisations saw sport as an environment in which anti-Semitism could be effectively challenged and undermined.

Jewish individuals

Sport – most especially professional boxing – has a long-established role within British Jewish history for providing an assertive response to anti-Jewish prejudice and stereotypes. During the late Georgian period, it was believed that Jewish prize-fighting was having a direct impact on levels of violence against the Jewish community. Renowned English social reformer, Francis Place (1771–1854), claimed that Jewish boxing success had the knock-on effect that 'the art of boxing as a science ... soon spread among the young Jews and they generally become expert at it'. This, according to Place, meant that

> the consequence was in a very few years seen and felt too. It was no longer safe to insult a Jew unless he was an old man and alone ... But even if the Jews were unable to defend themselves, the few who would be disposed to insult them merely because they are Jews would be in danger of chastisement from passers by and of punishment by the Police.[180]

Whilst only a small proportion of the Jewish community actually took up the sport, success in boxing created the perception that Jews were strong and willing to physically defend themselves. The achievements of boxers such as Daniel Mendoza helped to propagate the view that attacking Jews was both less socially and culturally acceptable and an increasingly dangerous proposition. In his history of *Anti-Semitic Stereotypes*, Felsenstein argues that the success of Mendoza and his contemporaries is 'one of the most pointed illustrations of the way in which accepted prejudices against the Jews could at least be implicitly challenged'. For Felsenstein, the fact that the Jewish community gained 'self respect' from Jewish boxing success meant that 'traditional antipathies' were, to a certain degree, 'assuaged'. The achievements of Jewish prize-fighters were a 'clear challenge ... [to] traditional allegations of Jewish cowardice'.[181]

Such ideas have been expressed with regard to American Jewish professional boxing in the early twentieth century. Historians have frequently referred to boxing participation as being a rejoinder to stereotypes and anti-Semitism within wider society. As Levine has argued, 'no other activity provided such a clear way to refute stereotypes of the weak, cowardly Jew that anti-Semites employed to deny Jewish immigrants and their children full access to American opportunities'.[182] Similarly, Riess has claimed that Jewish success in the American ring 'surprised Gentiles who accepted conventional stereotypes about Jewish manliness'.[183] Wider interest in the sport amongst American Jewry served as a fortifying factor in the minds of many youngsters, who were able to 'identify with Jewish boxers who personified the necessity of Jewish toughness in a threatening world'.[184]

These notions are reflected in the history of British Jewish boxing. Like their American counterparts, contemporary British Jewish pugilists were believed to provide a retort to Jewish stereotypes through their endeavours in the ring. In 1914, for instance, a full-page article entitled 'The Hefty Hebrew: The Shattering of a Silly Old Legend' was published in *Boxing*. The newspaper's correspondent recounted at length Jewish contributions both to professional boxing since the eighteenth century and to the armed forces during the early stages of the First World War. All this, he claimed, helped to undermine the 'old legend that, however the Hebrew may shine in finance, he can never, never has and never will display any real powers as a warrior in any capacity'. In contrast to popular stereotypes, *Boxing* argued that the evidence highlighted demonstrated that 'the Jew has always been a fighter'.[185]

Similar ideas concerning the effect of boxing on perceptions of the Jewish community surfaced during the 1930s. At a time when the anti-Semitic campaigns of groups such as the British Union of Fascists were beginning to gather pace, Jewish participation in the professional ring was claimed to be acting as a retort to right-wing notions of Jewish physical and moral cowardice and their supposed aloofness. An article in the *Jewish Chronicle* in 1934 claimed that Anglo-Jewish involvement in the 'pugilistic world' since the 1900s showed that Jews were a 'courageous and gallant race, cherishing the British ideals of fairplay, pluck, manliness and chivalry'. British Jewish success in the prize-ring apparently demonstrated that Jews were physically and psychologically strong and were willing to defend themselves with vigour when attacked. It was argued that Jewish involvement in the sport had 'done more than cartloads of oratory and writing to combat any tendency towards anti-Semitism that may have been sown by the unscrupulous and perverted devotees of the very un-English hate cult'.[186]

Whilst there is inevitably a degree of hyperbole in statements such as these, amongst the Jewish professional boxing community there is evidence of a much more assertive response to anti-Semitism and contemporary Fascism. Several Jewish boxers in the 1930s claimed that they took it upon themselves to directly challenge contemporary anti-Semitism through their endeavours in the ring. Harry Mizler, for example, recounted a bout during the late 1930s against a known supporter of the BUF where the referee was forced to stop the fight after seven rounds. Mizler, it transpired, 'wouldn't knock him out' as he wanted to inflict as much physical damage on his opponent as possible due to his political and racial opinions. Likewise, middle-weight boxer Jack Hyams recalled a successful fight at the same time against a German boxer who later went on to join the Gestapo. Hyams later claimed he 'gave him a good beating!' because he knew his opponent was an anti-Semite.[187]

Another professional boxer who responded to contemporary anti-Semitism in a similarly direct manner was Ted 'Kid' Lewis. Although Lewis was a supporter of Mosley during the embryonic stages of the British Union of Fascists, his biographer claims he abandoned the party in acrimonious circumstances when they turned to an openly anti-Semitic platform in late 1933.[188] Lewis apparently confronted the BUF leader at his office in London and asked him 'Is it true you're anti-Semitic? And I want the truth this time. Are you anti-Jewish?' to which Mosley simply replied 'Yes'. According to his son, 'Kid' Lewis then 'settled with Mosley in the only way he knew how' – attacking him and his four bodyguards and leaving the offices unscathed and 'grinning from ear to ear'. [189]

Amongst other Jewish sportsmen and women, the same resolute (yet much less physical) attitude towards anti-Semitism can be detected. As we have seen with regard to Harold Abrahams and Jewish golfers, many Jews remained determined to continue their sporting careers in the face of often severe racial prejudice. This determination can also be seen within tennis, another sport which saw relatively widespread discrimination of Jews. Angela Buxton, for example, despite success at the very highest level – she was French Open and Wimbledon ladies' doubles winner, and Wimbledon ladies' singles runner-up, in 1956 – often found herself marginalised due to her Jewish background.[190]

Throughout her career, Buxton faced anti-Semitism from both the tennis community and the British tennis establishment. A third generation immigrant Jew, Angela was born in Liverpool in 1934 to Violet and Harry Buxton, a successful businessman and entrepreneur. At boarding school, the Buxtons' only daughter took up tennis and during her teenage years was encouraged to move to London to aid her sporting development. When she attempted to join the prestigious Cumberland Lawn Tennis Club in north-west London, however, Buxton experienced her first taste of sporting anti-Semitism. After being initially accepted by the club, her application was eventually turned down, with Buxton being told by a Cumberland coach that 'you'll never make it … you're perfectly good, but you're Jewish. We don't take Jews here'.[191] Soon after, Angela's mother received a phone call from the Cumberland Club notifying her that her daughter had been removed from an upcoming junior county tournament: 'Oh, Mrs Buxton, I'm very sorry to tell you your daughter's been disqualified, so don't bother to come … we've heard on the grapevine that she doesn't really have Middlesex qualifications'.[192]

Angela faced a similar level of hostility during her adult playing career. After the Buxtons' move to Los Angeles in 1952, a move funded by Harry Buxton to help aid his daughter's career, Angela was summarily rejected from the Los Angeles Tennis Club – renowned at the time for its discrimination against potential members from minority backgrounds.[193] In England two years later, Buxton was forced to practise with a local journalist before a tournament held at the Southport Argyle Lawn Tennis Club. This was because members of the club, who would traditionally offer their services as 'hitting partners' to players entered in the tournament, refused to play with Buxton because she was Jewish.[194]

Buxton also encountered similar prejudice from the British tennis establishment. In later years, it was alleged that decisions taken by the Lawn Tennis Association during the 1950s not to pair Angela with several female British players in the international Wightman Cup tournament were driven by the fact she was Jewish.[195] Even after her impressive showings in singles and doubles competitions during 1956 – the latter in a pairing with the similarly marginalised African American player, Althea Gibson – Buxton faced rebuffs from both the Lawn Tennis Writers' Association and the All England Tennis Club.[196] Despite Buxton's success, the British Jewish player was placed on a 'waiting list' for membership of the prestigious club after her Wimbledon successes. In 2004, Buxton told the *New York Post*, with reference to the All England Club, that 'I think the anti-Semitism is still there … the mere fact that I'm not a member is a full sentence that speaks for itself. I wish it still wasn't such an elite sport'.[197]

Despite facing significant prejudice, Angela Buxton showed a determination which enabled her to carve out a highly successful career. Indirectly, she believed her sporting success provided a retort to the anti-Semitism she encountered. Although Buxton claimed she was anything but a 'crusader' for Jewish rights, she admitted many years later that the 'anti-Semitism ... made me more determined'.[198] Her resolve to offer a sporting counter to those who discriminated against her was apparent during Angela's teenage years. For example, after her rejection from the Cumberland Club in 1949, Buxton made it her personal mission to return to the club and win the Middlesex Junior Championships staged there annually: 'I made a point of going back to win their bloody tournament – twice – just to rub their noses in it – and they never gave me a cup of tea. Not even that'.[199]

Buxton's coach also showed pleasure in the fact that she experienced success in spite of anti-Semitism. On the eve of her Wimbledon doubles final appearance in 1956, her coach, Jimmy Jones, used his *Daily Mirror* column to indirectly attack the authorities who had discriminated against Buxton during her earlier years.[200] Although Buxton herself noted her disappointment over the indifferent response she received from the tennis establishment after her 1956 Wimbledon victory, she felt pleased to have gone a long way to realising her sporting ambitions in the face of racial prejudice. She claimed 'there wasn't much publicity about it, in fact I remember there was only one headline 'Minorities Win', a very small headline ... [however] as far as I was concerned, I had accomplished something that I had set out to do and it was a very good feeling'.[201]

Jewish organisations

A number of Jewish organisations also promoted a response to anti-Semitism through sporting means. In several instances, these groups did not necessarily endorse this approach simply to challenge sporting discrimination. It was also the case that they saw physical recreation as a useful medium for responding to anti-Semitism prevalent in wider society. This is especially true with regard to a number of 'grass-roots' organisations during the peak of Fascist activity in Britain in the mid-1930s. In 1938, for example, the

Jewish People's Council organised an anti-Fascist committee in conjunction with the London Amateur Football League. After an attack by BUF supporters on players on one football team, the Council worked with the League to arrange for speakers to visit all ninety-eight affiliated clubs to hold anti-Fascist meetings and lectures.[202]

Certain Jewish youth organisations also saw sport as a means of responding to contemporary anti-Semitism. Whilst members of clubs supported by the Jewish establishment were actively discouraged from becoming involved in Jewish 'defence' efforts, the British Maccabi Association placed a strong emphasis from its outset on working against anti-Semitism and using its programme to help undermine stereotypes and popular prejudice.[203] Indeed, many Maccabi club members were active in anti-Fascist organisations during the 1930s and were heavily represented in their ranks during the infamous Battle of Cable Street in October 1936.[204]

This reflected Maccabi's European roots, where Maccabi was partly founded as a sporting vehicle to respond to anti-Semitism.[205] Such actions were supported by British Maccabi leaders, many of whom were vocal in their belief that physical recreation could help to combat the growth of anti-Jewish sentiment in wider British society. When the *Jewish Chronicle* announced the formation of the British Maccabi Association in 1934, it applauded the organisation's aspiration to create a 'virile and sportsmanlike race of Jews'. It went on to highlight that the Association's understanding that 'anti-Semitism can be far more effectively combated by the younger generation on the field of play in friendly rivalry with non-Jewish sportsmen than by any amount of written propaganda' and noted 'it is for this reason, among others, that we welcome the progress of the Maccabi in Great Britain'.[206]

The notion of using sport to help combat anti-Semitism was a prominent theme in the BMA's press campaigns, public addresses and promotional literature during the 1930s. In 1935, the Chairman of the Association, Colonel J.H. Levey, stated that one reason his organisation focused on physical recreation was that 'meeting non-Jews on the sports field was one way of killing anti-Semitism'.[207] Similarly, one year later, against a backdrop of a worsening international and national context for the Jewish community, the BMA's first President, Henry Mond (the second Lord Melchett), affirmed his belief that the promotion of sport could help to challenge anti-Semitism as 'it [Maccabi] presented a field of contact which was of the best type, presenting opportunities of friendship and friendly rivalry of a kind that in England was particularly well understood'.[208] In 1947, in the face of growing popular anti-Semitism and violence against Jews, the sports director of Newcastle Maccabi reiterated the view that sport could help to alleviate racial tension:

> Sport, in my humble opinion, can bring out and develop a strong feeling of comrade and friendship between Jew and non-Jew, which in these troubled times can go far in combating the dread disease, anti-Semitism. The non-Jew idolises any form of sport, so I appeal to you all, whenever there is an interfunction, whether we or they be visitors, be it with Jews or non-Jew, Play the Game ... allow them to judge for themselves if Jewish youth is worthy of the name of Sportsmen [sic], a name which means as much to us as it does to them.[209]

Clearly, sport was also seen to be a medium for combating prejudice directed towards Jews in the post-war period. Although the 1930s are generally regarded as a peak of anti-Semitism and Fascism, historians have shown that both were also apparent during the Second World War and in the period immediately following the cessation of hostilities.[210] Against a background of worsening relations between the British Government and the *Yishuv* (Jewish community in Palestine), as well as post-war austerity, British Fascist organisations underwent a significant resurgence. Groups such as the British League of Ex-Servicemen and Women, headed by ex-Mosleyite Jeffrey Hamm, resumed the 'provocative street-corner anti-Semitism' prevalent during the 1930s.[211] Alongside events in Palestine and Fascist activities, a number of domestic factors also accounted for a post-war resurgence of anti-Jewish feeling, culminating in 1947 with widespread anti-Semitic rioting and violence in London, Leeds, Liverpool and Glasgow.[212]

Although the Jewish establishment remained reticent about confronting prejudice directly, some within mainstream British Jewry proved less willing to allow resurgent Fascism and anti-Semitism to go unchallenged. The 43 Group, for instance, was formed by a group of demobilised Jewish soldiers keen to confront resurgent Fascism head on.[213] Other Jewish ex-servicemen who wanted to tackle post-war anti-Semitism, however, turned their attention to sport. In 1946, Major Harry Sadow, George Hyams,

Asher Rebak and Frank Davis came together to form the Wingate Football Club in Hendon, north London. The club, named after Orde Wingate (1903–44), who worked with the Jewish Defence Forces and the 'Chindit' task force before and during World War Two, was formed partly for sporting motivations – the founders noting that they wanted to give other Jewish ex-soldiers the opportunity to continue playing the sport they enjoyed during their time in the army.[214]

The main factor in the creation of the club was a desire to use football as a means of challenging and undermining contemporary anti-Semitism. As was later noted, the four founding members felt that 'they could fight anti-Semitism better in sport than by talking about it'.[215] By entering a Jewish team, wearing blue and white kits emblazoned with the Star of David, into the amateur Saturday leagues, club officials hoped that increased sporting contact would be a source of good feeling and friendship. They believed that the club could 'foster between Jew and Gentile a greater spirit of comradeship' which would help to alleviate growing anti-Semitism.[216]

Wingate's officials also felt that football could serve as a useful means of altering contemporary negative perceptions of the Jewish community. Evidence from the Mass Observation surveys conducted during the Second World War found that derogatory stereotypes of Jews occasionally focused on their apparent lack of interest in sport and games.[217] Similarly, anti-Jewish sentiment both during and after the war was said to have partly concentrated on alleged Jewish 'bourgeois' ways, their 'non-physical' nature and 'economic opportunism' in the face of post-war austerity.[218] It was to combat these notions, according to one of the club's founder members, that Wingate was created. As Frank Davis noted several years later:

> Mosley was marching again in Ridley Road and the stereotyped image of the Jew was making a comeback …We decided to fight it by setting up our own football club and I think we did a very good job in proving that being a Jew didn't mean you were a little fat gown manufacturer. All right, so a Jew wasn't a coalminer – but he could be a sportsman who moved around with a great deal of grace.[219]

In order to help change Jewish stereotypes, the club's founder members stressed the need for Wingate's players to demonstrate exemplary sportsmanship on the field of play. Those representing Wingate were pro-actively encouraged during the club's early years to play fairly and build a positive reputation for the club – a policy which seemingly had much success. Wingate became synonymous with impeccable sportsmanship during its first two years and had the unique record of not conceding any penalties or having any players reprimanded, or even spoken to, by officials.[220] Wingate also won many awards and plaudits from within the footballing authorities. In 1957, the Secretary of the London League noted that Wingate had 'maintained a very high standard of sportsmanship and lived up to their motto of "Friendship through Sport"'.[221] As one club official reported in 1954: 'whether or not the club won its matches, it always won the esteem of the opponents and spectators'.[222] Founder member Frank Davis claimed many years later that 'everybody knew that if you played Wingate, you played the best sportsmen'.[223]

In later years, other avenues for using football to undermine anti-Semitic stereotypes and prejudice emerged. Despite being based in one of the largest areas of Jewish settlement in contemporary Britain, fewer Jewish footballers joined the north London club during the 1960s and 1970s – forcing Wingate to open its door to non-Jewish players. Although this was felt by some to be a move away from Wingate's original ideology, others welcomed the development as a positive step. Committee member, Sidney Burns, believed that 'playing on the same side as non-Jews does even more good than playing against them'. For the non-Jews that joined the club during this period, their experiences had often helped to rid them of negative preconceptions surrounding the Jewish community. One player claimed he was surprised to receive such a warm welcome from the team when he joined during the 1970s. Despite being non-Jewish in a still largely Jewish dressing room, he noted positively that 'no-one ever makes me feel like an outsider'. Similarly, another non-Jew believed playing for Wingate had significantly changed his opinion of Jews overall: 'before I mixed with Jews, I always felt that they thought themselves *it*. You know, they had this air of superiority. But I had that idea knocked out of my head the very first day I played for Wingate'.[224]

Wingate achieved a modest level of success – and became well known for philanthropic work – but its significance lay in its real and symbolic effort in tackling anti-Semitism.[225] Although relatively insignificant in the annals of football history, an examination of this small north London club provides another indication of the willingness of British Jewry to use sport to fight racial hostility.[226] Those behind the creation of the club did not pursue as 'direct' a line of action as other anti-Fascist and 'anti-anti-Semitic' organisations. They were, however, clearly equally as impassioned to see their community take positive measures to defend itself and work to undermine resurgent Jewish stereotypes. Although open to accusations of naïvety, Wingate's founders demonstrated a conviction that sport could be a weapon in the wider fight against discrimination and 'earnestly believed that one positive way of helping combat the ignorance and social evil of anti-Semitism was on the field of play'.[227]

The examples shown here give an indication that sections of the Jewish sporting community were often assertive when faced with anti-Semitism. A number of Jewish individuals and organisations showed resolve when they encountered prejudice in their sporting lives or when the wider community was faced with upsurges of racism or Fascist activity. Physical recreation could not prevent organised and social forms of discrimination from occurring, nor rid society of deep-rooted cultural, social, political and economic anti-Semitism. But a conviction clearly existed amongst certain sporting Jews that physical recreation could, in some small way, help to combat racial prejudice. Alongside wider social and political efforts to minimise anti-Semitism, sport clearly emerged during the first part of the twentieth century as one avenue through which Jews could respond to racial discrimination.

In many ways, sport provides a reflection of the dichotomy in approaches taken towards anti-Semitism by the Jewish establishment and the Jewish mainstream. In youth organisations controlled or supported by sections of the Jewish elites, sport was used in an indirect manner in an attempt to alleviate anti-Semitic prejudice. In stark contrast, individuals and organisations hailing from the rank and file of Jewish society were often more confrontational and direct in their sporting response to prejudice. Through sport, it is apparent that these Jews, either directly or indirectly, were challenging anti-Semitism and the organised and social discrimination faced by the wider Jewish community during this period.

It is difficult to claim that the Jewish sporting 'response' had anything resembling the effect on anti-Semitism and Fascism that wider Jewish 'self-defence' efforts had. Although there are indications that Jewish sporting responses could, in a much more limited way, help to change Jewish stereotypes, minimise the sporting impact of discrimination and improve interracial relations, there is insufficient evidence to show that sport had anything other than a marginal effect on contemporary anti-Semitism.

Significantly, however, a belief existed amongst part of the mainstream of British Jewry that sport was one way of combating prejudice and discrimination. For a growing number of Jews involved in British sport, there seemed nothing incongruous in trying to use a key facet of British national and cultural identity to combat 'un-British' anti-Semitism. This, in effect, is a reflection of the growing involvement and interest in physical recreation by Anglo-Jewry and further evidence of the development of a distinct Jewish sporting tradition during the early part of the twentieth century.

Conclusions: sport and anti-Semitism

From the late nineteenth century through to the 1960s, sport was inextricably linked to anti-Semitism within modern Britain. Sport was not only a vehicle which was used to define and exclude the Jewish 'other', it also proved to be a milieu in which the Jewish community could challenge stereotypes and prejudice. Whilst much has been written of 'organised' and 'social' forms of anti-Semitism faced by British Jewry, and also with regard to Jewish responses to discrimination, an examination of sport illuminates a great deal on the nature and form of anti-Jewish sentiment in its British context.

In terms of 'organised' hostility towards British Jewry, it is apparent that sport was utilised to reinforce anti-Semitic notions and ideas of Jewish racial and cultural 'otherness'. From the mid-1930s onwards, the British Union of Fascists turned to sport and sporting rhetoric in order to highlight the allegedly negative effect of British Jews on British culture, economics, politics and leisure. By utilising long-standing myths of Jewish 'difference' and influence, the BUF sought to create the image of a Jewish 'other' within British society which would contrast with the BUF's supposedly British values and ideology. In effect, sport formed one aspect of their propaganda campaign which was designed to further their policy of using the Jewish community as a political scapegoat.

With reference to 'social' discrimination, the form of hostility faced by socially mobile Jews in the spheres of employment, housing and leisure was also prominent in the middle-class sporting milieu. Within that environment, a powerful 'anti-Semitism of exclusion' existed whereby Jewish sportsmen and women were summarily excluded from membership of various private sporting clubs due to their ethnicity. This form of discrimination was especially prominent, and geographically widespread, within the sport of golf. Across the country, from the late Victorian period through to the 1960s, Jewish golfers were banned or subjected to quotas by a bigoted and ignorant golfing community. Such was the strength of this anti-Semitism that Jewish sportsmen were forced to create their own clubs and organisations to enable them to play the sport in an environment free of racism and hostility.

While one 'response' to discrimination can be seen with the creation of these kinds of Jewish sports clubs and organisations, it is also evident that sport was viewed in a more comprehensive manner as a vehicle for challenging anti-Semitism. At various points, participation in the British sporting world was seen by Jews as a means of directly and indirectly combating discrimination. In a reflection of an 'assertive' trend towards anti-Semitism prominent within the Jewish working classes, sport was used as a means of ideological self-defence – undermining and challenging racial stereotypes and prejudice. Whilst their success may have been limited to specific sporting or local contexts, the belief clearly existed that sport was a useful environment in which the battle against racism could effectively be waged.

A greater understanding of anti-Jewish sentiment and discrimination in its historical context can be gained by a broad analysis of Jewish involvement in sport. Whilst the sporting world has not previously received any significant attention from academics interested in British anti-Semitism, it is clear that themes and discourses within their research are linked in many ways to the world of physical recreation. It is apparent that 'organised' and 'social' forms of anti-Semitism clearly took on a sporting dimension during the period at hand, whilst wider attitudes and approaches to racism within British Jewry are also reflected within the sporting milieu. Through an examination of the sporting form of anti-Semitism, news areas of life where Jews experienced racism can be uncovered. However, it is also true that much is revealed and illustrated about the nature, expression and retort to racial discrimination amongst the community between the 1890s and the 1960s.

Notes

1 Endelman, *The Jews of Britain*, p. 4.
2 Julius, *Trials of the Diaspora*, p. liii. For instance, Cecil Roth's *History of the Jews in England* is often highlighted by recent historians of Anglo-Jewry for its general lack of reference to anti-Semitism and anti-Jewish sentiment. Instead, Roth talked of a 'gradual acceptance' of Jews and emphasised Jewish 'freedom' within British society in the period from the twelfth century through to Jewish Emancipation in the Victorian era. Roth, *A History of the Jews*, p. 270. More modern scholarship produced in a 'Neo-Rothian' vein also portrays the modern Jewish experience in an overly positive manner. Rubinstein, for instance, has written of the Anglo-Jewish 'success story' and claims that the history of Jews in Britain is 'astonishingly free of hostility'. He has argued that 'institutional and cultural forces' have helped to 'restrict anti-Semitism to the fringes' and that 'outbreaks of anti-Semitism ... almost always diminish and disappear very quickly'. Rubinstein, *A History of the Jews*, pp. 2, 8–9.
3 T. Endelman, 'Jews, Aliens and Other Outsiders in British History', *Historical Journal*, 37, 1994, pp. 959–969.
4 Holmes, *Anti-Semitism*, p. 7.
5 Ibid. p. 220; G. Lebzelter, *Political Anti-Semitism in England: 1918–1939* (London, 1978).
6 T. Kushner, *The Persistence of Prejudice: Anti-Semitism in British Society during the Second World War* (Manchester, 1989); T. Kushner, 'Anti-Semitism and Austerity: The August 1947 Riots', in P. Panayi (ed.), *Racial Violence in Britain in the Nineteenth and Twentieth Centuries* (London, 1996); Kushner, *We Europeans?*
7 Julius, *Trials of the Diaspora*, pp. lvii–lviii. See also, chapter 6: 'Contemporary Secular Anti-Zionisms'.
8 There has also been discussion amongst scholars of Anglo-Jewry concerning another form of anti-Semitism, the so-called 'anti-Semitism of tolerance'. In an article published in 1985, renowned scholar of Manchester Jewry, Bill Williams, put forward the idea that racism towards Jews could not solely be explained by referring to the failure of British liberalism. He claimed that the nature of liberalism itself, and the demands that it placed on Jewish 'conformity to the values and manners of bourgeois English society', were also a 'driving force of British racism'. See Williams, 'The Anti-Semitism of Tolerance', p. 94.

 9 T. Kushner, 'The Impact of British Anti-Semitism: 1918–1945', in Cesarani, *The Making of Modern Anglo-Jewry*, p. 201.
10 Panayi, *An Immigration History*, pp. 231–236.
11 John, 'Anti-Semitism', pp. 119–141.
12 P. Levine, '"Our Crowd at Play": The Elite Jewish Country Club in the 1920s', in Riess, *Sports and the American Jew*, pp. 162–168.
13 See G. Eisen, 'Jewish History and the Ideology of Modern Sport: Approaches and Interpretations', *Journal of Sport History*, 25, 3, 1998, p. 507; G. Eisen, 'Jews and Sport: A Century of Retrospect', *Journal of Sport History*, 26, 2, 1999, p. 236.
14 Lebzelter, *Political Anti-Semitism*, pp. 32–34. Kushner has examined the links between British sporting rhetoric and the exclusive 'clubland' ideology in his examination of Government attitudes towards internment during 1940. T. Kushner, 'Clubland, Cricket Tests and Alien Internment, 1939–1940', in D. Cesarani and T. Kushner (eds), *The Internment of Aliens in Twentieth Century Britain* (London, 1993), pp. 79–102.
15 See, for instance, T. Collins, 'Return to Manhood: The Cult of Masculinity and the British Union of Fascists', *International Journal of the History of Sport*, 16, 4, 1999; M.A. Spurr, '"Playing for Fascism": Sportsmanship, Anti-Semitism and the British Union of Fascists', *Patterns of Prejudice*, 37, 4, 2003.
16 Holmes, *Anti-Semitism*, p. 89.
17 Kushner, *The Persistence*, p. 9.
18 One of the earliest examples can be seen with the British Brothers' League, which was active in the period from 1901 to 1905. The League was a loosely constituted movement which wanted to 'draw together in one solid group' all who opposed Jewish immigration and to agitate for restrictive legislation. Although many of its leaders, including several prominent Conservative East End MPs, tried to steer the League away from an openly anti-Semitic stance, 'this was not completely successful'. B. Gainer, *The Alien Invasion: The Origins of the Aliens Act of 1905* (London, 1972), pp. 69–72; Holmes, *Anti-Semitism*, pp. 89–96.
19 P. Panayi, *The Enemy in Our Midst: Germans in Britain during the First World War* (Oxford, 1991), chapter 6: 'Anti-German Sentiment: Spy-Fever, Anti-Alienism and the Hidden Hand'.
20 T. Linehan, *British Fascism, 1918–1939: Parties, Ideology and Culture* (Manchester, 2000), chapter 7: 'British Fascism and Anti-Semitism'. Linehan notes that there were some right-wing organisations active during the 1930s who rejected anti-Semitism outright, such as the United Empire Fascist Party, and others whose leadership were known to be pro-Jewish, such as the Unity Band.

21 R. Thurlow, *Fascism in Britain: From Oswald Mosley's Blackshirts to the National Front* (London, 2006), p. 44; Holmes, *Anti-Semitism*, chapter 9: 'The Protocols and the Britons'; G. Lebzelter, 'Henry Hamilton Beamish and the Britons: Champions of Anti-Semitism', in K. Lunn and R. Thurlow (eds), *British Fascism: Essays on the Radical Right in Interwar Britain* (London, 1980), pp. 41–56.

22 J. Morell, 'Arnold Leese and the Imperial Fascist League: The Impact of Racial Fascism', in Lunn and Thurlow, *British Fascism*, pp. 57–75; Lebzelter, *Political Anti-Semitism*, chapter 4: 'Imperial Fascist League'.

23 Linehan, *British Fascism*, p. 195; Thurlow, *Fascism in Britain*, pp. 51–57. On the Right Club, see R. Griffiths, *Patriotism Perverted: Captain Ramsay, the Right Club and British Anti-Semitism, 1939–1940* (London, 1998).

24 Thurlow, *Fascism in Britain*, p. 61.

25 M. Pugh, *'Hurrah for the Blackshirts!' Fascists and Fascism in Britain between the Wars* (London, 2006), p. 218. Although there is evidence from speeches in late 1933 that Mosley held anti-Semitic views, the symbolic shift in Mosley's public attitude against the Jewish community is generally regarded to have come in 1934, in speeches given at the Albert Hall, London and Belle Vue, Manchester.

26 C. Holmes, 'Anti-Semitism and the BUF', in Lunn and Thurlow, *British Fascism*, p. 115.

27 For an overview of this historiography, see Linehan, *British Fascism*, pp. 187–193. On the history of the BUF see *inter alia*, Pugh, *'Hurrah'*; Thurlow, *Fascism in Britain*, chapter 3: 'The BUF and British Society: 1932–1939'; R. Benewick, *The Fascist Movement in Britain* (London, 1972); D.S. Lewis, *Illusions of Grandeur. Mosley, Fascism and British Society: 1931–1981* (Manchester, 1987); T. Linehan, *East London for Mosley: The British Union of Fascists in East London and South-West Essex, 1933–1940* (London, 1996).

28 R. Benewick, *Political Violence and Public Order* (London, 1969), p. 151; W. Mandle, *Anti-Semitism and the British Union of Fascists* (London, 1968), pp. 22–23; R. Skidelsky, *Oswald Mosley* (London, 1981), pp. 385–410.

29 Holmes, 'Anti-Semitism and the BUF', p. 128.

30 B. Cheyette, 'Hilaire Belloc and the Marconi Scandal: A Reassessment of the Interactionist Model of Racial Hatred', in T. Kushner and K. Lunn (eds), *The Politics of Marginality: Race, the Radical Right and Minorities in Twentieth Century Britain* (London, 1990), pp. 131–142.

31 Holmes, *Anti-Semitism*, pp. 143, 177–178.

32 Lebzelter, *Political Anti-Semitism*, p. 95.

33 Collins, 'Return to Manhood', p. 145. Collins claims that the BUF were 'consciously and aggressively masculine', using sporting partici- pation and rhetoric within their written and verbal propaganda as ways of improving the real and perceived strength and virility of the Fascist movement in Britain.

34 Spurr, '"Playing for Fascism"', pp. 362, 375.

35 Pugh, *'Hurrah'*, p. 220. The first of these was aimed at a more working-class audience, whereas *Action* was introduced in 1936 in an attempt to attract a 'more educated' readership and 'read more like a normal newspaper' covering themes and topics such as politics, the arts, film, women's issues and physical recreation. Both of these publi- cations included occasional columns with specific anti-Semitic reference to sport, whilst virulently racist regular correspondents such as A.K. Chesterton, Clement Bruning and A.G. Findley all sporadi- cally covered sporting issues linked to Jewish participants.

36 Lebzelter, *Political Anti-Semitism*, p. 13.

37 Endelman, *The Jews of Britain*, p. 202.

38 Kushner, 'British Anti-Semitism', p. 194; Pugh, *'Hurrah'*, p. 215. See also Kushner, *We Europeans?*, pp. 209–210, which highlights that notions of Jewish power and influence were also present within Britain during the Second World War.

39 Holmes, *Anti-Semitism*, pp. 176–178.

40 Pugh, *'Hurrah'*, p. 211. For more background on the growth of the notion of 'Jewish power' see Holmes, *Anti-Semitism*, chapter 5: 'Our New Masters?' and Lebzelter, *Political Anti-Semitism*, chapter 1 'The Myth of a Jewish World Conspiracy'.

41 See, for instance, Holt, *Sport and the British*, chapter 2: 'Amateurism and the Victorians'.

42 *The Blackshirt*, 1 November 1935, 6 December 1935.

43 Ibid. 13 December 1935.

44 Ibid. 5 September 1936.

45 *Action*, 4 June 1938.

46 Collins, 'Return to Manhood', pp. 156–158.

47 Ibid. p. 157.

48 *Action*, 21 February 1936.

49 Ibid. 10 July 1937.

50 Seemingly, much of the BUF discussion was drawn directly from the campaign mounted by the National Union of Boxers against the Devonshire Club during 1937. In March of that year, NUB officials criticised Solomons over the issue of 'seconds' money and the club was picketed on several occasions. Significantly, the Union staunchly defended itself against allegations that it had singled out Solomons due to 'anti-Jewish bias' and it was noted that the organisation had

also raised the issue with several other non-Jewish clubs and
promoters. See M. Taylor, 'Boxers United: Trade Unionism in British
Boxing in the 1930s', *Sport in History*, 29, 3, 2009, pp. 467–468.

51 *The Blackshirt*, 4 September 1937.

52 *Action*, 7 January 1939.

53 For an overview of Joyce's life, see M. Kenny, *Germany Calling: A
Personal Biography of William Joyce* (Dublin, 2003).

54 *Jewish Chronicle*, 8 December 1939.

55 LMA 4286/03/07/020, 'The MAL Story' [c.1970], p. 13.

56 Quoted in C. Cross, *The Fascists in Britain* (London, 1961), p. 127.

57 Lebzelter, *Political Anti-Semitism*, p. 96.

58 Holmes, *Anti-Semitism*, p. 189.

59 Spurr, '"Playing for Fascism"', p. 375.

60 Collins, 'Return to Manhood', pp. 145–146.

61 *Action*, 19 March 1936.

62 Ibid.

63 *The Blackshirt*, 18 September 1937.

64 *Action*, 27 August 1938.

65 Ibid. 6 February 1937.

66 This is what happened, although there is no evidence to suggest that
British golf clubs did this out of support of right-wing groups such as
the BUF. See the second section of this chapter.

67 *Action*, 24 June 1939.

68 Kushner, 'British Anti-Semitism', p. 193.

69 Ibid. pp. 193–194.

70 Pugh, *'Hurrah'*, p. 215.

71 Spurr, '"Playing for Fascism"', p. 375.

72 Kushner, 'British Anti-Semitism', p. 201; Julius, *Trials of the
Diaspora*, p. 379.

73 Kushner, 'British Anti-Semitism', p. 200; Holmes, *Anti-Semitism*, p.
204; Lebzelter, *Political Anti-Semitism*, p. 32.

74 See for example, Endelman, *The Jews of Georgian England*, pp.
270–271.

75 Kushner, 'British Anti-Semitism', pp. 200–201.

76 Kushner, *The Persistence*, p. 96. For working-class anti-Semitism see
Endelman, *Radical Assimilation*, p. 193.

77 Endelman, *The Jews of Britain*, p. 199. For example, openly discriminatory job adverts against Jews were regularly placed in the pages of
'respectable' newspapers during the 1920s and 1930s, whilst Jews
also 'faced discrimination from estate agents and hostility from neigh-
bours' when moving house. There are numerous examples of Jews
being banned from restaurants, hotels and boarding houses at this
time, whilst several colleges and public schools introduced quotas for

Jewish pupils. Jews were also refused insurance policies due to their apparently 'high-risk' status and also found 'formal and informal barriers' in place when trying to enter the 'various professions'. See, Kushner, 'British Anti-Semitism', pp. 200–201; Holmes, *Anti-Semitism*, p. 204; Lebzelter, *Political Anti-Semitism*, pp. 32–33.

78 Endelman, *The Jews of Britain*, p. 199.
79 Lebzelter, *Political Anti-Semitism*, p. 33.
80 *Jewish Chronicle*, 29 December 1933.
81 Lebzelter, *Political Anti-Semitism*, p. 33.
82 As Kushner has shown, it was this kind of 'clubland' discrimination which partly accounted for governmental attitudes towards refugees and internment during the Second World War. Kushner, 'Clubland', pp. 79–101.
83 The experiences of Angela Buxton – Wimbledon ladies' doubles champion in 1956 – would be typical for many Jews playing tennis during the mid-twentieth century. Buxton was frequently turned down for club membership and encountered problems in competition due to anti-Semitism. See B. Schoenfeld, *The Match. Althea Gibson and Angela Buxton: How Two Outsiders – One Black, the Other Jewish – Forged a Friendship and Made Sports History* (New York, 2004). See also, the third section of this chapter. Likewise, Jews interested in badminton also found themselves summarily excluded or banned by private clubs on account of their ethnicity. See, for example, the Sunderland Jewish Badminton Club, which was founded in 1954 due to anti-Semitism in local clubs. TWAS SX113/1, Constitution (1954). Similar problems were evident in squash. For instance, Jews in Birmingham playing squash in the 1950s were forced to create their own club, The Wingate Club, because they could not gain entry to local clubs due to their Jewishness. Correspondence of author with Michael Leek, 8 August 2009.
84 Eisen, 'Jewish History', p. 501.
85 Lowerson, *Sport*, p. 130.
86 G. Cousins, *Golf in Britain: A Social History from the Beginnings to the Present Day* (London, 1975), p. 139.
87 *Jewish Chronicle*, 10 July 1908, 26 July 1912.
88 For Goldsmid, see *Jewish Chronicle*, 9 October 1903. For Sassoon, see *Golf Illustrated*, 10 July 1908.
89 *Golf Illustrated*, 12 June 1908, 19 June 1908; *The Times*, 30 May 1908; *Bradford Daily Argus*, 29 May 1908, 3 June 1908.
90 Cousins noted in 1975 that the Royal and Ancient, the traditional governing body of the sport, 'has several Jewish members', whilst both the Oxford and Cambridge golfing societies also had several members throughout their history. Cousins, *Golf in Britain*, p. 142.

91 Lowerson, *Sport*, p. 22. For prejudice within the sport towards female golfers, see J. George, '"An Excellent Means of Combining Fresh Air, Exercise and Society": Females on the Fairways, 1890–1914', *Sport in History*, 29, 3, 2009, pp. 333–353.

92 Levine has shown that during the 1920s and 1930s many Jewish immigrants found their entry into American golf clubs blocked due to their religious background. Levine, '"Our Crowd at Play"', pp. 162–168. Likewise, Tatz has highlighted that similarly anti-Semitic membership policies were adopted by Australian golf clubs in the period from the early twentieth century through to the 1950s. C. Tatz, *A Course of History. Monash Country Club: 1931–2001* (Sydney, 2002), p. 28.

93 Lowerson, *Sport*, p. 22.

94 The term belongs to George Eisen and refers to Jewish sports clubs founded in Central Europe in the late nineteenth century due to anti-Semitism in Gentile organisations. See Eisen, 'Jewish History', p. 507.

95 *Jewish Chronicle*, 8 April 1960.

96 *Golf*, 11 May 1894.

97 *Golf Illustrated*, 17 February 1911.

98 Collins, 'Jews', p. 147.

99 *Golf Illustrated*, 4 February 1910.

100 Ibid. 25 October 1912. For other anti-Semitic cartoons see, Ibid. 11 February 1910, 15 April 1910, 6 May 1910.

101 Holmes, *Anti-Semitism*, pp. 19–21.

102 *Golf Illustrated*, 2 September 1910.

103 Ibid. 9 September 1910.

104 *Daily Mirror*, 9 July 1924.

105 Endelman, *The Jews of Britain*, pp. 198–201.

106 E. Krausz, 'The Economic and Social Structure of Anglo-Jewry', in Gould and Esh, *Jewish Life in Modern Britain*, p. 31.

107 See, for instance, R. Holt, 'Golf and the English Suburb: Class and Gender in a London Club, c1890–c1960', *Sports Historian*, 18, 1, 1998, p. 82. Holt notes that in 1950 the club captain of the Stanmore Golf Club, located in north London, minuted his opinion that 'a candidate shall not be refused election merely because of his Race'. Holt concedes, however, that the 'reason for widening access seems to have less to do with changing social attitudes after the horrors of Nazism than the immediate financial needs of the Club'. He claimed that the captain's statement demonstrated the club's desire for new membership after a decline in the number on the organisation's rolls during the Second World War. Endelman, *The Jews of Britain*, pp. 198–201.

108 *Jewish Chronicle*, 18 March 1960.

109 *Yorkshire Post*, 23 April 1923 quoted in T. Hyman, *A History of Moor Allerton Golf Club: 1923–2001* (Moor Allerton, 2001), p. 6.

110 *Hendon Times*, 1 April 1960.

111 G. Swift, *'Are You Made Up?' The Story of a Golf Club: Lee Park Golf Club, 1954–2004* (Liverpool, 2004), p. 4.

112 Interview with author, 29 July 2009.

113 *Hendon Times*, 1 April 1960. It was noted in the *Jewish Chronicle* that Hendon had a 5% cap on Jewish members. *Jewish Chronicle*, 4 March 1960.

114 *Jewish Chronicle*, 4 March 1960.

115 Ibid. 18 March 1960; Cousins, *Golf in Britain*, p. 140.

116 *Hendon Times*, 1 April 1960.

117 MJM J309, Interview with Sydney Lea.

118 UoSSC MS65, Correspondence between Council of Christians and Jews and English Golf Union, 23 June 1954, 27 July 1954, 23 September 1954.

119 *Jewish Chronicle*, 1 April 1960.

120 *Hendon Times*, 8 April 1960, 22 April 1960. Some Jewish golfers supported the right of private clubs to block entry of Jews. One correspondent to the *Jewish Chronicle* in 1960 claimed 'we may deplore their bigotry and bad manners, but there is nothing more we can or should do about it if we are to preserve our dignity. We cannot compel them to like us or want us'. *Jewish Chronicle*, 1 April 1960.

121 Cousins, *Golf in Britain*, p. 140.

122 For the article on anti-Semitism in golf clubs in Leeds see *Jewish Chronicle*, 13 April 1923.

123 Quoted in Hyman, *A History of Moor Allerton*, p. 7.

124 Swift, *'Are You Made Up?'*, p. 4.

125 SJAC, Interview with Philip Jacobson, 11 May 1989.

126 Cousins, *Golf in Britain*, p. 140.

127 *Jewish Chronicle*, 25 March 1960.

128 Quoted in Hyman, *A History of Moor Allerton*, p. 7. As we have seen, the alleged 'unsporting' nature of Jews was a recurring theme in the anti-Semitic propaganda of the British Union of Fascists and golf was one sport which did not escape their focus. See above, pp. 160–174.

129 Cousins, *Golf in Britain*, p. 140.

130 *Jewish Chronicle*, 25 March 1960.

131 *Hendon Times*, 31 May 1957.

132 B. Donoghue, 'Finchley', in D. Butler and A. King, *The British General Election of 1964* (London, 1965), pp. 241–253; Alderman, *Modern British Jewry*, pp. 336–337.

133 In June 1957, Finchley Golf Club made a press release stating that all questions regarding religion had been removed from application

forms. See *Hendon Times*, 28 June 1957.

134 As seen above, British Jews responded to anti-Semitism in a variety of middle-class sports by forming their own 'parallel institutions'. For instance, in Manchester, the Waterpark Club was founded after a local businessman's daughters had been refused entry to the Prestwich Tennis Club. Waterpark went on to become an important centre for sport and leisure for Manchester's Jewish youth. Williams, *Jewish Manchester*, pp. 138–139; *Jewish Chronicle*, 25 February 1927.

135 Eisen, 'Jews and Sport', p. 236.

136 Endelman, *The Jews of Britain*, pp. 196–197, 241.

137 Groups such as the Irish and West Indians generally occupied much lower parts of the social and economic ladder than Jews for the majority of the twentieth century. Panayi, *An Immigration History*, pp. 109–110, 117.

138 Hyman, *A History of Moor Allerton*, p. 16. Contemporary reports suggested that the first ever 'Jewish' golf club was founded in 1916 in Quaker Ridge, New York, United States of America.

139 Ibid. p. 14.

140 Ibid. pp. 33, 47.

141 Williams, *Jewish Manchester*, p. 138; *Jewish Chronicle*, 17 January 1936.

142 E. Schlesinger, *Creating Community and Accumulating Social Capital: Jews Associating with Other Jews in Manchester* (London, 2003).

143 *Jewish Chronicle*, 17 January 1936. By the end of its first year, Whitefield had a total of 406 members, growing to over 800 during the 1950s. Schlesinger, *Creating Community*.

144 Hyman, *A History of Moor Allerton*, p. 112; SJAC, Bonnyton Golf Club History brochure: 1957–2007, p. 3; TWAS SX124/2/1, North-Eastern Jewish Golfing Society AGM Minutes, 11 December 1967.

145 SJAC, Bonnyton History, p. 4.

146 Swift, 'Are You Made Up?', pp. 3–6. Liverpool Record Office, Liverpool 296JSC/1/7/1, 'Brochure announcing some details of the new Lee Park Golf Club' [c.1954].

147 Interview with Michael Leek, 28 July 2009. B. Hiscox, *Shirley Golf Club: The First 40 Years, 1955–1995* (Birmingham, 1995), pp. 36–37.

148 *Jewish Chronicle*, 19 November 1937.

149 Ibid. 25 March 1960.

150 Cousins, *Golf in Britain*, p. 142; *Jewish Chronicle*, 8 April 1960.

151 Hyman, *A History of Moor Allerton*, p. 16; Cousins, *Golf in Britain*, p. 141.

152 SJAC, Interview with Philip Jacobson, 11 May 1989.

153 Interview with William Hiscox, 28 July 2009; Interview with Michael Leek, 28 July 2009.

154 Despite the conscious policy of openness and inclusiveness, not all Jewish clubs attracted non-Jews in any significant number. The Bonnyton Moor Club, for example, may have publicly stated its desire to attract non-Jewish members, but for largely practical reasons the club initially drew a minimal number of golfers from outside the Jewish community. One member of Bonnyton claimed that the poor condition of the course, joined with the fact that the club was located at a considerable distance from Glasgow, meant that very few non-Jews joined. SJAC, Interview with Philip Jacobson, 11 May 1989.

155 *Yorkshire Evening News*, 21 February 1931.

156 Swift, *'Are You Made Up?'*, p. 33.

157 Interview with William Hiscox, 28 July 2009. In recent years, concerns have been raised of the decreasing number of Jewish members of the various Jewish golf clubs. Seemingly, the shrinking size of British Jewry as a whole, the temptation of alternative, cheaper sports and the cost of the sport itself and club membership has had the effect of lowering the number of Jews interested in joining Jewish clubs. *Jewish Chronicle*, 13 August 2010.

158 Cousins, *Golf in Britain*, p. 142.

159 *Jewish Chronicle*, 19 November 1937, 25 March 1960.

160 Hiscox, *Shirley Golf Club*, p. 84.

161 *Jewish Chronicle*, 9 April 1937.

162 Cousins, *Golf in Britain*, p. 141.

163 See, for instance, *Jewish Chronicle*, 22 September 1978; Cousins, *Golf in Britain*, pp. 140–141.

164 SJAC, Interview with Philip Jacobson, 11 May 1989.

165 *Jewish Chronicle*, 8 April 1960.

166 Shirley Golf Club, for instance, had over 70% non-Jewish membership by the 1970s. Hiscox, *Shirley Golf Club*, p. 84. Likewise, in 2004 Lee Park claimed it had only 25% Jewish membership, whereas Jewish golf clubs in Manchester have recently began campaigns to recruit young Jewish members due to the severe decline in Jews involved in the club. Swift, *'Are You Made Up?'*, p. 33; Schlesinger, *Creating Community*. In the interview with Michael Leek, 28 July 2009, he claimed, without going into specific details, that several current Jewish members of the Shirley Park Golf Club had been refused membership elsewhere. He claimed that it seemed anti-Semitic membership policies were still being practised in a number of organisations locally.

167 Cousins, *Golf in Britain*, pp. 140–141.

168 *Hendon Times*, 1 April 1960.

169 Holt, *Sport and the British*, p. 131.

170 See, for instance, Kushner, *The Persistence*, pp. 164–169; Julius,

Trials of the Diaspora, p. liii; E. Smith, 'Jewish Responses to Political Anti-Semitism and Fascism in the East End of London, 1920–1939', in K. Lunn and T. Kushner (eds), *Traditions of Intolerance: Historical Perspectives on Fascism and Race Discourse in Britain* (Manchester, 1989), pp. 60–67; Smith, 'Jews and Politics', p. 159; Cesarani, 'The East London', p. 51.

171 Kushner, *The Persistence*, p. 164; quoted in Smith, 'Jewish Responses', p. 60.

172 Julius, *Trials of the Diaspora*, p. liii.

173 In 1902, for instance, the Aliens Defence Committee was formed by Jewish and non-Jewish trade unionists to combat opposition to Jewish immigration. Kushner, *The Persistence*, p. 164. Similarly, it was immigrant and working-class Jews who defended Anglo-German and Anglo-Russian Jews during the Great War, who protested vigorously against the Holocaust and who formed Jewish defence organisations, such as the 43 Group, to combat Fascism and anti-Semitism in the early post- World War Two period. Julius, *Trials of the Diaspora*, p. liii; Endelman, *The Jews of Britain*, p. 171; R. Bolchover, *British Jewry and the Holocaust* (Cambridge, 1993), pp. 59–61; M. Beckman, *The 43 Group: The Untold Story of Their Fight Against Fascism* (London, 1993).

174 T. Endelman, 'English Jewish History', *Modern Judaism*, 11, 1981, p. 102; Cesarani, 'The East London', p. 51; Julius, *Trials of the Diaspora*, p. liii. The infamous Battle of Cable Street in 1936 'epitomised the diversity of opinion within the Jewish community' over how anti-Semitism should be tackled. Whilst the *Jewish Chronicle* and the Board of Deputies urged Jews to stay away from the march, groups such as the Communist Party encouraged them to 'counter-demonstrate' and 'fight' the Fascists both ideologically and physically. E. Smith, 'But What Did They Do? Contemporary Jewish Response to Cable Street', in T. Kushner and N. Valman (eds), *Remembering Cable Street: Fascism and Anti-Fascism in British Society* (London, 2000), pp. 49–50.

175 T. Kushner and N. Valman, 'Minorities, Fascism and Anti-Fascism', in Kushner and Valman, *Remembering Cable Street*, p. 1.

176 See above, Chapter 1.

177 The Manchester JLB group argued that the decision to withdraw from the competition for one year in 1936 was a 'sporting gesture', designed to 'encourage other units to enter' and prevent the Shield from becoming a 'closed' tournament. UoSSC MS223/4/14, *Annual Report of the Manchester Jewish Lads' Brigade* (Manchester, 1938), p. 7.

178 *Jewish Chronicle*, 8 May 1936; Kadish, *'A Good Jew'*, p. 126.

179 Collins, 'Jews', p. 151.
180 Quoted in Endelman, *The Jews of Georgian England*, pp. 219–220.
181 Felsenstein, *Anti-Semitic Stereotypes*, pp. 229–230.
182 Levine, *Ellis Island*, p. 162.
183 Riess, 'Tough Jews', p. 60.
184 Levine, *Ellis Island*, p. 167.
185 *Boxing*, 12 September 1914. There was a positive response to the 'Hefty Hebrew' article, not least from members of the Jewish community who felt that the assertions made by the *Boxing* correspondent would do a great deal to challenge and undermine contemporary racial stereotypes. See, for instance, *Boxing*, 19 September 1914.
186 *Jewish Chronicle*, 8 June 1934.
187 Ibid. 22 November 1968.
188 Lewis stood as a parliamentary candidate for Whitechapel, for Mosley's 'New Party' in the 1931 General Election. He polled just 154 votes. His son, Morton Lewis, claims that his father supported Mosley during the early 1930s because he was not fully aware of Mosley's political standpoint. He believes that Lewis' poor financial position, naivety and good nature explain why he was so trusting of Mosley and therefore slow to realise the increasingly anti-Jewish stance of the BUF and its supporters. Lewis, *Ted 'Kid' Lewis*, p. 226–230.
189 In later life, Lewis was said to have 'regretted deeply' his dealings with Mosley and the New Party, yet the association remains prominent in popular memory of the fighter. Ibid. p. 230.
190 On Buxton's career, see Siegman, *Jewish Sports Legends*, p. 174.
191 Schoenfeld, *The Match*, pp. 37–38.
192 *Observer*, 8 July 2001.
193 Schoenfeld, *The Match*, pp. 95–97.
194 BBC Radio 4 'Woman's Hour', Flic Everett Interview with Angela Buxton, transmitted 22 July 2004. www.bbc.co.uk/radio4/womanshour/2004_29_thu_02.shtml (accessed 12 August 2009).
195 *Observer*, 8 July 2001.
196 For Gibson, see F.C. Gray and Y.R. Lamb, *Born to Win: The Authorised Biography of Althea Gibson* (Hoboken, New Jersey, 2004).
197 *New York Post*, 13 June 2004.
198 BBC Radio 4 Interview, 22 July 2004.
199 *Observer*, 8 July 2001. In later years, Buxton had the chance to visit the club on several occasions when her son, Joseph, began his career as a tennis umpire. According to Schoenfeld, Buxton made as many people as possible aware of the club's anti-Semitic attitude to her

during her playing days. Schoenfeld, *The Match*, p. 39.
200 *Daily Mirror*, 6 July 1956. Jones claimed that Buxton's success proved that the Lawn Tennis Association had been wrong five years earlier to claim that 'she [Buxton] will never be any good' during a talent scouting session.
201 *Observer*, 8 July 2001.
202 *Jewish Chronicle*, 21 October 1938. A number of JPC leaders were also involved with the Communist Party, whose sporting wing, the British Workers' Sports Federation, was led by a number of second generation immigrant Jews. The Communist Party in Great Britain was also known for its direct approach towards Fascism and anti-Semitism in the 1930s and drew many Jewish members because of this. Collins, 'Jews', p. 151; J. Heppell, 'A Rebel, not a Rabbi: Jewish Membership of the Communist Party of Great Britain', *Twentieth Century British History*, 15, 1, 2004, pp. 28–50.
203 Bunt, *Jewish Youth Work*, pp. 20–23. Bunt notes that AJY leaders believed that Jews should not involve themselves with anti-Fascist groups as this 'ran counter to their policy of avoiding conspicuous and "un-English" behaviour'. The Board of Deputies continually urged current and former youth club members not to join groups such as the Communist Party – who they labelled a 'red, red herring'.
204 Ibid. 175; Green, *Social History*, p. 226.
205 Levine, *Ellis Island*, p. 264. Levine notes that Maccabi in Europe was an attempt to 'mobilise the physical prowess of middle-class Jewish youth in the face of increased opposition and violence throughout Eastern Europe'.
206 *Jewish Chronicle*, 8 June 1934.
207 Ibid. 9 August 1935.
208 Ibid. 4 December 1936. See also *East London Advertiser*, 23 February 1935.
209 TWAS S/MAC/3/1, *Maccabi News*, 1, 1947, p. 1.
210 See, for instance, Kushner, *The Persistence*; Thurlow, *Fascism in Britain*, chapter 8: 'New Wine for Old Bottles, 1945–1960'; R. Eatwell, 'Fascism and Political Racism in Post-War Britain', in Lunn and Kushner, *Traditions of Intolerance*, pp. 218–222.
211 Endelman, *The Jews of Britain*, p. 232.
212 Kushner, 'Anti-Semitism and Austerity', pp. 150–155.
213 Endelman, *The Jews of Britain*, p. 233. The 43 Group – so-called due to the number present at their first meeting – emerged in March 1946. The Group resolved to take a more assertive approach to the Fascist threat and broke up meetings, used covert tactics to infiltrate various groups and undertook 'defence' programmes. Although publicly condemned by the Jewish elite, the 43 Group grew to over five

hundred members and by the time of the organisation's dissolution in 1950, they had dealt a significant blow to contemporary Fascism. See Beckman, *The 43 Group*.

214 For Orde Wingate, see T. Royle, *Orde Wingate: A Man of Genius, 1903–1944* (London, 2010).

215 *Jewish Chronicle*, 11 November 1979.

216 Ibid. 14 March 1947.

217 Smith, 'Sex', p. 13. On anti-Semitism within the Mass Observation movement more generally, see Kushner, *We Europeans?*.

218 Kushner, *The Persistence*, chapter 4: 'The Jewish Image in the War'; Kushner, 'Anti-Semitism and Austerity', p. 155.

219 *Jewish Chronicle*, 22 November 1979.

220 A.H. Fabian and G. Green (eds), *Association Football* (London, 1960), p. 357.

221 *Hendon Times*, 17 May 1957. The club also won awards for its sportsmanship on several occasions during the 1940s, 1950s and 1960s.

222 Ibid. 14 May 1954.

223 *Jewish Chronicle*, 22 November 1979.

224 Dee, '"Your religion is football!"', pp. 58–61.

225 After starting off in the Middlesex League in 1946 and performing consistently, if somewhat unspectacularly, for six seasons, they won promotion to the London League in 1952, before going on to gain promotion to the Athenian League in 1964. Despite problems with their ground due to the M1 extension, Wingate's merger with Finchley FC in 1991 – and their move to the purpose built Abrahams Stadium – secured their future into the new millennium. See Wingate and Finchley FC 'Club History' www.wingatefinchley.com/history.html (accessed 10 December 2009). Away from football, the club was also heavily involved with charity work during the 1950s and 1960s, raising funds for a number of Jewish and non-Jewish causes across north London. See, for instance, *Hendon Times*, 11 January 1960, 11 March 1960.

226 Wingate itself achieved something nearing folkloric status within British Jewry for its efforts in disproving stereotypes and challenging anti-Semitism. See, for instance, C. Sinclair, 'Wingate Football Club', in B. Cheyette (ed.), *Contemporary Jewish Writing in England and Ireland: An Anthology* (London, 1998), pp. 89–101.

227 www.wingatefinchley.com/history.html (accessed 10 December 2009).

Conclusion

In July 2011, British television broadcaster ITV screened a programme entitled *Strictly Kosher*. Looking at the life of Jews in modern-day Manchester, the one-off documentary demonstrated that considerable religious, cultural and social differences are present within the distinctly heterogeneous community. The programme gave an indication of the nature of life for Jews in the city, especially with regard to religious practices followed by the city's growing Orthodox community – including Sabbath laws, *Shidduchim* (matchmaking), *mikveh* (the practice whereby female Orthodox Jews bathe after menstruation or childbirth) and customs surrounding traditional Jewish weddings. Significantly, at one such wedding featured in the programme, the father of the bride in an arranged marriage is asked what he 'expects' of his new son-in-law. He replies: 'The only thing I expect from him is to change from a Manchester United fan to a Manchester City one'.[1]

Such a statement perhaps would have surprised a mainstream, prime-time British television audience. Given the focus of much of the documentary on the traditions of the Orthodox community, a clear demonstration of a knowledge and interest in professional football – a sport regularly played on the Jewish Sabbath, no less – may have appeared bizarre. However, the man's light-hearted statement did illustrate that, against a backdrop of growing strict religious observance in the city, sport was an aspect of life for Jews in modern Manchester. As with the local non-Jewish population, supporting a local team was something which defined a Mancunian Jew's identity and gave them a topic for conversation and humour.

Similarly, *Sport and British Jewry* also reveals new and perhaps surprising detail about British Jews across a much larger timeframe and a broader geographical focus. Whilst traditional and stereotypical views of the Jewish community have not readily associated this population with sport and physical recreation, it is clear that a noticeable sporting tradition did emerge. Disproving perceptions surrounding British Jewry was not the primary objective of the preceding analysis and narrative. However, this book does go a long way towards painting a new, more accurate picture of the community from the late Victorian era through to the late 1960s – a picture of a population deeply involved and interested in sporting pastimes and distinctly 'sporting' in their attitudes, habits and tastes.

The complex relationship between Jews and sport documented in this volume can also tell us a great deal about the history of British Jewry itself. In 2008, leading historian of British sport, Martin Johnes, argued that sport had been an 'active rather than passive' agent in Britain's social and cultural life. Johnes claimed that 'rather than just reflecting society's wider structures and ideas', sport 'helped shape' how the British 'thought of the world'.[2] In reality, this volume proves that these statements also apply to *British Jewish* life during a large part of modern history. It shows how sport shaped the way Jews thought about themselves as individuals, how they felt about others within the community, how they viewed British society and how British society viewed them. Sport, in essence, tells us a great deal about what it meant to be British *and* Jewish from the 1890s through to the 1960s.

For instance, sport illuminates a great deal on the relationship between the Jewish establishment and the Jewish migrant population. During the late nineteenth and early twentieth century, sport was used as a panacea to help ease the growing anxiety of the Jewish elites caused by 'alien' migration to Britain. Concerned that their own position within British society was threatened by this immigration, they turned to sport to impart a condensed version of Britishness and national identity to immigrant children. In this mission, they found a receptive audience, with many young Jews taking up sport with enthusiasm and reaping the physical and psychological 'benefits' it offered. For other second generation Jews such as Harold Abrahams, sport acted as a personal catalyst for integration and acceptance – with Anglicisation and sporting participation going hand in hand.

Sport was an accessible and enjoyable feature of Britishness which aided the acculturation of aspects of British national identity amongst the immigrant population. In the lives of many immigrant Jews, sport aided integration into a variety of social, cultural and sporting milieus and hastened their Anglicisation. Importantly, for a community that has traditionally sought acceptance into the British mainstream through participation in the arts, business and politics, sport acted as another way in which the Jewish community tried to legitimate itself in the eyes of wider society.

Sport also exerted a powerful direct effect on the ethnicity of British Jewry. In many ways, interest in physical recreation played a significant role in catalysing the disappearance of immigrant culture and the creation of new, secularised Jewish identities. By undermining religious adherence and communal cohesion – and hampering attempts to promote these – sport helped to radically change the ethnic characteristics of a significant section of the Jewish population. Amongst the second and subsequent immigrant generations, sport changed the way in which Jewishness was both felt and expressed in its British context.

In essence, sport exacerbated a 'drift' of younger Jews away from their religious, cultural and communal identity. Far from just reflecting this trend, participation in physical recreation made a direct contribution to remarkable changes occurring in the cultural and religious profile of the community. As in America, sport proved to be an important factor in the destruction and 'redefinition' of Jewishness amongst second and third generation immigrant Jews.[3]

Jewish involvement in British sport also influenced and illustrated some of the most negative interactions with the wider non-Jewish population. Throughout much of the period between the 1890s and the 1960s, sport became a significant vehicle for the expression of racial hostility. Jewish sporting pastimes were linked inextricably to 'organised' and 'social' expressions of anti-Semitism originating from bigoted sections of the wider population. It was stressed that the Jewish 'other' existed within British sport and would only have a harmful influence on its development. Significantly, however, sport also provided a limited means of responding to this racial discrimination and challenging anti-Semitism prevalent within sport and wider British society. Through participation in physical recreation, Jews could disprove abhorrent stereotypes linked to the community and provide a retort to those who discriminated against them.

In many ways, sport served as a means for both the expression and rejection of supposed Jewish 'otherness'. During large parts of the twentieth century, British sport was an environment in which perceptions of Jews were formed and an arena in which anti-Semitism could have a powerful exclusionary effect. In reply to this discrimination, sport was also employed as a means of undermining various forms of racism. An analysis of British sport therefore reveals new avenues in British history in which racial discrimination towards Jews was both expressed and challenged.

This investigation into the sporting experiences of British Jewry has important scholarly implications. For historians of modern British Jewry, the preceding analysis of the Jewish sporting experience demonstrates effectively that leisure interests must be addressed if comprehensive social and cultural histories of the community are to be developed. In one sense, sport gives an important 'window ... onto the modern Jewish experience' and can tell the historian much about the general nature of British Jewish society and culture during the time period.[4] It is also true, however, that the impact of sport was such that many considerable social and cultural changes within the community can only be fully understood by examining the Jewish sporting experience.

Whilst this volume shows the considerable direct impact that sport had on the lives of many British Jews, it also opens up a previously unexamined perspective for the study of migration, ethnicity, minority identity and racial discrimination within modern Britain. Although it may not have been appreciated previously, an analysis of minority sporting participation can illuminate a great deal on the way immigrants formed their own identities. It also highlights much concerning the nature of internal interactions within minority communities and their relationships with wider society. Any social history which seeks to comprehensively analyse British minority communities, and which does not attempt to address these groups' links to sport and physical recreation, is effectively incomplete.[5]

This volume also bears much significance on the historical study of British sport. An investigation of Jewish participation in physical recreation reveals much on the nature and characteristics of British sporting traditions. Firstly, it is clear that an analysis of Jewish sporting involvement demonstrates both the inclusiveness *and* exclusiveness of the British sporting environment for outsiders and minorities. Whilst sport may have opened up opportunities for Jewish migrants to engage with an essential aspect of British culture and identity, it was also a milieu in which prejudice could be formed and mobilised. Secondly, it is also apparent that sport can have vast social and cultural importance for migrant and minority groups. Participation and interest in physical recreation, which was consciously promoted by the Jewish elites, offered Jews the chance to acculturate a hybridised form of 'Britishness'. Sporting interests also affected the development and cohesion of religious and ethnic identity.

Most simply, however, this particular examination highlights a fact popularly known, yet largely academically overlooked: namely that there has been a significant historical involvement in British sport by immigrants and minorities. Whilst social background, gender and nationality have all been seen and analysed by academics as important determining influences on sporting partici- pation, this is not true for immigration and race within their British context. This is an important omission from the canon of literature written on the history of British sport. It suggests, incorrectly, that British migrants and minorities have not historically engaged with the sporting traditions of the majority community nor developed their own sporting cultures.

Immigrant groups such as British Jews can have a significant impact on British sport, whilst sport can also considerably affect the minority community itself in many different ways. Studies of minority sporting involvement could, therefore, be the next logical step for a field which has long been concerned about being 'too narrow in our questions, our audiences and our constituency'. In essence, race and ethnicity could provide 'new' angles for historians interested in developing a broader understanding of the British sporting tradition. By turning to physical recreation within immigrant and minority ghettoes, the 'ghettoisation of the subject' – a fear prevalent within British sport history for over twenty years – may be avoided.[6] Such analyses would benefit this academic field, but would also add new depth to the wider understanding of the clear and complex relationship between British sport and British minority groups.

Notes

1 *Strictly Kosher* (dir. Chris Malone, 2011).
2 M. Johnes, 'British Sports History: The Present and the Future', *Journal of Sport History*, 35, 2008, p. 401.

3 Levine, *Ellis Island*, p. 271.

4 J. Kugelmass, 'Why Sports?', in Kugelmass, *Jews, Sports and the Rites of Citizenship*, p. 25.

5 Significantly, there does seem to be a growing awareness amongst scholars of British minority and immigrant history that sport and physical recreation are important themes to address. See, for instance, Panayi's volume entitled *An Immigration History*, published in 2010, which looks briefly at Jewish, German and Irish immigrant involvement in British sport and the impact that physical recreation had on the internal and external dynamics of these minority groupings. Panayi, *An Immigration History*, pp. 155, 168–169, 174, 179, 293, 313–315.

6 Johnes, 'British Sports History', p. 402. In 1984, James Walvin claimed that the field needed to 'make an impact beyond the pale of the specialism itself' in order to achieve a broader influence and stronger reputation within wider academic British history. J. Walvin, 'Sport, Social History and the Historian', *British Journal of Sport History*, 1, 1, 1984, p. 5.

Select bibliography

Primary sources

Archival sources
Churchill Archives Centre, Churchill College, Cambridge
NBKR Papers of Philip Noel-Baker

Liverpool Record Office
296JSC Jewish Sports Club Archives

London Metropolitan Archives
4286 Maccabi Union Great Britain
ACC2996 Victoria Jewish Lads' Club Archives
GLC Greater London Council

Manchester City Archives, Manchester Central Library
M130 Papers of the Grove House Lads' Club and the Manchester
   Jewish Lads' Brigade

Manchester Jewish Museum
Oral history archive

National Archives, Kew
MEPO Metropolitan Police Archives

Scottish Jewish Archives Centre, Glasgow
Archives of the Bonnyton Moor Golf Club
Glasgow Maccabi Archives

Tyne and Wear Archives Services, Newcastle upon Tyne
S/MAC Newcastle Maccabi
SX113 Sunderland Jewish Badminton Club
SX124 North-Eastern Jewish Golfing Society, 1963–76

University College, London, Library
Annual Reports of West Central Jewish Working Lads' Club

University of Birmingham, Special Collections
HA Harold Abrahams Collection

University of Southampton Special Collections
MS65 Archives of the Council of Christians and Jews
MS116/121 Notting Hill Jewish Lads' Club and the Stepney Jewish
   Lads' Club
MS116/138 Correspondence of R.J.D. Arcy Hart
MS126 Papers of the Ancient Order of Maccabaeans, 1891–1964
MS132 Henriques Papers, 1894–1970s
MS147 Papers of David Mellows
MS152 Papers of the West Central Jewish Working Lads' Club
MS172 Papers of the Stepney Jewish Lads' Club
MS223 Papers of Stanley Rowe
MS244 Papers of the Jewish Lads' and Girls' Brigade

Printed works
Parliamentary papers
Royal Commission on Alien Immigration, London: His Majesty's
   Stationery Office, 4 volumes, 1903.
*Report of the Inter-Departmental Committee on Physical
   Deterioration*, London: His Majesty's Stationery Office, 3
   volumes, 1904.

Newspapers and periodicals
Action
Athletics Weekly
The Blackshirt
Boxing
Boxing News
Boxing, Racing and Football
Bradford Daily Argus

Daily Express
Daily Mirror
Daily Telegraph
East London Advertiser
Golf
Golf Illustrated
Hendon Times
Jewish Chronicle
Jewish Echo
Jewish Graphic
Jewish World
Manchester Guardian
New York Post
Observer
Pall Mall Gazette
St James' Gazette
The Times
Yorkshire Evening News
Yorkshire Post

Contemporary books, articles and memoirs
Adam, Rosalind, *Jewish Voices: Memories of Leicester in the 1940s and 1950s*, Leicester: Leicester Writing School, 2009.
Adler, Henrietta, 'Jewish Life and Labour in East London', in Llewellyn Smith, Hubert (ed.), *The New Survey of London Life and Labour*, Volume VI, *Survey of Social Conditions, Part II: The Western Area*, London: P.S. King and Son, 1934.
Besant, Walter, *East London*, London: Chatto and Windus, 1901.
Booth, Charles (ed.), *Life and Labour of the People of London*, Volume I, *East London*, London: Williams and Norgate, 1889.
Dickens, Charles, *Oliver Twist*, London: Richard Bentley, 1837.
Finn, Ralph, *No Tears in Aldgate*, Bath: Redwood Press, 1973.
Goldman, Willy, *East End My Cradle: Portrait of an Environment*, London: Robson Books, 1988.
Henriques, Basil, *The Oxford and St George's Jewish Lads' Club*, London: Langley and Son, 1914.
——, *Club Leadership*, Oxford: Oxford University Press, Third Edition, 1943.
—— and Slotki, I.W., *The Jewish Sabbath*, London: FOM Publishing, 1940.

Jacobs, Joe, *Out of the Ghetto: My Youth in the East End, Communism and Fascism, 1913–1939*, London: Phoenix Press, 1991.

Llewellyn Smith, Hubert, 'Introduction', in Llewellyn Smith, H. (ed.), *The New Survey of London Life and Labour*, Volume IX, *Life and Leisure*, London: P.S. King and Son, 1935.

Maccabaeans, *Report of the Maccabaean Athletic Committee*, London: Pulman and Sons, 1901.

Potter, Beatrice, 'The Jewish Community', in Booth, Charles (ed.), *Life and Labour of the People of London*, Volume I, *East London*, London: Williams and Norgate, 1889.

Ribalow, Harold, *Fighter from Whitechapel: The Story of Daniel Mendoza*, New York: Jewish Publication Society, 1962.

Russell, Charles and Lewis, Harry Samuel, *The Jew in London: A Study of Racial Character and Present-Day Conditions*, London: Fisher and Unwin, 1901.

——, and Rigby, Lilian, *Working Lads' Clubs*, London: Macmillan, 1908.

Solomons, Jack, *Jack Solomons Tells All*, London: Rich and Cowan, 1951.

Stanley Hall, G., *Adolescence*, Volume I, New York: D. Appleton, 1904.

Stepney Jewish Lads' Club, *How a Jewish Working Boys' Club is Run: An Account of the Stepney Jewish Lads' Club*, London: Eden Fisher and Co., 1914.

White, Arnold, *The Problems of a Great City*, London: Remington, 1895.

——, *The Modern Jew*, London: William Heinemann, 1899.

Secondary sources

Published works

Alderman, Geoffrey, *The Federation of Synagogues, 1887–1987*, London: Federation of Synagogues, 1987.

——, *Modern British Jewry*, Oxford: Clarendon Press, 1992.

Back, Les, Crabbe, Tim and Solomos, John, *The Changing Face of Football: Racism, Identity and Multiculture in the English Game*, Oxford: Berg, 2001.

Beck, Peter, *Scoring for Britain: International Football and*

International Politics, 1900–1939, London: Routledge, 1999.

Beckman, Morris, *The 43 Group: The Untold Story of Their Fight Against Fascism*, London: Centerprise, 1993.

Benewick, Robert, *Political Violence and Public Order*, London: Allen Lane, 1969.

——, *The Fascist Movement in Britain*, London: Allen Lane, 1972.

Berkowitz, Michael, *Western Jewry and the Zionist Project: 1914–1933*, Cambridge: Cambridge University Press, 1997.

——, 'Jewish Blood-Sport: Between Bad Behaviour and Respectability', in Berkowitz, Michael and Ungar, Ruti (eds), *Fighting Back? Jewish and Black Boxers in Britain*, London: UCL, 2007.

——, and Ungar, Ruti (eds), *Fighting Back? Jewish and Black Boxers in Britain*, London: UCL, 2007.

Black, Eugene, *The Social Politics of Anglo-Jewry, 1880–1920*, Oxford: Basil Blackwell, 1988.

Black, Gerry, *Living Up West: Jewish Life in London's West End*, London: Jewish Museum of London Life, 1994.

——, *JFS: The History of the Jews' Free School, London since 1732*, London: Tymsder Publishing, 1998.

Blecking, Diethelm, 'Jews and Sports in Poland before the Second World War', in Mendelsohn, Ezra (ed.), *Jews and the Sporting Life*, Oxford: Oxford University Press, 2008.

Bodner, Allen, *When Boxing was a Jewish Sport*, London: Praeger, 1997.

Bolchover, Richard, *British Jewry and the Holocaust*, Cambridge: Cambridge University Press, 1993.

Borish, Linda, 'Jewish American Women, Jewish Organisations and Sports, 1880–1940', in Riess, Steven (ed.), *Sports and the American Jew*, New York: Syracuse University Press, 1998.

Braber, Ben, *Jews in Glasgow, 1879–1939: Immigration and Integration*, London: Vallentine Mitchell, 2007.

Brenner, Michael, 'Introduction: Why Jews and Sports?', in Brenner, Michael and Reuvani, Gideon (eds), *Emancipation Through Muscles: Jews and Sports in Europe*, London: University of Nebraska Press, 2006.

Brotz, Howard, 'The Outlines of Jewish Society in London', in Freedman, Maurice (ed.), *A Minority in Britain: Social Status of the Anglo-Jewish Community*, London: Vallentine Mitchell, 1955.

Bunt, Sidney, *Jewish Youth Work in Britain: Past, Present and Future*, London: Bedford Square Press, 1975.

Burdsey, Daniel, *British Asians and Football: Culture, Identity, Exclusion*, London: Routledge, 2007.

Carnes, Mark C., *Past Imperfect: History According to The Movies*, New York: Holt Books, 1996.

Carter, ed., '*Chariots of Fire*: Traditional Values/False History', *Jump Cut: A Review of Contemporary Media*, 28, April 1983.

Cashmore, Ellis, 'Bigotry, Manhood and Moral Certitude in an Age of Individualism', *Sport in Society*, 11, 2, 2008.

Cesarani, David, 'The East London of Simon Blumenfeld's *Jew Boy*', *London Journal*, 13, 1, 1987.

——, *The 'Jewish Chronicle' and Anglo-Jewry, 1841–1991*, Cambridge: Cambridge University Press, 1996.

——, 'A Funny Thing Happened on the Way to the Suburbs: Social Change in Anglo-Jewry Between the Wars, 1914–1945', *Jewish Culture and History*, 1, 1, 1998.

—— (ed.), *The Making of Modern Anglo-Jewry*, Oxford: Basil Blackwell, 1990.

Cheyette, Bryan, 'Hilaire Belloc and the Marconi Scandal: A Reassessment of the Interactionist Model of Racial Hatred', in Kushner, Tony and Lunn, Kenneth (eds), *The Politics of Marginality: Race, the Radical Right and Minorities in Twentieth Century Britain*, London: Frank Cass, 1990.

——, *Constructions of the 'Jew' in English Literature and Society: Racial Representations, 1875–1945*, Cambridge: Cambridge University Press, 1993.

Chill, Adam, 'The Performance and Marketing of Minority Identity in Late Georgian Boxing', in Berkowitz, Michael and Ungar, Ruti (eds), *Fighting Back? Jewish and Black Boxers in Britain*, London: UCL, 2007.

Clavane, Anthony, *The Promised Land: The Re-Invention of Leeds United*, London: Yellow Jersey Press, 2010.

Cohen, Norman, 'Trends in Anglo-Jewish Religious Life', in Gould, Julius and Esh, Shaul (eds), *Jewish Life in Modern Britain*, London: Routledge and Kegan Paul, 1964.

Cohen, Stuart, *English Zionists and British Jews: The Communal Politics of Anglo-Jewry, 1895–1920*, Princeton: Princeton University Press, 1982.

Collins, Tony, 'Racial Minorities in a Marginalised Sport: Race,

Discrimination and Integration in Rugby League, *Immigrants and Minorities*, 17, 1, 1998.

——, 'Return to Manhood: The Cult of Masculinity and the British Union of Fascists', *International Journal of the History of Sport*, 16, 4, 1999.

——, 'Jews, Anti-Semitism and Sports in Britain, 1900–1939', in Brenner, Michael and Reuvani, Gideon (eds), *Emancipation Through Muscles: Jews and Sports in Europe*, London: Nebraska, 2006.

Cooper, Zaki (ed.), *Living and Giving: The Jewish Contribution to Life in the UK, 1656–2006*, London: 350th Umbrella Group, 2006.

Cousins, Geoffrey, *Golf in Britain: A Social History from the Beginnings to the Present Day*, London: Routledge and Kegan Paul, 1975.

Cronin, Mike, *Sport and Nationalism in Ireland: Gaelic Games, Soccer and Irish Identity since 1884*, Dublin: Four Courts, 1999.

——, 'Playing Games? The Serious Business of Sports History', *Journal of Contemporary History*, 38, 3, 2003.

Cross, Colin, *The Fascists in Britain*, London: Barrie Books, 1961.

Crump, Jeremy, 'Athletics', in Mason, Tony (ed.), *Sport in Britain: A Social History*, Cambridge: Cambridge University Press, 1989.

Cunningham, Hugh, *Leisure in the Industrial Revolution*, London: Croom Helm, 1980.

Davis, Richard, *The English Rothschilds*, London: Collins, 1983.

Dee, David, '"Nothing Specifically Jewish in Athletics?" Sport, Physical Recreation and the Jewish Youth Movement in London, 1895–1914', *London Journal*, 34, 2, July 2009.

Donoghue, Brian, 'Finchley', in Butler, David and King, Anthony, *The British General Election of 1964*, London: Macmillan, 1965.

Eatwell, Roger, 'Fascism and Political Racism in Post-War Britain', in Lunn, Kenneth and Kushner, Tony (eds), *Traditions of Intolerance: Historical Perspectives on Fascism and Race Discourse in Britain*, Manchester: Manchester University Press, 1989.

Efron, John, '"When is a Yid not a Jew?" The Strange Case of Supporter Identity at Tottenham Hotspur', in Brenner, Michael and Reuvani, Gideon (eds), *Emancipation Through Muscles: Jews and Sports in Europe*, London: Nebraska, 2006.

Eisen, George, 'Jewish History and the Ideology of Modern Sport:

Approaches and Interpretations', *Journal of Sport History*, 25, 3, 1998.

——, 'Jews and Sport: A Century of Retrospect', *Journal of Sport History*, 26, 2, 1999.

Endelman, Todd, *The Jews of Georgian England: 1714–1830*, Philadelphia: Jewish Publication Society, 1979.

——, 'English Jewish History', *Modern Judaism*, 11, 1981.

——, *Radical Assimilation in English Jewish History*, Bloomington: Indiana University Press, 1990.

——, 'Jews, Aliens and Other Outsiders in British History', *Historical Journal*, 37, 1994.

——, *The Jews of Britain: 1656 to 2000*, London and Berkeley: University of California Press, 2002.

Fabian, A.H. and Green, Geoffrey (eds), *Association Football*, London: Caxton Publishing, 1960.

Feldman, David, 'Englishmen, Jews and Immigrants in London, 1865–1914: Modernization, Social Control and the Paths to Englishness', in Dotterer, Ronald, Dash Moore, Deborah and Cohen, Steven (eds), *Jewish Settlement and Community in the Modern Western World*, London: Associated University Presses, 1991.

——, *Englishmen and Jews: Social Relations and Political Culture, 1840–1914*, London and Tononto: Yale University Press, 1994.

Felsenstein, Frank, *Anti-Semitic Stereotypes: A Paradigm of Otherness in English Popular Culture*, Baltimore: Johns Hopkins University Press, 1999.

Finn, Ralph, *The Official History of Tottenham Hotspur Football Club, 1882–1972*, London: Robert Hale, 1972.

Frank, Stanley, *The Jew in Sport*, New York: The Miles Publication Company, 1936.

Gainer, Bernard, *The Alien Invasion: The Origins of the Aliens Act of 1905*, London: Heinemann, 1972.

Galily, Yair, 'The Contribution of the Maccabiah Games to the Development of Sport in the State of Israel', *Sport in Society*, 12, 8, 2009.

Garrard, John, *The English and Immigration: A Comparative Study of the Jewish Influx 1880–1910*, London: Oxford University Press, 1971.

Gartner, Lloyd, *The Jewish Immigrant in England, 1870–1914*, London: Vallentine Mitchell, Third Edition, 2001.

Gems, Gerald, 'The Rise of Sport at a Jewish Settlement House: The Chicago Hebrew Institute, 1908–1921', in Riess, Steven (ed.), *Sports and the American Jew*, New York: Syracuse University Press, 1998.

Gilman, Sander, *The Jew's Body*, London: Routledge, 1991.

Goodman, Paul, *Zionism in England: 1899–1949*, London: Zionist Federation of Great Britain and Ireland, 1949.

Gould, Julius and Esh, Shaul (eds), *Jewish Life in Modern Britain*, London: Routledge and Kegan Paul, 1964.

Gray, Francis Clayton and Lamb, Yanick Rice, *Born to Win: The Authorised Biography of Althea Gibson*, Hoboken, New Jersey: John Wiley and Sons, 2004.

Green, Joseph, *A Social History of the Jewish East End in London, 1914–1939: A Study of Life, Labour and Liturgy*, Lampeter: Edwin Mellen, 1991.

Griffiths, Richard, *Patriotism Perverted: Captain Ramsay, the Right Club and British Anti-Semitism, 1939–1940*, London: Constable, 1998.

Gurock, Jeffrey, *Judaism's Encounter with American Sports*, Indianapolis: Indiana University Press, 2005.

Hanak, Arthur, 'The Historical Background of the Creation of the Maccabi World Union', in Simri, Uriel (ed.), *Physical Education and Sport in the Jewish History and Culture*, Netanya, Israel: Wingate Institute for Physical Education and Sport, 1973.

Harding, John with Berg, Jack, *Jack 'Kid' Berg: The Whitechapel Windmill*, London: Robson Books, 1987.

Harif, Haggai, and Galily, Yair, 'Sport and Politics in Palestine, 1918–1948: Football as a Mirror Reflecting the Relations between Jews and Britons', *Soccer and Society*, 4, 1, 2003.

Harris, Bernard, 'Anti-Alienism, Health and Social Reform in late-Victorian and Edwardian Britain', *Patterns of Prejudice*, 31, 4, 1997.

Hart, Mitchell B., 'The Unbearable Lightness of Britain: Anglo Jewish Historiography and the Problem of "Success"', *Journal of Modern Jewish Studies*, 6, 2, 2007.

Helman, Anat, 'Zionism, Politics, Hedonism: Sports in Inter-War Tel Aviv', in Kugelmass, Jack (ed.), *Jews, Sports and the Rites of Citizenship*, Chicago: University of Illinois Press, 2007.

Heppell, Jason, 'A Rebel, Not a Rabbi: Jewish Membership of the Communist Party of Great Britain', *Twentieth Century British History*, 15, 1, 2004.

Hill, Jeff, '"Connie" – Local Hero, National Icon: Sport, Race and Politics in the Legend of Learie Constantine', *Sports Historian*, 22, 1, 2002.

Himmelfarb, Gertrude, 'Victorian Philanthropy: The Case of Toynbee Hall', *American Scholar*, 59, 3, Summer 1990.

Hiscox, Bill, *Shirley Golf Club: The First 40 Years, 1955–1995*, Birmingham: Shirley Golf Club, 1995.

Hochburg, Severin Adam, 'The Repatriation of Eastern European Jews from Great Britain: 1881–1914', *Jewish Social Studies*, 50, 1/2, Winter/Spring, 1988.

Hoffman, Joseph, *Ten Great Maccabians: A History of Maccabi for Young People*, London: Lotus Press, 1981.

Holland, Julian, *Spurs: A History of Tottenham Hotspur Football Club*, London: Phoenix, 1956.

Holmes, Colin, *Anti-Semitism in British Society: 1876–1939*, London: Edward Arnold, 1979.

——, 'Anti-Semitism and the BUF', in Lunn, Kenneth and Thurlow, Richard (eds), *British Fascism: Essays on the Radical Right in Interwar Britain*, London: Croom Helm, 1980.

Holt, Richard, *Sport and the British*, Oxford: Oxford University Press, 1989.

——, 'The Foreign Office and the Football Association: British Sport and Appeasement, 1935–1938', in Arnaud, Pierre and Riordan, James (eds), *Sport and International Politics: The Impact of Fascism and Communism on Sport*, London: Taylor and Francis, 1998.

——, 'Golf and the English Suburb: Class and Gender in a London Club, c1890–c1960', *Sports Historian*, 18, 1, 1998.

——, 'Great Britain: The Amateur Tradition', in Kruger, Arnd and Murray, William (eds), *The Nazi Olympics: Sport, Politics and Appeasement in the 1930s*, Chicago: University of Illinois Press, 2003.

Homa, Bernard, *Orthodoxy in Anglo-Jewry: 1880–1940*, London: Jewish Historical Society of England, 1969.

Huggins, Mike, *Flat Racing and British Society, 1790–1914: A Social and Economic History*, London: Frank Cass, 2000.

Hyman, Ted, *A History of Moor Allerton Golf Club: 1923–2001*, Moor Allerton: Moor Allerton Golf Club, Second Edition, 2001.

Ismond, Patrick, *Black and Asian Athletes in British Sport and*

Society: A Sporting Chance?, Basingstoke: Palgrave Macmillan, 2003.

Jacobs, Jack, 'The Politics of Jewish Sports Movements in Interwar Poland', in Brenner, Michael and Reuvani, Gideon (eds), *Emancipation Through Muscles: Jews and Sports in Europe*, London: Nebraska, 2006.

Johal, Sanjiev and Bains, Jas, *Corner Flags and Corner Shops*, London: Phoenix Press, 1999.

John, Michael, 'Anti-Semitism in Austrian Sports between the Wars', in Brenner, Michael and Reuvani, Gideon (eds), *Emancipation Through Muscles: Jews and Sports in Europe*, London: Nebraska, 2006.

Jones, Stephen, *Sport, Politics and the Working Class: Organised Labour and Sport in Interwar Britain*, Manchester: Manchester University Press, 1988.

Julius, Anthony, *Trials of the Diaspora*, Oxford: Oxford University Press, 2010.

Kadish, Sharman, *'A Good Jew and a Good Englishman': The Jewish Lads' and Girls' Brigade, 1895–1995*, London: Vallentine Mitchell, 1995.

Katz, David, *The Jews in the History of England: 1485–1850*, Oxford: Clarendon Press, 1994.

Kaufman, Haim, 'Jewish Sports in the Diaspora, Yishuv and Israel: Between Nationalism and Politics', *Israel Studies*, 10, 2, 2005.

——, and Bar-Eli, Michael, 'Processes That Shaped Sport in Israel during the Twentieth Century', *Sport History Review*, 36, 2, 2005.

Keddie, John, *Running the Race: Eric Liddell, Olympic Champion and Missionary*, London: Evangelical Press, 2007.

Kenny, Mary, *Germany Calling: A Personal Biography of William Joyce*, Dublin: New Island, 2003.

Kessler, Edward, 'Claude Montefiore and Liberal Judaism', *European Judaism*, 34, 1, 2001.

Korr, Chuck, *West Ham United: The Making of a Football Club*, Chicago: University of Illinois Press, 1986.

Krausz, Ernest, 'The Economic and Social Structure of Anglo-Jewry', in Gould, Julius and Esh, Shaul (eds), *Jewish Life in Modern Britain*, London: Routledge and Kegan Paul, 1964.

Kruger, Arnd, 'Germany: The Propaganda Machine', in Kruger, Arnd and Murray, William (eds), *The Nazi Olympics: Sport,*

Politics and Appeasement in the 1930s, Chicago: University of Illinois Press, 2003.

Kugelmass, Jack, 'Why Sports?', in Kugelmass, Jack (ed.), *Jews, Sports and the Rites of Citizenship*, Chicago: University of Illinois Press, 2007.

——, (ed.), *Jews, Sports and the Rites of Citizenship*, Chicago: University of Illinois Press, 2007.

Kushner, Tony, *The Persistence of Prejudice: Anti-Semitism in British Society during the Second World War*, Manchester: Manchester University Press, 1989.

——, 'The Impact of British Anti-Semitism: 1918–1945', in Cesarani, David (ed.), *The Making of Modern Anglo-Jewry*, Oxford: Basil Blackwell, 1990.

——, 'Clubland, Cricket Tests and Alien Internment, 1939–1940', in Cesarani, David and Kushner, Tony (eds), *The Internment of Aliens in Twentieth Century Britain*, London: Frank Cass, 1993.

——, 'Anti-Semitism and Austerity: The August 1947 Riots', in Panayi, Panikos (ed.), *Racial Violence in Britain in the Nineteenth and Twentieth Centuries*, London: Leicester University Press, 1996.

——, *We Europeans? Mass Observation, 'Race' and British Identity in the Twentieth Century*, Aldershot: Ashgate, 2004.

——, and Valman, Nadia, 'Minorities, Fascism and anti-Fascism', in Kushner, Tony and Valman, Nadia (eds), *Remembering Cable Street: Fascism and Anti-Fascism in British Society*, London: Vallentine Mitchell, 2000.

Lammers, Benjamin, 'The Birth of the East Ender: Neighbourhood and Local Identity in Interwar East London', *Journal of Social History*, 39, 2, Winter 2005.

——, '"The Citizens of the Future": Educating the Children of the Jewish East End, c.1885–1939', *Twentieth Century British History*, 19, 4, 2008.

Langton, Daniel, *Claude Montefiore: His Life and Thought*, London: Vallentine Mitchell, 2002.

Laqueur, Walter, *The History of Zionism*, London: Tauris Parke Publications, Third Edition, 2003.

Lazarus, Mark, *A Club Called Brady*, London: New Cavendish, 1996.

Lebzelter, Gisela, *Political Anti-Semitism in England: 1918–1939*, London: Macmillan, 1978.

——, 'Henry Hamilton Beamish and the Britons: Champions of Anti-Semitism', in Lunn, Kenneth and Thurlow, Richard (eds), *British Fascism: Essays on the Radical Right in Interwar Britain*, London: Croom Helm, 1980.

Levine, Peter, *Ellis Island to Ebbets Field: Sport and the American Jewish Experience*, Oxford: Oxford University Press, 1992.

——, "Our Crowd at Play": The Elite Jewish Country Club in the 1920s', in Riess, Steven (ed.), *Sports and the American Jew*, New York: Syracuse University Press, 1998.

Lewis, D.S., *Illusions of Grandeur. Mosley, Fascism and British Society: 1931–1981*, Manchester: Manchester University Press, 1987.

Lewis, Morton, *Ted 'Kid' Lewis: His Life and Times*, London: Robson Books, 1990.

Linehan, Thomas, *East London for Mosley: The British Union of Fascists in East London and South-West Essex, 1933–1940*, London: Frank Cass, 1996.

——, *British Fascism, 1918–1939: Parties, Ideology and Culture*, Manchester: Manchester University Press, 2000.

Lipman, Sonia and Lipman, Vivian (eds), *Jewish Life in Britain: 1962–1977*, London: K.G. Saur, 1981.

Lipman, Vivian, *Social History of the Jews in England: 1850–1950*, London: Watts and Co., 1954.

——, *A Century of Civil Service, 1859–1959: The History of the Jewish Board of Guardians*, London: Routledge, 1959.

Livshin, Rosalyn, 'Acculturation of Immigrant Jewish Children, 1890–1930', in Cesarani, David (ed.), *The Making of Modern Anglo-Jewry*, Oxford: Basil Blackwell, 1990.

Llewellyn, Matthew, 'Epilogue: Britannia Overruled', *International Journal of the History of Sport*, 28, 5, 2011.

Loewe, Lionel Lewis, *Basil Henriques*, London: Routledge and Kegan Paul, 1976.

Loewe, Raphael, 'The Bernhard Baron Settlement and Oxford and St George's Club', in Newman, Aubrey (ed.), *The Jewish East End: 1840–1939*, London: Jewish Historical Society of England, 1981.

London, Louise, *Whitehall and the Jews, 1933–1948: British Immigration Policy and the Holocaust*, Cambridge: Cambridge University Press, 2000.

Lowerson, John, *Sport and the English Middle Classes 1870–1914*,

Manchester: Manchester University Press, 1993.

Lunn, Kenneth, 'The Ideology and Impact of the British Fascists in the 1920s', in Lunn, Kenneth and Kushner, Tony (eds), *Traditions of Intolerance: Historical Perspectives on Fascism and Race Discourse in Britain*, Manchester: Manchester University Press, 1989.

Magnusson, Sally, *The Flying Scotsman: The Eric Liddell Story*, London: Quartet, 1981.

Malcolmson, Richard, *Popular Recreations and English Society, 1700–1850*, Cambridge: Cambridge University Press, 1973.

Mandell, Richard, *The Nazi Olympics*, London: Souvenir Press, 1971.

Mandle, William, *Anti-Semitism and the British Union of Fascists*, London: Longman, 1968.

Mangan, J.A., *Athleticism in the Victorian and Edwardian Public School*, London: Frank Cass, 1981.

Marvin, Caroline, 'Avery Brundage and American Participation in the 1936 Olympic Games', *Journal of American Studies*, 16, 1, 1982.

Mason, Tony, *Association Football and English Society, 1863–1915*, Brighton: Harvester, 1980.

——, and Holt, Richard, *Sport in Britain: 1945–2000*, Oxford: Blackwell Publishing, 2000.

McCasland, David, *Eric Liddell: Pure Gold*, London: Discovery House, 2003.

McIntosh, Peter, *Physical Education in England since 1800*, London: G. Bell and Sons, 1968.

McKibbin, Ross, *Classes and Cultures: England, 1918–1951*, Oxford: Oxford University Press, 2000.

McWhirter, Norris, 'Abrahams, Harold Maurice (1899–1978)', *Oxford Dictionary of National Biography*, Oxford: Oxford University Press, 2004.

Meacham, Standish, *Toynbee Hall and Social Reform: 1880–1914*, London and New Haven: Yale University Press, 1987.

Mendelsohn, Ezra , 'Preface', in Mendelsohn, Ezra (ed.), *Jews and the Sporting Life*, Oxford: Oxford University Press, 2008.

——, (ed.), *Jews and the Sporting Life*, Oxford: Oxford University Press, 2008.

Morell, John, 'Arnold Leese and the Imperial Fascist League: The Impact of Racial Fascism', in Lunn, Kenneth, and Thurlow,

Richard (eds), *British Fascism: Essays on the Radical Right in Interwar Britain*, London: Croom Helm, 1980.

Mosse, George, 'Max Nordau, Liberalism and the New Jew', *Journal of Contemporary History*, 27, 4, 1992.

Panayi, Panikos, *The Enemy in Our Midst: Germans in Britain during the First World War*, Oxford: Berg, 1991.

——, *Immigration, Ethnicity and Racism in Britain, 1815–1945*, Manchester: Manchester University Press, 1994.

——, *An Immigration History of Britain: Multicultural Racism since 1800*, London: Pearson, 2010.

Pollard, Stephen, 'Sport', in Cooper, Zaki (ed.), *Living and Giving: The Jewish Contribution to Life in the UK, 1656–2006*, London: 350th Umbrella Group, 2006.

Polley, Martin, 'The British Government and the Olympic Games in the 1930s', *Sports Historian*, 17, 1, 1997.

——, *Moving the Goalposts: A History of Sport and Society since 1945*, London: Routledge, 1998.

Postal, Bernard, Silver, Jesse and Silver, Roy (eds), *Encyclopaedia of Jews in Sport*, New York: Bloch, 1965.

Presner, Todd, *Muscular Judaism: The Jewish Body and the Politics of Regeneration*, Abingdon and New York: Routledge, 2007.

Pugh, Martin, *'Hurrah for the Blackshirts!' Fascists and Fascism in Britain between the Wars*, London: Pimlico, 2006.

Ribalow, Harold, *The Jew in American Sport*, New York: Bloch, 1948.

Richards, Huw, 'Lawson, Harry Lawson Webster Levy, Viscount Burnham (1862–1933)', *Oxford Dictionary of National Biography*, Oxford: Oxford University Press, 2004.

Riess, Steven, 'Tough Jews: The Jewish American Boxing Experience, 1890–1950', in Riess, Steven (ed.), *Sports and the American Jew*, New York: Syracuse University Press, 1998.

——, (ed.), *Sports and the American Jew*, New York: Syracuse University Press, 1998.

Riordan, Jim, 'The Hon. Ivor Montagu (1904–1984): Founding Father of Table-Tennis', *Sport in History*, 28, 3, 2008.

Roberts, Randy, 'Eighteenth Century Boxing', *Journal of Sport History*, 4, 3, 1977.

Rosenberg, Edgar, *From Shylock to Svengali: Jewish Stereotypes in English Fiction*, Stanford: Stanford University Press, 1960.

Rosenthal, Michael, *The Character Factory: Baden-Powell and the*

Origins of the Boy-Scout Movement, New York: Pantheon, 1986.

Roth, Cecil, *A History of the Jews in England*, Oxford: Clarendon Press, Third Edition, 1964.

Royle, Trevor, *Orde Wingate: A Man of Genius, 1903–1944*, London: Frontline, 2010.

Rubinstein, William, *A History of the Jews in the English Speaking World: Great Britain*, London: Macmillan, 1996.

Ryan, Mark, *Running with Fire: The True Story of 'Chariots of Fire' Hero*, London: J.R. Books, 2011.

Samuel, Raphael (ed.), *East End Underworld: Chapters in the Life of Arthur Harding*, London: Routledge and Kegan Paul, 1981.

Sashon, Moshe and Schrodt, Barbara, 'The Maccabi Sports Movement and the Establishment of the Maccabiah Games, 1932', *Sport History Review*, 16, 1, 1985.

Schlesinger, Ernest, *Creating Community and Accumulating Social Capital: Jews Associating with Other Jews in Manchester*, London: Institute of Jewish Policy Research, 2003.

Schoenfeld, Bruce, *The Match. Althea Gibson and Angela Buxton: How Two Outsiders – One Black, the Other Jewish – Forged a Friendship and Made Sports History*, New York: HarperCollins, 2004.

Searle, Geoffrey, *The Quest for National Efficiency. A Study in British Politics and Political Thought: 1899–1914*, Oxford: Blackwell, 1971.

Shimoni, Gideon, 'Poale Zion: A Zionist Transplant in Britain, 1905–1945', *Studies in Contemporary Jewry*, 2, 1986.

Shipley, Stan, 'Boxing', in Mason, Tony (ed.), *Sport in Britain: A Social History*, Cambridge: Cambridge University Press, 1989.

Siegman, Joseph, *Jewish Sports Legends*, Washington: Potomac Books, Fourth Edition, 2005.

Silman-Cheong, Helen, *Wellesley Aron: A Rebel with a Cause*, London: Vallentine Mitchell, 1992.

Simri, Uriel (ed.), *Physical Education and Sport in the Jewish History and Culture*, Netanya, Israel: Wingate Institute for Physical Education and Sport, 1981.

Sinclair, Clive, 'Wingate Football Club', in Cheyette, Bryan (ed.), *Contemporary Jewish Writing in England and Ireland: An Anthology*, London: Peter Halbern, 1998.

Skidelsky, Robert, *Oswald Mosley*, London: Macmillan, 1981.

Slater, Robert, *Great Jews in Sports*, New York: Jonathan David, 2003.

Smith, Elaine, 'Jewish Responses to Political anti-Semitism and Fascism in the East End of London, 1920–1939', in Lunn, Kenneth and Kushner, Tony (eds), *Traditions of Intolerance: Historical Perspectives on Fascism and Race Discourse in Britain*, Manchester: Manchester University Press, 1989.

——, 'Jews and Politics in the East End of London, 1918–1939', in Cesarani, David (ed.), *The Making of Modern Anglo-Jewry*, Oxford: Basil Blackwell, 1990.

——, 'But What Did They Do? Contemporary Jewish Response to Cable Street', in Kushner, Tony and Valman, Nadia (eds), *Remembering Cable Street: Fascism and Anti-Fascism in British Society*, London: Vallentine Mitchell, 2000.

Smith, Sally, 'Sex, Leisure and Jewish Youth Clubs in Interwar London', *Jewish Culture and History*, 9, 1, 2007.

Spencer, Paul, 'A Discussion of Appeasement and Sport as Seen in the *Manchester Guardian* and *The Times*', *Australian Society for Sports History Bulletin*, 2, 1996.

Springhall, John, *Youth, Empire and Society*, London: Croom Helm, 1977.

Spurr, Michael A., '"Playing for Fascism": Sportsmanship, Anti-Semitism and the British Union of Fascists', *Patterns of Prejudice*, 37, 4, 2003.

Stedman Jones, Gareth, *Outcast London: A Study in the Relationship between Classes in Victorian Society*, Oxford: Clarendon Press, 1971.

Stoddart, Brian, 'Sport, Cultural Relations and International Relations: England versus Germany, 1935', *Soccer and Society*, 7, 1, 2006.

Swift, Geoff, *'Are You Made Up?' The Story of a Golf Club: Lee Park Golf Club, 1954–2004*, Liverpool: Lee Park Golf Club, 2004.

Tananbaum, Susan, '"Ironing Out the Ghetto Bend": Sports and the Making of British Jews', *Journal of Sport History*, 31, 1, 2004.

Tatz, Colin, *A Course of History. Monash Country Club: 1931–2001*, Sydney: Allen and Unwin, 2002.

Taylor, Matthew, *The Association Game: A History of British Football*, London: Longman, 2008.

——, 'Boxers United: Trade Unionism in British Boxing in the 1930s', *Sport in History*, 29, 3, 2009.

——, 'Round the London Ring: Boxing, Class and Community in Interwar London', *London Journal*, 34, 2, 2009.

Thurlow, Richard, *Fascism in Britain: From Oswald Mosley's Blackshirts to the National Front*, London: I.B. Tauris, 2006.

Ungar, Ruti and Berkowitz, Michael, 'From Daniel Mendoza to Amir Khan: Minority Boxers in Britain', in Berkowitz, Michael and Ungar, Ruti (eds), *Fighting Back? Jewish and Black Boxers in Britain*, London: UCL, 2007.

Vamplew, Wray, 'Gold, Sir Arthur Abraham (1917–2002)', *Oxford Dictionary of National Biography*, Oxford: Oxford University Press, 2009.

Wagstaffe Simmons, G., *History of Tottenham Hotspur Football Club 1882–1946*, London: Thomas Knight, 1947.

Walters, Guy, *Berlin Games: How Hitler Stole the Olympic Dream*, London: John Murray Publishers, 2006.

Walvin, James, *The People's Game*, London: Allen Lane, 1975.

——, 'Sport, Social History and the Historian', *British Journal of Sport History*, 1, 1, 1984.

Wasserstein, Bernard, *Britain and the Jews of Europe: 1939–1945*, Oxford: Clarendon Press, Third Edition, 1979.

Weber, Thomas, *Our Friend 'The Enemy': Elite Education in Britain and Germany before World War I*, Stanford: Stanford University Press, 2008.

White, Jerry, *Rothschild Buildings: Life in an East End Tenement Block 1887–1920*, London: Routledge, 1980.

Wilberforce, Richard, 'Cohen, Lionel Leonard, Baron Cohen (1888–1973)', *Oxford Dictionary of National Biography*, Oxford: Oxford University Press, 2004.

Wilcock, Evelyn, 'The Reverend John Harris: Issues in Anglo-Jewish Pacifism, 1914–1918', *Jewish Historical Studies*, 30, 1987/88.

Williams, Bill, 'The Anti-Semitism of Tolerance: Middle-Class Manchester and the Jews, 1870–1900', in Kidd, Alan and Roberts, Kenneth (eds), *City, Class and Culture*, Manchester: Manchester University Press, 1985.

——, *Manchester Jewry, A Pictorial History: 1788–1988*, Manchester: Archive Publications, 1988.

——, '"East and West" in Manchester Jewry, 1850–1914', in Cesarani, David (ed.), *The Making of Modern Anglo-Jewry*, Oxford: Basil Blackwell, 1990.

——, *Jewish Manchester: An Illustrated History*, Derby: Breedon Books, 2008.

Williams, Jack, *Cricket and Race*, Oxford: Berg, 2001.

Unpublished works

Dee, David, '"Your religion is football!" Soccer and the Jewish Community in London, 1900–1970', De Montfort University, MA, 2007.

——, 'Jews and British Sport: Integration, Ethnicity and anti-Semitism, c1880–c1960', De Montfort University, Ph.D., 2011.

Rosen, Michael, 'The Maccabi Movement in Great Britain in 1934–1948', University College, London, MA, 2001.

Websites

www.bbc.co.uk.

BBC Radio 4 'Woman's Hour', Flic Everett Interview with Angela Buxton, transmitted 22 July 2004.

W. Gallagher, 'Review of *Chariots of Fire*', 14 August 2001.

www.jewishagency.org.

Jewish Agency for Israel, 'The Story of Sport in Israel', chapter 6: 'Rule Britannia! The British Influence and the Maccabiah Games' (accessed 30 March 2009).

www.maccabigb.org.

'About' Maccabi GB (accessed 12 September 2009).

www.wingatefinchley.com.

Wingate and Finchley FC 'Club History' (accessed 17 September 2008).

Index

Note: 'n' after a page reference indicates the number of a note on that page; page numbers in *italic* refer to illustrations

AAA *see* Amateur Athletics Association
aaliyah 126
Aaron, Barney 3
Aarons, Marilyn 138
Aarons, Sam *see* Furness, 'Kid' (Sam Aarons)
Abrahams, Adolphe 58
Abrahams, Esther 57
Abrahams, Harold 8, 11n17, 17, 71, 82n153, 87n232, 179, 200, 225
    Anglicisation 60–63, 69–70, 168
    anti-Semitism 54, 56–57, 58–59, 60, 69, 83n163, 83n165
    Berlin Olympics 55, 61, 64, 67–68
        actions regarding boycott movement 65–67, 86n212, 86n215
    family background 57–58, 62
    sporting career 54, 60
    see also Chariots of Fire; Ryan, Mark
Abrahams, Isaac 57–58, 59
Abrahams, Lionel 58
Abrahams, Sidney (Solly) 58
Action 160–161, 163, 213n35
    Jewish 'Hidden Hand' in British sport 165, 166, 167, 168
    Jewish sporting 'difference' 170, 171
Acts of Parliament
    Aliens Act (1905) 14, 39–40, 43
Adler, Henrietta 142n18
Adler, Herman 27
adolescence, 'problem' of 23–24
AJY *see* Association for Jewish Youth

Albert Hall 150n144, 169
Al-Fayed, Mohammed 56
Allison, George 99
Amateur Athletics Association 59, 65, 68–69, 82n153
American Jewry 2, 19, 125, 176, 226
    Americanisation of migrants through sport 16
    anti-Semitism and sport 159, 175, 193–194, 216n92
    boxing 111, 112, 113–114, 115, 116, 122, 146n92, 148n109, 148n115, 198–199
    boycott movement for Berlin Olympic Games 64, 86n215
    decline of Jewish sport in 7, 13n31
    historiography concerning sport 5, 89, 159
    Maccabi movement in 152n166
    see also Chicago; Gurock, Jeffrey; Levine, Peter; New York City; *New York Post*; Riess, Stephen
Anglicisation, policy of 7, 8, 15, 16, 20–21, 40–41, 71–72, 72n9, 74n27, 102–103, 225–226
    historiography 15–16, 73n10
    see also girls and Anglicisation
anti-alienism 19–20, 26, 30–31, 39–40, 43–44, 76n56, 211n18
    aloofness, accusations of immigrant 8, 38, 39–40, 52
anti-Semitism 6, 8, 15, 46, 95, 158–159, 160, 162–163, 175,

196–197, 204, 207–209, 214n77, 226
historiography 158–159, 174–175, 204, 209, 210n2, 210n8
myths and stereotypes 2, 8, 20, 163–164, 170, 177–179, 185–187, 205–206
'hidden hand', myth of 161, 162, 163–169, 170, 173, 208
sport undermining 3, 6, 9, 31, 42, 43–44, 46, 51, 61, 198–199, 203–204, 205–206, 225
unsporting, Jews as 1, 2, 3, 27, 61, 112, 169–172, 205
weak, Jews as 2–3, 18, 26–27, 28, 29, 43, 198–199
sport combating 51, 126, 160, 196–208, 209, 218n134
see also anti-alienism; British Union of Fascists
Aron, Wellesley 134
Arsenal Football Club 2, 13n32, 24, 98–99, 101, 145n53
Ashe-Payne, William 24
Association for Jewish Youth 49, 105, 125, 135–136, 222n203
Association of Jewish Golf Clubs and Societies 192
athletics 2, 13n32, 24, 42, 53–72, 59
see also Abrahams, Harold; Chariots of Fire; Liddell, Eric
Australian Jewry 114, 124, 176, 216n92

badminton 175, 215n83
Balfour, Arthur 40
Bar Cochba
Glasgow 124, 130
London 124
Baron, Bernhard 117–118
basketball 50, 107
Battle of Cable Street 203, 220n174
BBC see British Broadcasting Corporation
BBBoC see British Boxing Board of Control
Beckett, Joe 166

Bedford 57
Belfast 189
Bennett, Sol 186
Berg, Jack 'Kid' (Judah Bergman junior) 110, 114, 115, 122, 140
career 113
family background 113, 147n106
Jewishness and self-promotion 115–116, 148n118
Bergman, Judah (junior) see Berg, Jack 'Kid' (Judah Bergman junior)
Bergman, Judah (senior) 113
Berkowitz, Michael 11n17, 132, 148n115, 149n124
Berliner, Victor 110
Besant, Walter 40–41
Beter 134
billiards 95, 100
Birmingham 137, 189–191, 192, 215n83
see also Shirley Golf Club
blackballing 172, 182
Black, Eugene 24, 73n14
The Social Politics of Anglo-Jewry, 1880–1920 73n14
Blackpool 184, 189
Blackshirt 160–161, 163, 171, 213n35
Jewish 'Hidden Hand' in British sport 165, 167–168
Jewish sporting 'difference' 171
BMA see British Maccabi Association
Board of Deputies 67, 86n219, 196, 220n174, 222n203
board schools 21, 32, 38, 40–41, 48, 49, 50–51
Bobker, Martin 95
Bonnyton Moor Golf Club 190, 192, 193, 219n154
boxing 2, 5, 146n92, 166–169
challenging anti-Semitism 198–200, 221n185
Georgian period 3, 10n14, 115–116, 198
Jewish youth movement 38, 41, 42, 44–47, 52–53, 117–118, 197
spectating 118–121
twentieth century 13n32, 111–122,

140, 147n93, 149n124,
  149n136, 151n152, 213n50
see also Berg, Jack 'Kid' (Judah
  Bergman junior); Lewis, Ted
  'Kid' (Gershon Mendeloff);
  Mendoza, Daniel; Prince of
  Wales' Boxing Shield; *individual
  boxing halls*
Boxing 119, 147n93, 199, 221n185
Bradford 176
Brady Street Club for Working Boys 22,
  23, 31–32, 34, 41, 42, 96, 104
Bradian 34
Brentford Football Club 95
Brighton 171–172
Bristol 22
British Boxing Board of Control
  147n93, 167
British Broadcasting Corporation 64,
  67, 86n221
British Brothers' League 162, 211n18
British Fascisti 161
British League of Ex-Servicemen and
  Women 204
British Maccabi Association 63,
  85n199, 123–141, 129, 140,
  153n183, 156n235, 203–204
  policy 126, 128, 132, 135, 136
  criticism of youth clubs and
    Association for Jewish Youth
    135–136
  see also Gildesgame, Pierre; Gradon,
    Kurt; Sportsmen's Century Club;
    individual clubs
British Olympic Association 64–66,
  86n209
  see also Hunter, Evan
British Union of Fascists 8, 160–174,
  199, 200, 203, 208, 213n33,
  213n35, 213n50, 221n188
  anti-Semitic propaganda 161,
    162–163, 164–173, 212n25
  background 161–162
  historiography 160, 162, 173,
    212n27
British Workers' Sports Federation 65,
  85n207, 165, 222n202

see also Communist Party Great
  Britain
Britons 159, 161
Brodetsky, Selig 96, 134
Brodie, Israel 116, 126
Bromhead, John 87n232
Broughton Rangers Rugby League
  Football Club 94, 96
Bruce, Morys (Lord Aberdare) 130
Brundage, Avery 86n215
Bruning, Clement 167
BWSF *see* British Workers' Sports
  Federation
BUF *see* British Union of Fascists
Bunt, Sidney 34, 78n106, 222n203
Burns, Sidney 206
Bushey Hall Golf Club 183
Butler Street Jewish Girls' Club 22, 29
Buxton, Angela 128, 200–202, 215n83,
  221n199

Cambridge University 54, 56–57,
  58–60
  Caius College 57
  Hawks Club 83n163
  University Athletics Club 60
Carnes, Mark
  *Past Imperfect: History According To
    The Movies* 69
Carter, Ed 56
Cashmore, Ellis 11n21, 55–56
  Black Sportsmen 11n21
Cesarani, David 89–90, 93, 109
Chapman, Herbert 99
Chariots of Fire 54, 55–57, 69,
  82n162
  scholarly critiques of 55–56
  see also Abrahams, Harold; Liddell,
    Eric
Chesterton, Arthur Kenneth 165
Cheyette, Bryan 2, 162
Church Lads' Brigade 21, 76n61
Clavane, Anthony 11n17, 146n86
Clifton College 22
Cohen, Lionel Leonard 54
Collins, Tony 11n17, 16–17, 213n33
Communist Party Great Britain 65,

85n207, 144n45, 165, 220n174, 222n203
see also British Workers' Sports Federation
Conservative Party 40, 130, 187, 211n18
see also Thatcher, Margaret
Coombe Hill Golf Club 191, 193
Cooper, Zaki
  Living and Giving: The Jewish Contribution to Life in the UK, 1656–2006 1–2
Council of Christians and Jews 184
Cousins, Geoffrey 186, 194
  Golf in Britain: A Social History from the Beginnings to the Present Day 194
Coussin, Brian 153n180
CPGB see Communist Party Great Britain
cricket 24, 25, 32, 54, 93, 96, 137
  Jewish youth movement 34, 35–36, 41, 50, 52, 103–104
Cumberland Lawn Tennis Club 201, 202
Cussins, Manny 13n32

dancing 93, 110, 130–131, 147n106, 154n193, 156n240
Davis, Frank 205, 206
day schools (Jewish) 21, 24
decline of Jewish sport in Britain 7, 13n32
Devonshire Club 118, 120, 167–168, 213n50
see also Solomons, Jack
Dickens, Charles
  Oliver Twist 2
dog-racing 95
double-sessions 50–51, 81n143
drinking 23, 26, 120, 186, 194

Eisen, George 159, 216n94
Elias, Sam 3
Emmanuel, Edward 119
Endelman, Todd 3, 11n18, 15, 72n9, 88–89, 109, 175

Radical Assimilation in English Jewish History, 1656–1945 11n18, 88–89, 109
The Jews of Britain: 1656–2000 11n18
Englander, David 142n23
England, national football team game against Germany (1935) 86n213, 97–98, 144n46, 164–165
English Golf Union 184
ethnicity/ethnic identity 4, 6, 8, 88–90, 109, 139–140, 226
Evers, Sybil 62
expulsion of Jews from Britain (1290) 9n1

Fagin 2, 10n6
Federation of Synagogues 92
Feldman, David 22, 73n10, 74n27
Felsenstein, Frank 198
  Anti-Semitic Stereotypes: A Paradigm of Otherness in English Popular Culture 198
Finchley Golf Club 183
  political controversy surrounding anti-Semitism (1957–1964) 187–188, 217n133
Findlay, Archibald 170–171
Finn, Ralph 147n104
Folkard, W. G. L. 184
football 2, 5, 11n17, 13n32, 13n52, 24, 25, 32, 94–95, 96, 142n21, 151n159, 170–171, 203, 204–207, 224
  Jewish youth movement 34, 35, 36, 41, 50, 52, 103–104, 106–108
  Maccabi 128, 137
  supporting/spectating 95–102, 107–108, 144n45, 145n55, 146n83
see also Wingate Football Club; individual clubs
43 Group 204, 220n173, 222n213
Frais, Abraham 188
Furness, 'Kid' (Sam Aarons) 112

gambling 23, 26, 106, 117, 118, 119,

120, 140, 149n124, 149n138
Garman, Joe 95
Gartner, Lloyd 4, 15, 72n7, 73n10
  *The Jewish Immigrant in England,
    1870–1914* 4
Germany 64–69, 86n213, 97, 144n46,
    164–165, 167, 169, 171
Gibson, Althea 201
Gildesgame, Pierre 126, 133, 135, 136,
    137, 169
Gilman, Sander 2
Ginsberg, Morris 106
girls and Anglicisation 22, 23, 29, 32,
    41, 49, 50, 51, 52, 102–103
Glasgow 189–190, 219n154
  Maccabi 130, 131, 156n239
Gleskie, Reuben 94
Goldman, Willy 94, 143n30
Goldsmid, Albert 21, 25, 51, 176
Goldstone, Abraham 94
golf 5, 8, 54, 93, 172, 174–195, 200,
    209, 216n107, 219n166
  growth of Jewish interest in 175–176
  openness of Jewish clubs 192–193,
    216n166
  response to anti-Semitism in 188–194
  see also individual clubs
Golf 176–177
Golf Illustrated 177–180
  anti-Semitic cartoons *178*, *180*
Goodwin, Jack 110
Gradon, Ken (Kurt Gradenwitz) 126,
    133, 152n172, 155n210
Green, Geoffrey 97, 142n19, 148n120
Grove House Jewish Lads' Club 23,
    106–108, 118
  Sabbath football, criticism
    concerning (1931–1932)
    106–108
Gurock, Jeffrey 16, 89, 141n5
  *Judaism's Encounter with American
    Sports* 89
gymnastics 24, 26, 38, 41, 79n116,
    80n117, 130
  as a retort to anti-alienism 43–44,
    52–53

Habonim 134
Hampstead Golf Club 181
Hapoel 124
Harris, John 93, 143n26
Hartsbourne Country Club 191
Harvey, Len 166
Haw-Haw, Lord *see* Joyce, William
Headingley stadium 96
Heaton Park Golf Club 183
Helfgott, Ben 128
Helman, Anat 152n166, 156n240
Hendon Golf Club 181, 217n113
Hendon Times, investigation into golf
    club anti-Semitism by 181–182,
    183, 184, 187, 194
Henriques, Basil 29, 32, 47, 77n81,
    104, 106, 117
Henriques, Eric 197
Herzl, Theodor 151n157
  see also Zionism
Highgate Golf Club 183
Hiscox, William 192
historiography 227–228
  British-Jewish history 4, 10n14,
    11n18, 15, 16, 71, 73n10,
    73n14, 88–90, 109, 140–141,
    158–159, 173, 174–175, 227
    New school 15, 158
    Whig school 3, 15, 158
  British sport history 5, 12n22, 225,
    227–228
  Jewish sport history 5, 6, 11n17,
    12n27, 12n29, 16, 89–90
Hitler, Adolf 64, 66
hockey 50, 103
Holmes, Colin 158, 162
  *Anti-Semitism in British Society:
    1876–1939* 158
Holt, Richard (Dick) 5, 59, 65,
    154n190, 216n107
  Sport and the British 5, 12n23
horse-racing 3, 4, 165–166
Hudson, Hugh 55
  see also Chariots of Fire
Huggins, Mike 3–4
Hunter, Evan 66
  see also British Olympic Association

hunting 10n12
Hutchison House Jewish Boys' Club
    78n82, 149n127
Hyams, George 204
Hyams, Jack 200

immigration (Jewish) to Britain
    Ashkenazi (pre-1880) 14, 19
    Central European (1930s) 15
    Russo-Jewish and Eastern European
        6, 8, 14, 15–16, 17, 19, 57
    social problems allegedly arising
        from 19–20
    Sephardic (pre-1880) 14, 19
Imperial Fascist League 161
Inter-Departmental Committee on
    Physical Deterioration (1904),
    report of the 28, 30
International Olympic Committee 64
Irish 6, 116, 148n120
Isaacs, Rufus 29
Israel 5, 12n27, 128, 132, 133,
    156n240, 204

JAA see Jewish Athletic Association
Jacobs, Harry 110, 120, 150n144
Jacobs, Lawrence 135
Jacobs, Joe 144n45
    Out of the Ghetto: My Youth in the
        East End, Communism and
        Fascism, 1913–1939 144n45
Jakobovits, Immanuel 141n13
Jay, Allan 128
Jewish Athletic Association 53, 61, 62,
    102, 135
    foundation 38–39, 48–49
    membership 49, 50
    policy 48, 102
    praise from established Jewish
        community 51, 52
Jewish Chronicle 50, 92, 97, 98, 99,
    101, 175, 187, 189, 193, 199, 203
    and Anglicisation campaign 20–21,
        24, 25, 30, 42–43
    concerns over sport's effect on ethnic
        identity 103, 104, 105, 107,
        110, 116, 119

and Harold Abrahams 56–57, 61,
    65, 67, 68
investigation in anti-Semitism in golf
    (1960) 181, 184, 186, 187,
    217n120
Jewish Lads' Brigade 30, 35, 134, 169,
    220n177
    foundation 21
    sport 24–25, 32, 44–46, 103,
        106–107, 197
    see also Prince of Wales' Boxing
        Shield
Jewish Literary Congress (1907) 103
Jewish People's Council 203, 222n202
Jewish World 28, 43–44, 50–51,
    61–62, 63, 96
Jews' Free School 21
Jockey Club 166
    see also horse-racing
Johnes, Martin 225
Jones, Jimmy 202
Jones, Stephen 12n22
Joyce, William 169
Judæans Athletic and Social Club
    118–119, 144n150
Judaism see religious observance
Julius, Anthony 4, 59
    Trials of the Diaspora: A History of
        Anti-Semitism in England 4

Kadish, Sharman 20, 35, 46
Kaye, Moss 183
Kinsey, Jack 165
Kushner, Tony 173, 211n14, 215n82

Labour Party 65
Laski, Neville 67
Lassen, Eric 176
Lawn Tennis Association 201–202
Lawson-Levy, Harry 43
Lazar, Harry 151n152
Lazar, Lew 151n152
Lea, Sydney 99–101, 183–184
Lebzelter, Gisela 158, 159
    Political Anti-Semitism in England:
        1918–1939 158
Leeds 19, 188–189, 192, 204

Leeds Parish Church Rugby League
    Football Club 95
Leeds United Football Club 13n32,
    99
Leek, Michael 182, 192
Lee Park Golf Club 190, 192, 219n166
Leicester Maccabi 131, 138
Lesser, Algernon 96
Levey, J.H. 136, 203
Levine, Peter 2, 5, 89, 148n109,
    152n166, 159, 198–199, 216n92
  *Ellis Island to Ebbets Field: Sport
    and the American Jewish
    Experience* 5, 89
Lewis, David 177
Lewis, Harry 27
Lewis, Ted 'Kid' (Gershon Mendeloff)
    80n121, 112, 114, 115, 117–118,
    122, 140, 149n127, 200
  family background 112–113,
    147n105
  involvement with British Union of
    Fascists 166, 200, 221n188,
    221n189
Leyton Orient Football Club 13n32
Liberal Party 187
Liddell, Eric 54, 84n198
  see also Chariots of Fire
Linehan, Thomas 211n20
Lipman, Vivian 14
Liverpool *see* Merseyside
Livshin, Rosalyn 89, 145n71
London 19, 21–22, 25, 28, 30, 41, 43,
    45, 46, 50, 52, 97–99, 104, 106,
    111, 112, 113, 118, 120, 121, 124,
    126, 129,130, 136, 144n46,
    144n49, 168, 169, 171, 172, 183,
    187, 191, 201, 203, 204–205,
    206–207
London County Council 50, 51, 120,
    121
London Federation of Working Boys'
    Clubs 41–43, 79n111
Los Angeles Tennis Club 201
Lowerson, John 142n20

Maccabaeans Society 48–49, 61, 62

Maccabaeans Athletic Committee 49
Maccabeus, Judas 126, *127*
Maccabiah 128
Maccabi Association, London 124,
    126, 128, 129–130, 136, 169
Maccabi Code 126, *127*, 132
Maccabi Great Britain *see* British
    Maccabi Association
Maccabi World Union 124, 128, 133,
    152n163, 155n213
  membership 124
McKibbin, Ross 142n21
Macmillan, Monty 153n159
McWhirter, Norris 83n163, 87n232
Magnus, Katie 22
MAL *see* Maccabi Association, London
Manchester 19, 21, 23, 45–46, 80n121,
    94, 95–96, 99–100, 106–107,
    110–111, 112, 145n55, 145n71,
    164, 165, 177, 183–184, 189, 197,
    218n134, 219n166, 220n177, 224
  Jewish Museum 99
  Jews' School 124n71
  Maccabi 137
Manchester City Football Club 95,
    99–101, *100*, 224
Manchester Guardian 65, 86n212
Manchester United Football Club 99
  see also Bobker, Martin; Garman,
    Joe; Goldstone, Abraham; Grove
    House Jewish Lads' Club; Lea,
    Sydney
Mandell, William 65, 68
Mangan, James Anthony 33
Mansfield, Alf 111–112
Mass Observation 2, 10n7, 205,
    223n217
Maurice, Frederick 30
Melchett, Alfred (Alfred Mond) 124,
    135
Melchett, Henry (Henry Mond) 124,
    203
Melnikoff, Pamela 57
Mendeloff, Gershon *see* Lewis, Ted
    'Kid'
Mendeloff, Solomon 113
Mendoza, Daniel 3, 4, 116, 198

Merseyside 19, 93, 103, 182, 189, 190, 192, 200–201, 204
  Liverpool Jewish Social Club 93
  see also Lee Park Golf Club
Merthyr Tydfil 57
Metropolitan Police 121
Middlesbrough 175
Millwall Football Club 95
Mizler, Harry 150n151, 200
Mizler, Moe 112
Mond, Alfred *see* Melchett, Alfred
Mond, Henry *see* Melchett, Henry
Montagu, Lily 22
Montagu, Samuel 92
Montefiore, Claude 52
Montefiore, Leonard 86n212
Morris, Albert 13n32
Morris, David (Hyman Morris) 94–95
Mosley, Oswald 161–162, 164, 169, 173, 200, 205, 212n25
  see also British Union of Fascists; New Party
Mosse, George 151n159
muscular Christianity 31
muscular Judaism 123–124, 125–126
  see also Nordau, Max; Zionism
MWU *see* Maccabi World Union
Myers, Simon 103
Myrdle Jewish Girls' Club 103

National Socialist German Workers' Party (Nazi Party) 15, 64, 65, 66–67, 68, 167, 172, 200
National Sporting Club 119
Nazi Party *see* National Socialist German Workers' Party
Netherlands 14
Newcastle
  Maccabi 128, 130, 138, 204
New Party 161
  see also British Union of Fascists; Mosley, Oswald
Noel-Baker, Philip 65–66, 86n212, 86n213
Nordau, Max 123–124, 151n159
  see also muscular Judaism
Nordic League 161

Norman, Henry 43
Northamptonshire County Cricket Club 54
Nottingham 189
Notting Hill Jewish Lads' Club 36

Oberlander, Fred 128
Olympic Games
  Antwerp (1920) 84n179
  Berlin (1936) 55, 64–69, 84n198
  Garmisch-Partenkirchen (Winter 1936) 64
  Paris (1924) 54, 60–61
  Stockholm (1912) 58
Oxford and St George's Jewish Lads' Club 28–29, 102, 117
  see also Henriques, Basil
Oxford University 54, 56, 58–59, 60, 71, 83n163

Pale of Settlement 27, 110, 112, 123
Palestine 15, 132, 133, 152n166, 156n240, 204
Panayi, Panikos 88, 141n12, 229n5
Paragon Hall 118, 120
pedestrianism 59
Place, Francis 198
Poland 32
Pollard, Stephen 1
Potters Bar Golf Club 191, 193
Pottle, Sue 82n162
Premierland 117, 118, 120–121, 122, 149n136, 150n144
Prince of Wales' Boxing Shield 45–46, 197, 220n177
Prince of Wales (later Edward VIII) 45, 45
public-schools, links to 19, 22, 31, 33–34

Raphael, John 54
rational recreation 16, 18, 23
readmission to Britain (Jewish) 1, 9n1
Rebak, Asher 205
re-emigration of Russo-Jewish migrants 20, 74n24
religious observance 6, 16, 90–92,

104–105, 108, 140, 141n13, 224
concerns over decline of 91–92,
    103–105, 135–136, 141n13
repatriation of Russo-Jewish migrants
    20, 74n24
Repton School 58, 59, 83n165
Riess, Stephen 199
Right Club 161
Ring, The 150n144
Rosenberg, Edgar 2
Roth, Cecil 10n14, 210n2
    A History of the Jews in England
    210n2
Rothman, Benny 85n207
    see also British Workers' Sports
        Federation; Communist Party
        Great Britain
Rothschild, Constance 27
Rothschild, Emma 22, 41
Rothschild, Nathaniel 10n12
Rothschild, Nathaniel Mayer (Victor) 54
Rothschild, Nathan Mayer 22, 43
Royal Commission on Alien
    Immigration (1903) 32, 40
Rubinstein, William 4, 10n14, 210n2
    *A History of the Jews in the English
        Speaking World: Great Britain* 4
rugby league 94, 95
    see also Broughton Rangers Rugby
        League Football Club; Leeds
        Parish Church Rugby League
        Football Club
rugby union 96, 137
    see also Raphael, John
Russell, Charles 27, 76n52
    Working Lads' Clubs 76n52
Russo-Jewish Committee 74n24
Ryan, Mark 11n17, 82n154, 86n215
    *Running with Fire: The True Story of
        'Chariots of Fire' Hero Harold
        Abrahams* 11n17, 82n154,
        83n163

Sabbath observance 142n18, 142n19
    decline of 91
    preventing Jewish involvement in
        sport 48, 49, 50, 53, 62–63,

142n21, 146n86
Sadow, Harry 204
Samuel, Herbert 51
Samuels, Lester 94
Sassoon, Edward 176
Schmeling, Max 167
Schoenfeld, Bruce 221n199
schools 21, 24, 32, 40–41, 48, 50
    see also board schools, day schools
        (Jewish)
Sebag-Montefiore, Cecil 25
Shakespeare, William 2
    Shylock 2
Sheffield 189
Shipley, Stan 142n21
Shirley Golf Club 190–191, 192, 193,
    219n166
Silver, Leslie 13n32
Smith, Elaine 146n89
Smith, Sally 16
Simon, John 86n221
smoking 23, 26, 100–101
social mobility 3–4, 6, 19, 35, 89, 97,
    98, 114, 122, 131, 174–175,
    180–181, 188, 209
Solomons, Jack 110, 120, 151n152
    attacks on by the British Union of
        Fascists 167–168, 213n50
Southport 189
Southport Argyle Lawn Tennis Club
    201
Southport Golf Club 201
Spain 14
Sportsmen's Century Club 153n183
squash 175, 215n83
Stanmore Golf Club 216n107
Stepney Jewish Working Lads' Club 25,
    27, *33*, 34, 36–37, 102, 103,
    118
    Stepney Jewish Club Chronicle
        34–35
stereotypes *see* anti-Semitism
Stern, Leonard 104
Stern, R. F. 103
Stockwood, Mervin 183
Strictly Kosher 224
swimming 25, 32, 50, 128

Swindon Town Football Club 95

table tennis 128, 13n32
Tananbaum, Susan 11n17, 16, 74n17
Tatz, Colin 216n92
Taylor, Matthew 12n22, 149n138
tennis 92, 93, 128, 175, 200–202,
    215n83, 218n134
    see also Buxton, Angela
Thatcher, Margaret 187
Times, The 66, 82n153, 86n212, 86n213
Tottenham Hotspur Football Club
    13n32, 143n44
    Jewish support for 96, 97–98, 101,
        144n45
    criticisms by British Union of
            Fascists 164–165, 170–171
Trades Union Congress 165

Ungar, Ruti 11n17
United Synagogue 105

Vansittart, Robert 86n221
Victoria Jewish Lads' Club 22, 29, 35
    gymnastics team 43–44

Waley-Cohen, Felix 51
Walvin, James 229n6
Wars
    Boer 27–28
    First World War 14, 161, 199,
        220n173
    Second World War 15, 158–159,
        168–169, 173, 204–205
Waterpark Club 218n134
Weber, Thomas 58, 83n164
Welland, Colin 55
    see also Chariots of Fire
West Central Jewish Girls' Club 22
West Central Jewish Working Lads'

Club 22, 25, 26, 28, 36, 41, 42,
    80n117
White, Arnold 39–40
    The Modern Jew 39–40
Whitefield Golf Club 184, 189,
    218n143
White, Jerry 28
Wignall, Trevor 97
Williams, Bill 110, 210n8
Wimbledon 200, 201–202
    see also Buxton, Angela; tennis
Wingate Football Club 204–205,
    223n225, 223n226
Wingate, Orde 205
Wingate Squash Club 215n83
Wonderland 118, 119
Worcestershire 182
wrestling 128
Wright, Billy 99

Young Poale Zion 134
youth movement 16, 18, 22, 32,
    102–108, 135–136
    fears over lack of interest in sport
        amongst migrant children 31–32
    membership 21–22
    physical success of sporting
        programme 29–30
    significance of sport within 25, 32,
        78n82
    see also Jewish Lads' Brigade;
        individual clubs

Zionism 123, 131–135, 140, 151n157,
    155n210, 155n213
    Zionist Congress, Karlsbad (1921)
        124
Zionist youth organisations 134–135
Zussman, Harry 13n32